DATE DUE

OCT 2 8 1994	
JAN 3 1 1995	
NOV 2 3 1995	
NOV 2 6 1996	
FEB 25 1998	
JAN 2 2 2002	

Perversions and

Near-Perversions in

Clinical Practice

New Psychoanalytic Perspectives

Perversions and Near-Perversions in Clinical Practice

New Psychoanalytic Perspectives

Edited by

Gerald I. Fogel, M.D.

Wayne A. Myers, M.D.

Yale University Press

New Haven and London

Designed by Barbara Werden.
Set in Linotron Times Roman type by The Composing Room
of Michigan, Inc.
Printed in the United States of America by Vail-Ballou Press,
Binghamton, New York.

Library of Congress Cataloging-in Publication Data

Perversions and Near-Perversions in Clinical Practice / edited by
Gerald I. Fogel, Wayne A. Myers
p.   cm.—(New psychoanalytic perspectives)
Includes bibliographical references.
Includes index.
ISBN 0-300-04829-7
1. Psychosexual disorders.   2. Sexual deviation.
3. Psychoanalysis.   I. Fogel, Gerald I.   II. Myers, Wayne A.
III. Series.
[DNLM: 1. Paraphilias—psychology.   2. Psychoanalytic Theory.
3. Psychoanalytic Therapy.   WM 610 P471]
RC556.P44   1991
616.85'83—dc20
DNLM/DLC
for Library of Congress   90–12584
CIP

10 9 8 7 6 5 4 3 2 1

Contents

Contributors and Editors

JACOB A. ARLOW, M.D.
Past president, American Psychoanalytic Association; former editor in chief, *Psychoanalytic Quarterly;* clinical professor of psychiatry, New York University School of Medicine.

SHELDON BACH, PH.D.
Faculty, New York Freudian Society and New York University Postdoctoral Program in Psychoanalysis; clinical professor of psychology, New York University Postdoctoral Program in Psychoanalysis; author, *Narcissistic States and the Therapeutic Process.*

ARNOLD M. COOPER, M.D.
Training and supervising analyst, Columbia University Center for Psychoanalytic Training and Research; professor of psychiatry and associate chairman for psychiatric education, Cornell University Medical College; past president, American Psychoanalytic Association.

GERALD I. FOGEL, M.D.
Training and supervising analyst, Columbia University Center for Psychoanalytic Training and Research; associate clinical professor of psychiatry, College of Physicians and Surgeons, Columbia University; coeditor, *The Psychology of Men: New Psychoanalytic Perspectives.*

LOUISE J. KAPLAN, PH.D.

Association for Child Psychoanalysis and the Margaret S. Mahler Research Foundation; author, *Oneness and Separateness: From Infant to Individual, Adolescence: The Farewell to Childhood, The Family Romance of the Imposter Poet, Thomas Chatterton, Female Perversions;* coeditor, *American Imago.*

OTTO F. KERNBERG, M.D.

Training and supervising analyst, Columbia University Center for Psychoanalytic Training and Research; associate chairman and professor, Department of Psychiatry, Cornell University Medical College; author, *Severe Personality Disorders: Psychotherapeutic Strategies.*

JOYCE MCDOUGALL, D.ED.

Full member, Paris Psychoanalytic Society; author, *Plea for a Measure of Abnormality, Theaters of the Mind, Theaters of the Body.*

HELEN C. MEYERS, M.D.

Assistant director and training and supervising analyst, Columbia University Center for Psychoanalytic Training and Research; clinical professor of psychiatry, College of Physicians and Surgeons, Columbia University; editor, *Current Issues in Transference and Countertransference.*

WAYNE A. MYERS, M.D.

Training and supervising and admitting psychoanalyst, Columbia University Center for Psychoanalytic Training and Research; clinical professor of psychiatry, Cornell University Medical College; author, *Dynamic Therapy of the Older Patient;* coeditor, *New Concepts in Psychoanalytic Psychotherapy.*

ELLEN HANDLER SPITZ, PH.D.

Visiting lecturer of aesthetics in psychiatry, Cornell University Medical College; author, *Art and Psyche.*

GEORGE STADE, PH.D.

Professor of English and comparative literature, Columbia University; editor in chief, *European Writers* (thirteen vols.); author, *Confessions of a Lady-Killer.*

ROBERT J. STOLLER, M.D.

Member, Los Angeles Psychoanalytic Society and Institute; professor of psychiatry, University of California, Los Angeles, School of Medicine; author, *Sex and Gender: On the Development of Masculinity and Femininity, Splitting, The Transsexual Experiment: Sex and Gender,* vol. 2, *Perversion: The Erotic Form of Hatred, Observing the Erotic Imagination, Presentations of Gender.*

Perversions and

Near-Perversions in

Clinical Practice

Introduction

Perversity and the Perverse

Updating a Psychoanalytic Paradigm

Gerald I. Fogel, M.D.

T HE traditional psychoanalytic definition of perversion stresses
sexual deviance and abnormality, often with an emphasis on the
abhorrent and bizarre. There is a sharp line implied between perversion and neurosis. As Freud first noted, however, polymorphous perverse sexual elements are components of everyone's sexual life, and the
line between normal and abnormal is often difficult to draw. Yet such
categories as transvestism, fetishism, sexual sadomasochism, exhibitionism, voyeurism, pedophilia, and bestiality have dominated the treatment literature in the past, offering clinicians understandings and treatment approaches that did not always take into account the frequency with
which perverse fantasies and behaviors appear in the everyday life of
everyday patients, including, therefore, many so-called normal people.

Today we would say that Freud used perversion as a paradigm to
demonstrate the unique importance of infantile sexuality in psychic development and unconscious life when he aphoristically defined neurosis
as the negative of perversion. But perversion has retained an aura of

1

something apart from both normality and neurosis, something "other," despite Freud's later work and that of subsequent generations of ego psychologists demonstrating that this conception is far too simple. The classical literature is thoroughly reviewed by various authors in this volume, and neurotic and perverse characteristics, behaviors, and syndromes are compared and contrasted where it is important and useful to do so. It is sufficient to say at this point that, as a paradigm, the perverse has attracted a great deal of new attention in recent years. Many, in fact, see it as the latest frontier in psychoanalysis, replacing the borderline and narcissistic as the area in which the most exciting new work and thought are being accomplished with the greatest impact on the advance of clinical and theoretical knowledge.

The contributors to this volume explore the latest perspectives on the perverse as it commonly appears in clinical practice today. New theoretical vantage points (such as object relations theory, self theory, separation-individuation and other developmental theories, and observational studies of sexual and gender development) implement classic views and offer new understandings and treatment approaches.

Certain themes recur frequently. Many authors point out that it is often useful to view perverse fantasies and enactments as complex adaptive and defensive compromise formations that may serve multiple functions over a wide range of diagnoses and degrees of psychopathology, just as any character trait or neurotic symptom may do. For example, fantasies or behaviors that serve only to enhance ego integration and intimacy or to facilitate sexual potency and pleasure in a normal or neurotic character may be necessary to stabilize ego boundaries, allow limited object relating, secure a sense of self, and bind primitive aggression in less stable, more severe character disorders. New theoretical perspectives also offer new ways to define health and pathology beyond that of manifest genital functioning. Some of the significant issues are the importance of primitive aggression, the related subject of power over and control of objects, dehumanization of self and others, stages on the way to object and self constancy and other separation-individuation issues, the warding off and control of underlying painful feelings, such as depression, alienation, deadness, or fragmentation, the role of early sexuality in identity formation, the role of trauma in etiology, sexualization as a defense, and the relation of perversion to healthy psychic development, creativity, imagination, and play.

Of course, most psychotherapists work all the time with perverse themes in the form of fantasies, symbolic enactments, and intermittent symptoms. These themes pervade the conscious and unconscious lives of patients, although they vary widely in their frequency and obligatory quality from case to case and time to time within a particular case. They are a common feature in the characterological syndromes seen frequently in clinical practice. In addition, many of the so-called character perversions can be more readily defined in terms of a pathognomonic underlying personality structure than the presence or absence of sexual symptoms.

Popular culture also floods us with perverse themes and images. In advertising, rock videos, and film, for example, we see evidence of a greater acceptance of and widespread taste for what was once considered esoteric or deviant. When changes in predominant psychopathology, psychoanalytic theory, and culture occur concurrently, we must consider the relationships among them.

Many psychoanalysts follow Freud's example by defining perversion as a value-free "scientific" category rather than adopting common usage, which takes the literal view: the perverse is that which is turned away from what is right, reasonable, or good. But it is almost impossible to evade the ethical dimension today; many of our contributors point out the bias that may be contained in diagnoses, treatment goals, and even what is taken as ordinary therapeutic attitudes. Ideas of good and bad are inherent in the maturational sequences of developmental schemas. For example, if the terms *narcissistic* and *primitive object relationship* may function as clinical concepts to be applied nonpejoratively, they also imply moral valuations: thou shalt not be greedy, hateful, or narcissistic, nor treat others as part objects. The term *perverse* also contains this inevitable double edge.

So, despite frequent exposure to perverse images and themes in their practices and daily lives, many therapists are not confident of their theoretical grasp and depth of experience in this area. Countertransference anxieties, moral aversions, and clinical, theoretical, sociocultural, and moral ambiguities contribute to the difficulties. Additionally, many therapists have seen few full-blown clinical perversions, and many may be subtly influenced by the traditional pessimism regarding dynamic therapy with such patients. Some are unaware of the resurgence of interest in and the wealth of new findings about the perverse or uncertain of how to apply these findings in their everyday practices or in understanding dominant elements in the personalities and cultural trends of our times. Considering the importance of and wide interest in the subject, there is an astonishing lack of published data available that bring together the diversity and richness of the advances in the psychoanalytic conception of perversions and the perverse over the past thirty years.

The editors hope that this volume will help rectify that situation. The subject of the perverse in everyday practice leads to that of full-blown sexual perversion, on the one hand, and to the nonsexual so-called character perversions, on the other. Together with cultural issues, it defines broad subject areas that are addressed in varying degrees by all contributors. Some of the important questions in these areas include:

1. When do fantasies and enactments of normal polymorphous perverse sexuality become pathologic? Can lines be drawn between a perverse symptom and a normal variation? What are the possible treatment approaches to such fantasies and behaviors? Should therapeutic choices be influenced by this ambiguous boundary?

2. What role do perverse elements play, and what functions may they serve, in those with borderline, narcissistic, neurotic, and normal characters? Can, or should, we distinguish sharply between full-blown clinical perversion and other characterological syndromes with perverse elements? By what criteria do we identify a "perverse structure" in a difficult character disorder in the absence of a full-blown clinical syndrome? What is the relationship between character perversion and the preoedipal and narcissistic character? Are all these distinctions meaningful in the clinical setting? And where they are, what are the differences in treatment approach?

3. What special pressures, tensions, and blind spots exist for the therapist working with perverse material, and what are some ways to increase clinical competence and self-awareness?

4. What can perverse sexuality teach us about the normal, about healthy development, and about artistic creation, play, and other meet-

ing grounds for the often ambiguous relationship between reality and illusion?

5. What is the significance of the greater influence of such themes in our current culture? Is there a correlation with a challenge to traditionally defined values, forms, and roles? Do we discern liberation or decay? Are ritualization of sex, sexualization of power, and the objectification of bodies signs of a perverse society? Can dehumanization and the rise of materialism legitimately be called "perverse"?

6. What is the significance of the fact that many traditional perversions occur only in males? Are there perversions or equivalents that are characteristically female?

The Plan of the Book

This book comprises four sections. The first, "The Perversions: Definitions and Overviews," focuses primarily on those syndromes that are full-blown perversions in the traditional sense. We soon see, however, that traditional nosology offers us few solid guidelines. In "The Unconscious Core of Perversion," Arnold M. Cooper provides a skilled, selective review of the literature and demonstrates how, with changing and competing theoretical paradigms and cultural norms, clear definitions are now difficult to find. He notes that *perversion* may be a term that like the terms *narcissism* and *masochism* must be defined each time it is used if we are to understand each other. He finds surprising continuities among the varying historical and current approaches, but a field greatly expanded, especially by our greater appreciation of narcissistic, pre-oedipal, and object relational issues. Cooper believes that there is a core trauma and three core unconscious fantasies in all perversions. The core trauma is "the experience of terrifying passivity in relation to the pre-oedipal mother perceived as dangerously malignant, malicious, and all-powerful, arousing sensations of awe and the uncanny." The core fantasies use dehumanization as the "ultimate strategy against the fears of human qualities." Two detailed examples from fiction vividly illustrate his thesis.

Cooper takes what he calls a "dimensional" rather than a "categorical" view of perversion, and Robert J. Stoller, in "The Term *Perver-*

sion," finds that categories, especially traditional psychoanalytic ones, are altogether useless, that it is essentially impossible to classify perversions into discrete syndromes. Perversions are not entities, he says, but are rather "behaviors in which all kinds of folks indulge."

But though it may not be possible to draw clear diagnostic distinctions between the so-called normal and abnormal, Stoller nevertheless has some criteria that distinguish a perversion per se from what he calls a variant. He also finds certain dynamic and structural factors that are always present in perversity, though he stresses strongly and repeatedly that these factors do not compose the whole person and that people who share these characteristics and behaviors are not necessarily alike in all ways. He emphasizes the attempt to repair a core trauma, the conversion of trauma to triumph, the replacement of spontaneity with a habitual fantasy scenario, and the invariable presence of risk, mystery, sin (the wish to harm and control), and subversion—an antisocial and anti-authoritarian factor. Having described the limitations (and sins) of psychoanalytic categorizing, especially in the realms of diagnosis, etiology, and prognosis (psychoanalysis is a "moral order trying to transform itself into . . . a science"), Stoller provides his own multifactorial schema for understanding the etiology of perversion.

In Part II, "Applications: The Perversions of Everyday Clinical Practice," the focus shifts from description and definition to treatment. Here, several highly experienced and articulate clinicians demonstrate from varying theoretical points of view the ways in which perverse fantasies and behaviors underlie, overlap, interrelate with, and sometimes obfuscate other important elements in the character structures and transferences of their everyday patients. Their various approaches to the ubiquity of such phenomena nicely illustrate the changes and expansion of theoretical views in recent years.

In "Derivative Manifestations of Perversion," Jacob A. Arlow stresses the ubiquity of persistent underlying unconscious fantasies in all thought and behavior and the value of the dynamic point of view, which sees all mental products as the result of forces in conflict. He provides rich clinical examples to illustrate his concept of character perversions. These are characterological traits or styles that are revealed in analysis to have originated as perversions or tendencies to perversion—usually in late latency or adolescence. Some of these adult character syndromes include unrealistic characters, petty liars, practical jokers, and petty swindlers. The underlying fearful conflicts are classical: such things as the need to avoid the unbearable evidence of the reality of castration in the sight of the female genital or the furtive enactment of a disavowed passive homosexual fantasy. Underlying perverse tendencies are also inevitably present in moral masochism in men. Arlow notes and illustrates the dynamic interaction between intrapsychic life and interpersonal relations as well as the relation of an individual to his culture. In such phenomena as men's fashion and pornography (which he calls "borrowed perversion") he demonstrates the relationship between cultural variations and intrapsychic attitudes and solutions to conflict.

Sheldon Bach, in "On Sadomasochistic Object Relations," also speaks to the ubiquity of perverse phenomena in clinical practice, but from an alternate theoretical perspective. He shows how sadomasochistic object relating is frequently used to replace a missing piece of a patient's ego structure. It is easier for many patients, he says, to use or exploit another person than to understand that person, which requires a dialogue. These pathologies present across a wide range of traditional nosologies and, like traditional perversions, may be viewed as a defense against and attempt to repair a traumatic loss not adequately mourned.

Bach states that these syndromes may express failure in many developmental lines: drive, ego, superego, self, and object relations. Although he emphasizes structural deficits and deficiencies in object relations, he also finds a way to integrate these perspectives with more classical conceptions of drive, defense, and conflict. The relationship of drive to object is complex and variable: some patients idealize drives and deny the significance of objects; others idealize objects and deny their own drives. In every instance, tact and the clinical data will determine the correct approach.

In "Perversion in Fantasy and Furtive Enactments," Helen C. Meyers takes on the difficult task of trying to map out the territory of this group of clinical presentations in relation to the traditional literature, in a sense to find the common ground between Arlow and Bach. Perverse dynamics, she points out, have always existed in *every* patient who gets analyzed. Perverse *structures* traditionally appear in classic perversions, and most think that it still makes sense (scientifically, not as a moral judgment) to speak of perversions as distinct syndromes, where such distinctions as that between conscious and unconscious fantasy or fantasy and action are usually meaningful.

She defines a new clinical area: "Halfway between perversion in fantasy and perversion in behavior are furtive enactments—not just fantasy, yet not quite fully perverse acts." Some clinical examples illustrate her ideas. She suggests that this not uncommon clinical phenomenology reveals a link between her patients and the classic perversions: an inhibition in the effective use of fantasy and symbolization. Many of these patients must "learn" how to masturbate creatively, to employ perverse fantasy in the service of psychosexual maturity. Thus her "halfway zone" seems to overlap considerably with the patients described by both Arlow and Bach. In fact, Bach is probably on precisely the same ground when he contrasts fetishistic or "play-acting" fantasy and action, on the one hand, with creative symbolic imaginative play and object relating, on the other.

Finally, in "A Case History of a Man Who Made Obscene Telephone Calls and Practiced Frotteurism," Wayne A. Myers presents a single case analyzed in detail. The telephone and subway travel—essential elements in the structure of his patient's perverse symptoms—in themselves lend a modern note to the analysis. The reader will have been prepared by the preceding theoretical essays for the admixture of conflicts, developmental levels, drives, mental structures, and structural deficits that are ultimately revealed to be layered into this patient's perverse scenario. We see, for example, castration anxiety, developmental trauma, the pre-oedipal mother, unresolved grief, passive homosexual longings, primitive aggression, oedipal drama, primal scene, and massive self-esteem issues. All these elements are significant and must be analyzed. This is a typical patient in many ways. The case illustrates how ambiguous the line is between the so-called classic perversion and perversity as analysts see it currently in their everyday practice. As Myers points out, in our culture the subway and the telephone have become common instruments for furtive enactments of perversity, so this is a fitting case example to conclude this section.

Part III is entitled "Wider Applications: Women, Couples, and Psychoanalysts." Although the reader will find much here that is clinically relevant, the focus enlarges beyond the patient in therapy.

In "Women Masquerading as Women," Louise J. Kaplan's major thesis is that "perversions, insofar as they derive a great deal of their emotional force from social gender stereotypes, are as much pathologies of gender identification as they are pathologies of sexuality." Her chapter therefore ranges widely over both individual and societal psychopathology and the interplay between them. She draws many interesting parallels between typical male and female regressive compromises that utilize "perverse strategies" to solve (and also shape) the universal crisis of oedipality. Many of these strategies utilize "exalted gender ideals of infancy," in essence preoedipal and presexual (in the adult genital sense) identifications, caricatures of mature sexuality that actually represent flight from neurotically or societally prohibited oedipal aspirations.

Convincing examples from classic literature, modern culture, and the psychoanalytic literature demonstrate the intricate web of personal conflict, familial necessity, and societal reinforcement that draws women into perverse solutions and also show how society serves its own distorted purposes by defining these complex characterological personal pathologies as normal. Kaplan documents in fascinating detail, for example, her provocative thesis that *stereotypic* femininity in women often has the same underlying structure and analogous purposes as classic perversions in males—that is, it is perverse. The perverse strategy, as she defines it, exploits biological differences to accomplish manifold conscious and unconscious purposes.

In "Aggression and Love in the Relationship of the Couple," Otto F. Kernberg continues the exploration of normal and abnormal love relations that has engaged him in recent years. The understanding of perversion and perversity has been crucial to this work, for he defines perversity as the "recruitment of love in the service of aggression, the consequence of a predominance of hatred over love." Perversions are syndromes characterized by a specific restriction of the normal range of sexual experience. But perversity and its manifestations characterize all loving relationships and serve a wide range of functions within couples and groups as well as in the individual. The most successful relationships will have worked through and integrated aggression in the service of love, intimacy, and social and cultural diversity and freedom.

Kernberg's emphasis is on "the interplay of love and aggression at the level of the couple's emotional relationship rather than at the level of their sexual interaction." Couples attempt through their relationships to work out deep, universally conflictual infantile taboos and to overcome pathological "discontinuities" and universal preoedipal and oedipal "triangulations." Various common forms of perversity are illustrated in rich detail, such as aggressive elements predominating and controlling sexual excitement, sadomasochistic patterns dominating and controlling the emotional relationship, dominance and control by persecutory and sadistic aspects of mutually projected superego functions, and the freezing of the relationship in one pattern of actualized unconscious complementary object relationship from the past. Kernberg utilizes and successfully integrates a vast amount of recent work in the field—his own and others'—on the psychology of individuals, couples, and groups.

In "Perversions and Deviations in the Psychoanalytic Attitude: Their Effect on Theory and Practice," Joyce McDougall focuses on the analyst in the analytic situation. Of all our contributors, she most sensitizes the reader to the ethical bias that may be contained in any definition of perversion or perversity. It is frequently the analyst's unanalyzed perversity that leads to categorizing and furtive countertransference enactments and a "return of the perverse." She notes that "the pervert is always someone else" and shows how the value judgments of theoreticians and practitioners may subvert the ideals and goals of analysis. She states that ideally "an analyst shall never wittingly impose upon his patients *his* system of values, *his* sexual preferences, *his* political opinions—or the theoretical convictions of *his* particular school of psychoanalytic thought. Any other attitude is a perversion of the analytic role."

McDougall's prior work on perversion is well known, as is her unique sensitivity to the pain and problems in living with what she calls the neosexualities and her gift for working analytically with these patients. But she also believes strongly that there are ambiguous and sometimes very thin lines between perversity and creativity or sublimation and that the most brutalizing and dehumanizing perversities may be hidden in the so-called normal. Further, these unhappy patterns may be institutionalized in social systems. She wants analysts not to look away from perversity in their patients and themselves but to examine the "psychic survival" that such adaptation always signals, and she summarizes vividly the traumata with which the perversities seek to cope. She also reminds analysts unceasingly of the ethical imperative at the heart of their work that is contained in the pledge to approach patients with an unswerving attitude of nonjudgmental neutrality. "Is it not a major perversion, then," she asks, "for an analyst to believe that he holds the key to the *Truth*?"

The final part of the book is entitled "Cultural and Literary Issues." Both authors adapt a broad cultural perspective to demonstrate that the issues analysts struggle with in their work with perverse patients resonate profoundly with universal human needs, fears, and tasks as revealed through a study of literature. The literature referenced is both sacred and profane: to illustrate the omnipresence of the perverse in the ongoing human drama, one author turns to Euripides, the other to Mickey Spillane.

Many other contributors have pondered, at least in passing, the ambiguity where personal and societal adaptation meet in perversity. If perversity denies culturally stable forms, even challenges the universality of the sexual and generational difference in the service of personal psychopathology, it is still true that in culturally rigid or unstable lives and times, perverse solutions may be adaptive, creative—a necessary regression and reminder of the stultification that may be the price of oedipal order. Ellen Handler Spitz, in "Reflections on the Smile of Dionysus: Theatricality, Specularity, and the Perverse," finds much to ponder in this regard in Euripides' play, and her essay evokes for the reader a vision she herself once had while viewing the drama: "Onstage throughout, a great bronzed disk caught and reflected the lights. Continuously in view, it glowed, glowered, leered, grinned, and grimaced at both audience and players. Seductive and unsettling, its haunting presence seemed to blur comedy and tragedy. Although it was meant perhaps as an amalgam of the two suns over Thebes, I saw in it only the diabolical smiling mask of Dionysus."

Spitz covers much ground. She is especially interested in how the play reflects "a world in which cultural upheaval engenders perverse enactments as attempted solutions to the paradoxes of human sexuality and generation." She also considers at length the theme of the birth trauma and the great difficulties and paradoxes in the mother-son dyad in the play, the problem of *recognition* of maternity. She notes the emphasis on representation by visualization and spectacle in perversion and in the play, and compares and contrasts it to representation by word alone. Throughout she stresses the intimate relations of paradox and the "centrality of double vision" to perversion, the eternal ambiguity and irony: man or woman, leader or led, revolution or order, natural or unnatural, moral or immoral?

George Stade, in "The Hard-Boiled Dick: Perverse Reflections in a Private Eye," casts his sardonic eye on the astonishingly popular detective novelist Mickey Spillane and his archetype hero, Mike Hammer. Stade believes that both Hammer and his audience define themselves by what they insist they are not. Hammer is "all man. Never is he more polemically a man than when confronted by his moral opposites, or negative definers. These are criminals, forward women, and perverts, all of whom, by the end of the novel, have been equated."

Stade points out that Spillane is unaware of the perverse core in his ethos or of the return of the perverse expressed in the actions of his sadistic, self-righteous hero or through the dreaded, enticing phallic heroines who haunt him. Spillane's law-and-order man, Hammer, prevails, unlike Euripides' law-and-order man, Pentheus, who is destroyed and drags the whole moral order he represents down with him because he would not see. Let us hope that Euripides conveys the true mythic reality and Spillane is merely a fable for the fifties.

Conclusion

As the reader will see from this volume, there is much that is new in the world and also much that is new in psychoanalysis since Freud and classical ego psychology. Especially in the past thirty years, valuable theoretical breakthroughs have added considerably to analysts' ability to understand and treat their patients, breakthroughs that take into account not only new perspectives on character and pathology but also the new world they actually live in.

I believe that psychoanalysis has always been characterized by non-reductionism, especially the kind that takes the form "them" as opposed to "us." Freud showed that neurotic and normal were false categories in important respects. In recent years, character disorders, borderline, narcissistic, and masochistic phenomena and many other categories of experience and behavior have been subjected to careful psychoanalytic scrutiny. The result has been not only a more sophisticated attitude toward these entities when we approach them therapeutically but also a fuller understanding of normal psychology and, of course, ourselves. A recent trend has been to do the same for the archetypal "other," the pervert, to show the logic of perversity and its necessary and ubiquitous role in human psychology. By drawing together in one volume an array of experts and a range of diverse perspectives, we hope to provide an up-to-date, thorough introduction and a number of useful therapeutic approaches to the eternally interesting, problematic, and paradigmatic subject of perversion and the perverse.

Most of the chapters in this volume derive from papers presented at a symposium sponsored by the Association for Psychoanalytic Medicine in collaboration with the Columbia University Center for Psychoanalytic Training and Research.

Part I
The Perversions
Definitions and Overviews

Chapter One

The Unconscious
Core of Perversion

Arnold M. Cooper, M.D.

T is characteristic of psychoanalysis today that concepts that once
seemed clear and precise are, in a pluralistic theoretical framework,
now diffuse or expanded, often beyond definition, although analysts
continue to speak and write as if they all know what they are talking
about. It would be surprising if the idea of perversion did not show some
of these attributes, since perversion not only is one of the earliest analytic
concepts but is highly bound both to theory and to cultural norms. I will
begin by giving some samples of attempts at definition that may illumi-
nate the domain of our interest, omitting some major contributors as I
illustrate the shifting meanings of perversion. I will then discuss the core
conflict of passivity and the three fantasies that are always present in
perversion, the male-female difference in perversion, and a bit about
perverse play and the range of perverse life.

In the "Three Essays on the Theory of Sexuality" Freud announced a
number of the themes that concern us here. He began with a clear sense
of what should be called perversion: "Perversions are sexual activities

which either (a) extend, in an anatomical sense, beyond the regions of the body that are designed for sexual union, or (b) linger over the immediate relations to the sexual object which should normally be traversed rapidly on the path towards the final sexual aim" ([1905] 1953, 150). He formulated perversion as the primacy of a partial sexual instinct, and neurosis as its negative (165). We might note the ambiguity that cultural inventiveness has provided concerning what the regions designed for sexual union are and what constitutes lingering rather than rapid traverse. Freud stressed this point when he said, "The most striking distinction between the erotic life of antiquity and our own no doubt lies in the fact that the ancients laid the stress upon the instinct itself, whereas we emphasize its object. The ancients glorified the instinct and were prepared on its account to honour even an inferior object; while we despise the instinctual activity in itself, and find excuses for it only in the merits of the object" (149). In this footnote, added in 1910, not only does Freud emphasize the looseness of the ties of the sexual instinct to the (expected) sexual object, but one might, reading between the lines, suggest that he considered the ancients as having the better of the argument from the viewpoint of pleasure. (Norman O. Brown took this comment of Freud's seriously; in *Life against Death* (1959) he argued that humans would be better off with instinctual freedom from society's guidance—that is, with freedom for perversion.) Freud went on to emphasize the role of disgust in determining what it is that we choose to call perverse (152), and the need for shame and disgust to constrain the sexual instincts within bounds considered normal (162).

Simultaneously, he held that perversion is the base for the most valued human constructions:

> What we describe as a person's "character" is built up to a considerable extent from the material of sexual excitations and is composed of instincts that have been fixed since childhood, of constructions achieved by means of sublimation, and of other constructions, employed for effectively holding in check perverse impulses which have been recognized as being unutilizable. The multifarious perverse sexual dispositions of childhood can accordingly be regarded as the source of a number of our virtues, insofar as through reaction-formation it stimulates their development. (238)

Perversions—disavowed or repressed, or, perhaps most important, sup-pressed—were surely part of everyday life, and it is clear that, for Freud, defenses against perverse impulses were a bedrock of human civilization.

Finally, it may be worth reminding ourselves of Freud the moralist who, when discussing "'Civilized' Sexual Morality and Modern Nervous Illness" in 1908, expressed some views that he never changed—on the one hand, the relentless antagonism between the demands of culture and those of the sexual instincts, and on the other, his own view of the true aims of sex. Referring to the perverse versions of intercourse, he said, "These activities cannot, however, be regarded as being . . . harmless . . . in love-relationships. They are ethically objectionable, for they degrade the relationships of love between two human beings from a serious matter to a convenient game, attended by no risk and no spiritual participation" ([1908] 1959, 200). Freud was serious in claiming love as a criterion of normality, and the perverse is objectionable—or the perverse is perverse—because it trivializes or degrades love. He objected to mas-turbation, for example, because it made it too easy to obtain sexual pleasure and because it led to an excessive and facile idealization of the love object without its being measured against the struggle of obtaining satisfaction within the limitations of real people.

Laplanche and Pontalis echo Freud, adding, "In a more compre-hensive sense, 'perversion' connotes the whole of the psychosexual behavior that accompanies such atypical means of obtaining sexual plea-sure" ([1967] 1973, 306). They also make the very important point that "in psychoanalysis, the word 'perversion' is used exclusively in relation to sexuality. Where Freud recognises the existence of instincts other than sexual ones, he does not evoke perversion in connection with them" (307). Today some of us consider aspects of aggressive and narcissistic activities as the major source of behaviors we would label perverse. Focusing on the inherent problems of conceptualizing perversion, Laplanche and Pontalis attempt to find the guiding normative principle for Freud in his concept of sexual development and its completion only in the genital phase, but they acknowledge the many difficulties with this view.

The Laplanche and Pontalis book sounds old-fashioned, perhaps, and we might be tempted to think of the *Diagnostic and Statistical Manual*

(3rd ed., rev.) as its polar opposite. The difference is surprisingly small, however, and resides more in the details of social politics than in principle. Having abolished the term *perversion* in favor of *paraphilia*, the manual says, "The Paraphilias are characterized by arousal in response to sexual objects or situations that are not part of normative arousal-activity patterns and that in varying degrees may interfere with the capacity for reciprocal, affectionate sexual activity" (279). The authors' morality is precisely the same as Freud's, but they differ in not attempting a developmental or structural understanding of the phenomenon. The manual continues, "The essential feature of disorders in this subclass is recurrent, intense sexual urges and sexually arousing fantasies, generally involving either (1) non-human subjects, (2) the suffering or humiliation of oneself or one's partner (not merely simulated), or (3) children or other non-consenting persons. The diagnosis is made only if the person has acted on these urges, or is markedly distressed by them." It has never been a secret that the manual's view of perversion, right or wrong, was powerfully shaped by the politics of gay liberation, which in turn has influenced analysts' ideas of the everyday perversions.

The effort to escape from the uncomfortable idea of perversion as cultural deviation is well illustrated by Stoller. In an important paper in 1974 and in a major set of works since then, he stressed that everyone is more or less perverse (1974, 432), and he distinguished "perversion" as a diagnosis applied to a personality dominated by a sexual fantasy versus "perversion mechanisms" universally applied in the attempt to preserve sexual gratification against trauma; the difference is quantitative. Perversion consists of the pursuit of gratification through hostility and vengeance designed to deny and defend against the frightening sexual curiosity, mystery, and danger that surround the traumatic attachment to mother. And very important, he suggested that "in men, perversion may at bottom be a gender disorder," reflecting the difficulty for men in establishing masculine identity after their primary feminine identification with their mothers (429). Stoller emphasized that without the energizing force of hostility, we are in the realm of mere deviance.

Stoller's work is especially important because it melds concepts of sexuality and the older emphasis on castration and fetishism in forming a perversion with newer concepts derived from the understanding of pre-oedipal narcissistic and safety needs and the problems of separation and individuation. He also touches on the idea that the male-female perversion difference derives from these earlier states rather than from the anatomical difference alone.

Person and Ovesey (1983), in a series of careful and penetrating studies of gender differentiation, have shown that normal core gender identity is a function of sex assignment and rearing, basically non-conflictual. Gender-role identity, however, is a product of many conflictual issues, involving problems of separation-individuation, complex body perceptions, and all the conflicts of the Oedipus phase. They reject Stoller's concept of primary femininity and stress that where core gender identity of the male is tenuous as a result of disturbances of separation, there is a greater incidence of some forms of perversion. Discussing transvestism, they emphasize that this perversion "is not simply a sexual disorder, but is best understood as primarily a disorder of the sense of self" (Ovesey and Person 1976, 219). They demonstrate that this disorder of the self is a result of an ego split of male and female gender identities secondary to unresolved separation anxiety occurring during infantile separation-individuation. Person and Ovesey emphasize "that gender precedes sexuality in development and organizes sexuality, not the reverse" (1983, 221).

Khan went further in taking the definition of perversion away from the sexual and toward the object-relational. He said, "The pervert puts an *impersonal object* between his desire and his accomplice: this *object* can be a stereotype fantasy, a gadget or a pornographic image. All three alienate the pervert from himself, as, alas, from the object of his desire. Hence the title of the book, *Alienation in Perversions*" (1979, 9).

Another step leading analysts far from their original definitions of perversion is illustrated in Arlow's 1971 paper "Character Perversion." Briefly, he described individuals with an original perversion or tendency toward perversion who replace the symptomatic activity with a character trait. For example, he described characters whose capacity for everyday reality testing was damaged secondary to defenses against voyeuristic and fetishistic perverse needs. Arlow emphasized that in these male patients the root trauma involved exposure to the female genital and consequent discovery of the missing phallus. Here, then, in the concept of perverse character, we have come the full distance toward the idea of perversion as a mechanism without a symptom.

I will mention only two more workers in tracing the changed ideas of perversion. Chasseguet-Smirgel has been influential in understanding perversion as a magical attempt to deny the inevitable infantile traumas to omnipotent fantasy in the discovery of the difference between the sexes and the difference between the generations. This disavowal is achieved by the creation of an anal-sadistic universe in which distinctions are erased (penis = feces = child), differentiation from mother is unnecessary, father is nonexistent, pregenitality is idealized, and sublimation is impossible and unnecessary (1984, 141). In this view, although the psychodynamic premises could not be more different from Kohut's, perversion is an attempted repair of a narcissistic pregenital injury, probably reflecting significant failures in maternal care.

Finally, McDougall describes the neosexualities, emphasizing the desperate inventiveness that characterizes perversion. She stresses that "the leading theme of the neosexual plot is invariably castration. . . . the triumph of the neosexual scenario lies in the fact that the castrative aim is only playfully carried out. . . . [Perversions] are all substitute acts of castration and thus serve to master castration anxiety in illusory fashion, at every conceivable level" (1985, 252). She also emphasizes that in the neosexualities the patient is unendingly involved in hatred and envy toward the breast-mother while attempting to idealize a maternal image that allows no place for the difference between the sexes (249). "Neosexualities, then, serve not only to maintain libidinal homeostasis but narcissistic homeostasis as well" (251).

Let me briefly summarize this summary. Over time analysts have changed both their definition of perversion and their theories of perversion. The original definition referred to a sexual action carried out with the wrong body parts (not heterosexual genitalia) and with the wrong sexual ideas (not heterosexual adult loving union). The definitions today vary. Some would retain the original definition intact while others would modify it "slightly" to permit the use of same-sex genitalia. Another group would stress the contamination of the sexual act, however it is carried out, by rage and hostility; still others would see the essence of perversion in the mode of sexual fantasy, which may be expressed in character traits regardless of the form of sexual action. There is no agreement on whether they should be defining a disorder or a universal psychodynamic mechanism. For the sake of brevity I am omitting a largely nonanalytic group who would maintain that the essence of the definition involves labeling for the purpose of social control.

Theories of perversion today reflect the multiple psychoanalytic points of view—ego psychological, object relational, and self psychological—that must be considered in describing a complex psychological construction such as perversion. As a result, the universe of the perverse has expanded enormously. Once simply unrepressed or undeveloped pregenital activities, the perverse now includes elaborate fetishistic constructions for healing castration anxiety, attempts to cope with the stresses of gender differentiation, failures to overcome severe narcissistic injury involving generational and sexual difference, failure to separate from early terrifying maternal representations, the characterologic expressions of perverse desires, and expressions of rage and vengeance via sex. Analysts emphasize the fear and aggression, with primitive splitting mechanisms or overdimensional castration fears and disorganizing rage, that derail the capacity for benign object ties. Following the hint of Laplanche and Pontalis when they spoke of Freud's not evoking the concept of perversion in connection with nonsexual instincts, many later workers have seen perversion primarily or equally as a miscarriage of narcissistic development and consequent aggression, rather than as a primarily libidinal deviation. Within this multiplicity of views, there is remarkable agreement among analysts on the psychodynamics of perversion, focusing on issues of narcissism.

In elaborating this view of the narcissistic base of perverse development I want to emphasize that the core trauma in many if not all perversions is the experience of terrifying passivity in relation to the preoedipal mother perceived as dangerously malignant, malicious, and all-powerful, arousing sensations of awe and the uncanny. The development of a perversion is a miscarried repair of this injury, basically through dehumanization of the body and the construction of three core fantasies designed to undo the intolerable sense of helpless passivity. Stoller and Khan have taught us about dehumanization in perversion and its relation to fetishism, and I will briefly elaborate their themes. Dehumanization is the ultimate strategy against the fears of human qualities—it protects against the vulnerability of loving, against the possibility of human unpredictability, and against the sense of powerlessness and passivity in comparison to other humans. In every perversion there is the interposition of a nonhuman quality in the otherwise human loving relationship; this may be a fetish object, a rigid routine not subject to emotional influence, or a demonstration of the inhumanity of the seemingly human. The hostility that Stoller correctly identifies as a core of perversion is an aid to the maintenance of dehumanization, not its cause. All attempts to abolish difference—whether of gender, physical size, maturational level, developmental level, power and control, and so on—have dehumanization, the absence of individuation, as one of their goals and consequences.

The attempt to dehumanize is carried out through the use of three specific fantasies. Regardless of which perverse role is adopted in action or conscious fantasy, the perversion is always a result of mixtures of three key unconscious fantasies constructed in the perverse defense against fears of passivity when confronted with maternal malevolence. These fantasies are all efforts to deny the experience of being the helpless, needy baby at the mercy of a frustrating, cruel mother. First fantasy: "I need not be frightened because my mother is really nonexistent; that is, she is dead or mechanical, and I am in complete control." Second fantasy: "I need not be frightened because I am beyond being controlled by my malicious mother because I am myself nonhuman—that is, dead and unable to feel pain—or less than human, a slave who can only be acted upon rather than act." And third: "I triumph and am in total control because no matter what cruelty my squashing, castrating, gigantic monster mother-creature visits upon me, I can extract pleasure from it, and therefore she (it) is doing my bidding." Differing mixtures of these three unconscious fantasies account for different presentations, but they are always present in perversion. They erase passivity by denying human maternal control of oneself as human, by defensively converting active to passive, and by extracting pleasure out of being controlled. These three fantasies deny that mother has hurt or can hurt the child. In effect the infant says, "(1) She doesn't exist, (2) I don't exist, (3) I force her—now a nonhuman 'it'—to give me pleasure." Regardless of whether sexual pleasure is consciously an aspect of the activity and regardless of the prominence of the fetish object, the perversion dynamic is in action whenever the body is treated as not human and mixtures of these three fantasies are present. I will illustrate these themes with two examples from fiction.

The Secret History of the Lord of Musashi by Tanizaki (1982), an eminent contemporary Japanese writer, provides a vivid and deep description of the development of a perversion.* At the age of six, young Lord Musashi was sent as a hostage to the home of a superior lord who brought him up, part prisoner, part noble. When he was twelve, the castle in which he lived was under siege, and though he was too young to be involved in the battle, he was emotionally caught up in it. Young Musashi is befriended by an older woman who says that she has been close to battle, and she agrees to permit him secretly to view how the women attend to the enemy heads taken in battle. The women's nightly task after the day of battle is "dressing" the heads—cleaning them, arranging the hair, touching up the dye on the teeth, applying some light cosmetic to make the heads presentable, and generally making them look as if they were alive. The primal scene aspects of Musashi's curiosity are powerfully conveyed as the author describes how, while the castle sleeps, he and the woman creep silently through the dark chambers: the woman leading him "no longer looked like the refined, warmhearted matron that he was used to seeing by daylight. The deep shadows in her sunken flesh gave her the haggard look of a demon mask. . . . The night light made . . . the old woman's face so unearthly" (22). He is terrified. He is then led to the room where the women are working. Musashi "riveted his eyes on the most terrifying objects in the room, determined to let nothing frighten him. . . . The heads themselves did not make a strong impression, but the contrast between the heads and the three women awakened a strange excitement in him. Compared to the pallor of the lifeless heads, the women's hands and fingers looked strangely vital, white, and voluptuous. . . . They worked mechanically and impassively, their faces as cold and unfeeling as stone. But somehow their impassivity was different from that of the heads. The one was hideous, the other sublime" (23–24). The fantasy of the female with total power, handling the passive dead male head, the fetishistic object, becomes exciting. Beauty equals cruelty. He finds it all "alluring" (25).

* I am indebted to Dr. Theodore Shapiro for telling me about this book.

The youngest of the three women—she is fifteen or sixteen—is described as having a natural charm; "as she gazed at a head an unconscious smile would play about her lips. It was this smile that attracted [Musashi] to her. At such moments, a guileless cruelty showed in her face. And her hands were more supple, more graceful. . . . To [Musashi] she was irresistibly beautiful" (25). Musashi realizes "he had witnessed an extraordinary scene. . . . To a boy of twelve, it must have seemed that a separate, hidden world had unfolded before him for a moment and then abruptly disappeared" (26). The next day he is not certain that it was not all a dream, but he cannot free himself of the images of the night, and he feels himself falling in love with the young woman. "Hers was a bewitching beauty, spiced with the bitterness of cruelty." He "envied the head placed before the beautiful girl. He was jealous. . . . He wanted to be killed, transformed into a ghastly head with an agonized expression, and manipulated in the girl's hands. Becoming a severed head was a necessary condition. He found no pleasure in imagining himself alive at her side; but if he could become such a head and be set before her in all her charm, how happy he would be!" (30). This is obviously the core of perversion—to become the passive, manipulated, dead, and deformed object of the malicious female.

As he discovers these feelings in himself he realizes that something diseased and malignant is going on in him; contrary to his outward boldness, bravery, and aggression, he has discovered his inner passivity in the identification with the mutilated, dead object of his passion. These strange feelings reach a climax on the third night of watching, when the girl he is in love with has before her the head of a young samurai whose nose has been cut off, a so-called woman-head. "As a result the face was uglier and more comical than those of ordinary ugly men. The girl . . . as she always did, gazed at the center of the face where the nose should have been and smiled. Juxtaposed with the mutilated head, the girl's face glowed with pride and joy of the living, the embodiment of flawless beauty and her smile, precisely because it was so girlish and unaffected, now appeared to be brimming with the most cynical malice and provided the boy with a wheel on which to spin endless fantasies. . . . The fantasies it inspired were inexhaustible and before he was aware of it had lured his soul away to a land of ambrosial dreams where he himself had become this noseless head and was living with the girl in a world inhabited only by the two of them" (33). The double castration and the sense of womanly malevolence arouse him to heights of masochistic pleasure.

Thinking to please the girl, and wishing to again have the pleasure of watching her with a "woman-head," he tries to capture one himself but is unable to sever the head of his enemy, managing only to sever the nose, which he carries around with him, not knowing why. The "secret paradise" of his perversion has been discovered (54).

Later, as a young samurai, Musashi learns that the wife of his lord is the daughter of the man whose nose he cut off. She believes the deed was done by her husband and has asked an admirer of hers to cut off her husband's nose as a humiliating vengeance. Musashi, discovering a woman with such capacity for cruelty, falls instantly in love with her. Her husband, comically, is bit by bit deformed by partial castrations—the loss of an ear and of a part of his lip as a result of arrow wounds from the eager-to-please suitor, who keeps just missing his target, the nose. Musashi establishes forbidden contact with his love by hiding in the shit pit of her toilet, climbing in through that tunnel to her room. The anality of perversion is made literal. Musashi plots with her to cut off her husband's nose, since he is eager to see another noseless head beside the woman, and he accomplishes this deed. The full-fledged perversion that emerges later involves Musashi's need to threaten violent castration (cutting off the nose) of a man in order to achieve arousal. But the author makes clear that the aggression masks the masochistic identification with the castrated object. His secret desire is to be the victim of the woman's cruelty. "His secret desire is to see the noseless husband beside his incomparably beautiful wife" (101).

The novel contains all the elements of the development of a perversion: parental abandonment, exposure to violence during childhood or adolescence and reexposure as a young adult, confirmation of the fantasies of the cruelty of women, a lost struggle against his own castration fears and terror of passivity, the equation of beauty with lust and cruelty, and the inability to maintain a sexual self-representation apart from the representation of the male as the victim of female cruelty. Incidentally, I find that this is the case in all sadistic perversions. In sadistic perversion, the perverse sadistic humiliating act conceals the underlying masochistic identification. All three of the fantasies I described—mother is not human, I am not human, I enjoy torture—are illustrated in Musashi's perversion. The female is demonic, the man is a fetish object, and being tortured by the demonic mother is an exquisite pleasure. These fantasies are the bedrock out of which the perversion is formed. This novel portrays the child's awe of the mysteries of mother and the arousal of the sense of both beauty and the uncanny, what Freud described as "that class of the terrifying which leads back to what is known of old and long familiar to us" in the perverse. The experience of awe and the uncanny, so common in perversion, is, of course, part of the construction of art and literature, and its exploration is one of the paths Freud alluded to when he spoke of the perverse as the stimulus for our virtues. Beautiful objects are perhaps created in part to allay the fear of passivity—the object of art is not alive. But that is another topic.

The Piano Teacher, a novel by Elfrieda Jelinek ([1983] 1988) illustrates some of the differences between male and female perversion. Erica Kohut, a thirty-five-year-old piano teacher who failed to make it as a concert pianist, is totally and hopelessly enmeshed in her dependency on and rage against a ferociously intrusive narcissistic controlling mother. She is friendless and sexless but harbors secret fantasies. Periodically she buys extravagant, wildly colored outfits that she doesn't wear; many nights she walks in the park observing and disturbing sexual couples, and she participates in a peep show along with the male voyeurs. She is secretly exhibitionistic, overtly voyeuristic. She is also a secret cutter. "She sits alone in her room. . . . She gingerly tests the edge; it is razor sharp. Then she presses the blade into the back of her hand several times but not so deep as to injure tendons. It doesn't hurt at all. The metal slices her hand like butter. . . . She makes a total of four cuts. That's enough, otherwise she'll bleed to death" (43). Erica is frigid, feels nothing sexually. Her life is dedicated to appearing superior and sabotaging those of her students who might be successful. She places broken glass in the coat pocket of a young woman flutist who shows great promise, is the pride of the school, and is about to give a recital. When the young musician puts her hand in her pocket, she is badly cut and unable to perform. Erica, incidentally, breaks the glass while she is in the toilet, again the anal theme. The hatred motivating Erica to such perverse violence is, it is clear, the consequence of her inability to separate herself from the feeling of total control by her mother. "Her mother demands obedience. If you take a risk, you perish. That advice comes from mother too. When she is home alone she cuts herself, slicing off her nose to spite other people's faces. . . . She sits down in front of the magnifying side of the shaving mirror, spreading her legs, she makes a cut, magnifying the aperture that is the doorway into her body. She knows from experience that such a razor cut doesn't hurt. . . . Her hobby is cutting her own body" (86).

A young student of hers, a narcissistic body builder, forms a plan to seduce her, and she becomes interested. She sends him a letter telling him what he must do in order to possess her. The letter is an elaborate, detailed, obsessive description of the forms of bondage and beating and torture that she wants him to put her through, including when and at what commands he is to perform which acts. He is completely repelled by her assuming control over his seduction and is made impotent by her demand-ingness and provocation. Their mutual perversions finally take the form of rape. He, to recover his potency, becomes enraged and beats her, breaking her nose and ribs, bloodying her, and penetrating her with a triumphant erection. She, in response to the rape, is briefly angry, takes her razor to pursue him, and ends up cutting herself again, somewhat depersonalized.

In this novel, issues of conquest and control have totally replaced anything resembling human love, and perversion is one aspect of the heroine's pathology. We have here a different arrangement of the core fantasies. Never having separated from mother, she manages to avoid total passivity by hating all living creatures, manifested partly in her self-mutilation, and dehumanizing her mother and herself. Still merged with the mother, she proves by a single act—cutting without feeling—that both mother and child are nonhuman. Remnants of sexuality are used defiantly, and the masochistic pleasure she pleads for from her would-be lover is denied her in the form that she demands—with herself in control of her victimization—and is instead carried out with herself totally pas-sive. One might note that in both novels, the perverted characters are concerned with beauty—Erica is a serious musician, although we never learn that she has been moved by music.

The differences between Lord Musashi and Erica Kohut lead us to a difficult theme—the male-female differences in perversion. Most authors who have written about perversions seem agreed that "the leading theme of the neosexual plot is invariably castration" (see McDougall 1985, 252).

In an earlier paper, "What Men Fear: The Façade of Castration Anxiety," I noted that the seemingly central role of castration anxiety in male character and symptom formation most often disguises underlying preoedipal anxieties of the loss of narcissistic well-being, as represented in feelings of safety, adaptive organization, and continuing attachment to mother (Fogel, Lane, and Liebert 1986). Castration anxiety, I tried to demonstrate, represents an escape to a cognitively more organized fear—fear of the loss of a body part—that displaces an unbearable tension of annihilation or disorganization. Person has emphasized that before castration anxiety appears, the boy's inability to secure his mother's love and prove adequate to her are predisposing narcissistic traumas that heighten later castration anxiety (1986, 20). It is McDougall's view also that the evils of maternal attachment are condensed in the castration anxiety involved in perversion, and she emphasizes the narcissistic as well as libidinal trauma in perversion.

The assumption that castration anxiety is a façade may help us understand why women seem less involved or at least less overtly involved in sexually perverse activities. In the absence of the direct symbolic castrative object, as embodied in the creation of the fetish, women's perversions take more subtle forms. Although women are not usually accused of perverse exhibitionism, much of women's fashion and the peek-a-boo game that is played with the breast are, for certain women, an opportunity to enact a female version of the "flasher." It may be that it is women's perversions, not their superegos, as Freud thought, that lack crispness and definition because of their attenuated castration anxiety. The perverse exhibiting woman uses her capacity to excite a male by the sight of her breast or body to overcome her own sense of smallness and unfemininity compared to her mother, as well as to demonstrate the greater power of her breast or whole body compared to the male penis. The sexual excitement she experiences in this triumph involves dehumanization of her own body and the male's and murder of the mother. The fetishistic object is not a phallus but a breast. In fact, one can raise the question whether fantasies of the huge breast do not underlie the fantasies of the phallus in fetishism. A homosexual patient described that he would much rather caress a man's penis than a woman's breast because the penis was larger. When asked to describe how he was conducting his measurements, he explained that he was comparing the nipple of the breast to the entire penis, a clear denial of the full breast. Another homosexual male speaks of his requirement that his pick-up partner have "perfect good looks, be like a perfect meal or a great wine." The oral reference is not accidental.

We also are quite unknowing, I believe, of the extent of female perverse activity. Late-night television and dirty-talk telephone numbers indicate that some women seem quite eager to tease men with their exhibitionistic activities. The classic striptease represents an exhibitionistic frustration and the teasing, not the gratification, of male voyeurism. Intermittent homosexual relations are carried out by women far more casually than by men, and vibrators and dildos are common apparatuses of many female sex lives. Many women reveal during the course of an analysis that they routinely check men's crotches, becoming aroused by looking at the outline of the genitals. Adolescent girls, however, seem not to spend the hundreds of hours that adolescent boys devote to trying to glimpse the mysterious forbidden body of the opposite sex. Numbers of normally functioning women periodically prefer intercourse tied spread-eagle to the bed or wish to be slapped on the buttocks. Some of the recent sex scandals that have emerged in nursery schools indicate that women also seem involved in a variety of pedophiliac activities. Which of these activities should be considered perverse is answerable only by knowing the extent to which they dehumanize actual relationships. Although female perversion is certainly present, it may be quantitatively less of an issue either because of the constancy of gender identification, as Stoller has indicated, or because of the greater difficulty the male experiences in gender-role establishment.

The point I want to stress is that female perversion may show less fetishistic focus and clearer central emphasis on struggles over passivity and control. Women are perhaps at less risk for the violent terrors the boy experiences as he realizes his need to establish masculinity. The female inability to separate from the mother is the entirety of the rage, whereas

for the male that rage is compounded by the need for male gender definition in face of the awe and wonder excited by the sense of the mother as
different, alien, as well as proof of the reality of castration. Much of the
history of Western culture and religion includes the relentless effort of the
male to tame, control, and demystify the female to relieve his anxiety.

Finally, I want to stress the difference between perversion as play within
the culture and perversion as pathology. As play, perversion carries into
life some of the spice of the forbidden, the mysterious, and the dangerous
in forms allowed by society although not always recognized as perverse.
Freud took it for granted that remnants of infantile sexuality can always
be found in adult life, and we would surely consider that ordinary rather
than pathological. I take it for granted that each of us has secrets, that
some secrets relate to the perverse, and that they help provide us with
individual boundaries and identity. The question is never whether but
how much.

Fashion provides one example of perversion as play, creeping into the
forms of daily life. Transvestism, a recognized paraphilia in the *Diagnostic Manual,* has clearly been a major theme of fashion and of rock
musicians in recent years. This play with sexual ambiguity, combined with
a spirit of aggression and potential violence, fits very well into the scheme
of the perverse attempt to erase difference and to dehumanize. Similarly,
the popularity of films like *Blue Velvet* or *The Night Porter* demonstrates
that the ordinary citizen is pleased to have a chance to play with perversion and enjoy its forbidden fruits without having to be perverse. Reading
or viewing porn is another instance of playing with perversion, and the
apparently common practice of couples using porn movies on the VCR to
assist in increasing sexual excitement can also be considered the playful
use of perversion. In these senses we may view our society as dedicated to
playing with perversion. But, we may not be different from other societies in the past. From the point of view, for example, of the exhibitionistic need to show something and the voyeuristic need to be frustrated
in the desire to see something, it probably matters little whether the game
is being played with an ankle or a breast or the genitalia.

The severe inhibition of these forms of play—the inability to engage
in the touchings and suckings and odd kissings of foreplay, or the inability

to tolerate perverse play in society—is another outcome of conflict over perversion. Individuals in whom the shame and disgust needed to over-come perverse impulses are so overwhelming that they are forced to regard the body as humanly unacceptable and beyond human play are thereby paradoxically succumbing to the perverse need to dehumanize.

In between play with perversion and obligatory perversion we can place the facultative, or occasional, pervert. The majority of perverse individuals, which may be the majority of people, feel the pressure for perverse action primarily when there is an additional stress to their nar-cissistic well-being. Beginning a creative work, preparing for an examina-tion, being away from home and spouse, are typical occasions for per-verse actions—masturbation with pornographic movies or magazines, calls to porn hotlines, visits to homosexual bars, dealings with prostitutes. Some men report compulsive masturbation after seemingly satisfying sex with their wives; some others report that their sex lives are entirely satisfactory—provided that there is no demand on them for any kind of tender or affectionate interaction, or provided that the routine never changes. In all these instances, fears of ultimate passivity are aroused by the task or by the absence of a supporting selfobject or by the evidence of the woman as independent, with a capacity to make demands and to have her own feelings. These perverse acts deny the woman's existence and the man's need for her. Again, these acts seem more prevalent among men than women, but we may know less about the female versions.

Perversion has become somewhat like masochism and narcissism in that the term needs to be described in each usage if we are to understand each other. I have stressed the common psychological mechanism at work in all those situations in which, however briefly, the body is dehumanized and in which mixtures of three defensive fantasies—mother is not human, I am not human, and I enjoy victimization—are constructed in the effort to avoid the fear of infantile passivity. I have taken a dimension-al rather than a categorical view of perversion. Within that broad spec-trum it remains important to specify our quantitative differences. As with all aspects of character, playing games with perverse mechanisms, stop-ping short of serious damage to the object or the relationship, needs to be sharply distinguished from malignant sexual perversions that destroy the object. A quantitative assessment of the extent of perverse encroachment on all aspects of character function is essential. The overt obligatory pervert is hugely different from the playful pervert, but realizing what they have in common will help analysts both to better understand and empathize with the severely ill pervert and to recognize the amount of perverse activity in everyday lives. At certain points quantitative differences lead to qualitative distinctions, and we need different names for the different activities; but my aim, at this moment, is to stress the psychodynamic commonality of our perverse activities.

The perversion dynamic is present whenever an action or fantasy is dominated by the denial of unconscious passivity through the triple fantasies of dehumanizing the object, dehumanizing the self, and securing masochistic pleasure. This dynamic is universal, with huge and important quantitative differences in individuals and in the same individual in different circumstances. Differences between male and female perversion may reside in the diminished awe and castration anxiety experienced by the female in gender definition and separation-individuation. Understanding the ubiquity of perversion ought to help analysts empathize with very damaged perverse patients and to understand the role in everyday life of the perverse aspects of our psychic structures.

References

Arlow, J. 1971. "Character Perversion." In *Currents in Psychoanalysis,* ed. I. Marcus. New York: International Universities Press, 317–36.

Brown, N. O. 1959. *Life against Death.* Middletown, Conn.: Wesleyan University Press.

Chasseguet-Smirgel, J. 1984. *Creativity and Perversion.* New York: W. W. Norton.

Fogel, G.; Lane, M.; and Liebert, R. S., eds. 1986. *The Psychology of Men: New Psychoanalytic Perspectives.* New York: Basic Books.

Freud, S. [1905] 1953. "Three Essays on the Theory of Sexuality." In *Standard Edition,* 7:125–245.

———. [1908] 1959. "'Civilized' Sexual Morality and Modern Nervous Illness." In *Standard Edition,* 9:181–204.

Jelinek, E. [1983] 1988. *The Piano Teacher.* New York: Weidenfeld and Nicolson. English translation.

Khan, M. M. R. 1979. *Alienation in Perversions*. New York: International Universities Press.

Laplanche, J., and Pontalis, J.-B. [1967] 1973. *The Language of Psychoanalysis*. New York: Norton. English translation.

McDougall, J. 1985. *Theaters of the Mind: Illusion and Truth on the Psychoanalytic Stage*. New York: Basic Books.

Ovesey, L., and Person, E. 1976. "Transvestism: A Disorder of the Self." *International Journal of Psychoanalytic Psychotherapy* 5:219–36.

Person, E. 1986. "Male Sexuality and Power." *Psychoanalytic Inquiry* 6:3–25.

Person, E., and Ovesey, L. 1983. "Psychoanalytic Theories of Gender Identity." *Journal of the American Academy of Psychoanalysis* 11:203–26.

Stoller, R. J. 1974. "Hostility and Mystery in Perversion." *International Journal of Psychoanalysis* 55:425–34.

Tanizaki, J. 1982. *The Secret History of the Lord of Musashi*. Putnam, N.Y.: Wideview/Perigee.

Chapter Two

The Term *Perversion*

Robert J. Stoller, M.D.

T HE first thesis is this: what are called "the perversions" are not entities but simply behaviors in which all kinds of folks indulge. Let me take that idea apart.

We need a vocabulary exercise: consider the terms *perversion, aberration, variant, diagnosis, syndrome, sin. Perversion* is not a well-received word any more; educated laypeople bristle at its pejorativeness, and many professionals, also alert to the name-calling, have long looked for a kinder, more objective terminology: *aberration, deviation, variant, paraphilia.* One rarely sees or hears the word now outside of psychoanalytic or religious circles, and analysts have—sometimes with justification—been accused of hiding their prejudices therein. I, however, with the idea that hostility in some form and degree is present in perversions, feel that the very opprobrium in which *perversion* soaks expresses a dynamic essential for those enjoying these aberrant erotic excitements. (That I suspect there are no nonaberrant excitements, once one finds people's fantasies, I have discussed elsewhere [1975, 1979, 1985a].)

Here (with a few details changed) is a quote from my earlier work that still pretty much represents my sense of *perversion* and some of the words associated with it:

> By *aberration* I mean an erotic technique or constellation of techniques that one uses as his or her complete sexual act and that differs from his or her culture's traditional, avowed definition of normality. Sexual aberrations can be divided into two classes: variants (deviations) and perversions.
>
> By *variant* I mean an aberration that is not primarily the staging of forbidden fantasies, especially fantasies of harming others. Examples would be behavior set off by prenatal hormones; abnormal brain activity, as with a tumor, experimental drug, or electrical impulse from an implanted electrode; an aberrant act that one is driven to *faute de mieux;* or sexual experiments one does from curiosity and finds not exciting enough to repeat.
>
> *Perversion,* the erotic form of hatred,* is a fantasy, usually acted out but occasionally restricted to a daydream (either self-produced or packaged by others—that is, pornography). It is a habitual, preferred aberration necessary for one's full satisfaction, primarily motivated by hostility. By *hostility* I mean a state in which one wishes to harm an object; that differentiates it from *aggression,* which often implies only forcefulness. The hostility in perversion takes form in a fantasy of revenge hidden in the actions that make up the perversion and serves to convert childhood trauma to adult triumph. To create the greatest excitement, the perversion must also portray itself as an act of risk taking. (Stoller 1975, 1985a)

In other words, *sin.* That is, the excitement comes from an awareness—conscious or unconscious—that one is harming, *needs* to harm, *wants* to harm. More precisely, the harm done is an act of humiliating in revenge for one's having been humiliated.

The second issue: are perversions clear-cut diagnoses whose practitioners look much the same clinically, express the same dynamics, and

---

* I now feel that *hatred* is not quite the right word here. Though the conscious experience may be hatred (e.g., in rape), it usually is not (e.g., in exhibitionism, fetishism). The unconscious affect nonetheless is, I think, hatred or rage.

emerge from the same etiologic factors?* No. I do not think psychoanalysts even know enough yet to correctly label them "syndrome"; they are, rather, complex behaviors, no more worthy of classification than such conditions as suicidal behavior; dislike of zucchini; being a composer, a circus clown, a student, a chiropractor's patient, a goldfish swallower; or the desire to be a psychoanalyst. No doubt these just-named states have their etiologies, dynamics, and phenomenology; but no two zucchini haters need have much in common beyond gagging. Simply put and obvious: "we cannot really classify behavior" (Foucault 1982–83).

I used to have no question that, say, transvestism was a diagnosis and then, on my becoming more sophisticated, that it was at least a syndrome (a constellation of related signs and symptoms). And the same holds true for homosexuality, fetishism, pedophilia, sadomasochism, and others. Having now talked with lots of people with these propensities—sometimes for years, and sometimes in treatment—I no longer see these states as any more homogeneous than, say, voyeurism, frotteurism, zoophilia, coprophilia, klismaphilia. (Why are our colleagues not embarrassed to aspire to science with such dreadful Greek/Latin/French neologisms? *Mysophilia!*)

This nonhomogeneity is apparent when we know that a person with a particular perverse desire may have other perverse desires. For instance, a fetishistic cross-dresser who enjoys being enchained while at the same time hanging himself may also be borderline, depressive, compulsive; on Fridays he may rob banks and buy a week's supply of crack; he may vote Libertarian, weigh three hundred pounds, have intercourse only with his wife and always, to her distress, in the missionary position, and love his five cats and his motorcycle.

Foucault quotes Borges pretending to quote "a 'certain Chinese encyclopedia' in which it is written that 'animals are divided into: (a) belonging to the Emperor, (b) embalmed, (c) tame, (d) sucking [*sic*] pigs, (e) sirens, (f) fabulous, (g) stray dogs, (h) included in the present classification, (i) frenzied, (j) innumerable, (k) drawn with a very fine camelhair

---

* These three criteria are necessary in the rest of medicine if one is to speak of "diagnosis" (Goldman 1973).

brush, (l) *et cetera,* (m) having just broken the water pitcher, (n) that from a long way off look like flies.' In the wonderment of this taxonomy, the thing we apprehend in one great leap, the thing that, by means of the fable, is demonstrated as the exotic charm of another system of thought, is the limitation of our own, the stark impossibility of thinking *that*" (1970, xv).* To attempt to classify people's personalities, including their erotic desires, is a hopeless job (and lends itself to instantaneous trial and conviction); analysts should, rather, settle for descriptions (Colby and Spar 1983) even if, thereby, they seem less wise.

Nonetheless, the experts have for decades written as if each perversion is a homogeneous state. When, for instance, we read about homosexuality, we are told about "the homosexual," as if homosexuals are all the same—for example, "prepsychotic" or "prenarcissistic." We are then presented with a theory that accounts for all homosexuality, as if there were such a *thing* as homosexuality, rather than—more simply and more accurately—innumerable homosexual behaviors, each different in appearance, structure, and origins. (I am dramatizing a bit here, for I do know that no one is totally different from everyone else and that sometimes similar behaviors have *some* similar origins.)

Recently, I have been talking with consensual sadomasochists. No one of them is very much like another except in their powerful commitment to getting erotic pleasure from giving or receiving pain. In their professions, hobbies, personality structures, empathy toward others, preferences in eating, television viewing, interest in sports, reading, clothes, optimism or pessimism, susceptibility to cigarette ads, insight into human behavior, use of recreational drugs, and psychiatric symptomatology—in short, in any behavior and desire that reflects underlying character structure—they differ. They say that, except for their erotic compatibilities, they may have little in common with their erotic partners. Given such immense differences, we shall not allege, via our "diagnoses," that these people are really much the same, that they are governed by the same dynamics coming out of the same early childhood experiences, condition-

---

* Colby and Spar (1983) found this directly in Borges (in slightly different form). It is worth repeating, I think.

ing experiences, synaptic chemistry, genes, or evolutionary ancestry. To claim they are greases the slide to prejudice: all Frenchmen are (or do) the same, all Chinese, all blacks, all psychiatrists, all cops, all women.

A colleague and I once tried to devise a final examination for a clerkship in psychiatry. The following technique was used:

> In order to provide a standardized representation of an evaluative interview with emotionally ill patients, spontaneous 30-minute psychiatric interviews were filmed so that the viewer sees the patient from the perspective of the interviewing psychiatrist. Then, hundreds of statements from the psychiatric domain were collected that would permit the clinical description of various patients with any type of psychopathology and which would cover all conceivable (and some inconceivable) areas that experts would consider when confronted by patients in a clinical situation.
>
> In using expert opinion to select a criterion, a group of psychiatrist-experts (usually the course instructors in the case of examination construction) were shown a filmed interview and asked to rate each of the statements as to its appropriateness in regard to the patient shown. A scale ranging from 0 to 5 was used to represent six degrees of appropriateness. Only those items on which the experts evidenced substantial agreement were retained for the examination procedure. An average of the experts' ratings on each of these items determined the criterion array of ratings.
>
> In the examination situation the students view the film and rate the patient on all the items agreed on by the experts. Each student's array of ratings is correlated with the criterion array to produce a single score which reflects the amount of agreement between the student's ratings and the criterion. (Stoller and Geertsma 1963, 58)

We stumbled unhappily—it wrecked the project—on the fact that the psychiatrists did not agree with each other on much of anything, clinically or theoretically. And this regardless of their years of experience, training, or type of practice (such as psychoanalysis or "eclectic").

This position is not nihilistic—that nothing is known, nothing is true, no theory helps, no treatment works. I am, instead, simply saying that when analysts have little or no evidence, they do best, regarding theory making, to tread lightly, and when they recognize the low quality of their evidence, they should go out and collect better, as many are well prepared to do.

It is also wrong to conclude that I believe the erotic behaviors I study are no more than "variants" or "alternate life-styles." Given the connotations and political implications of those phrases—they are not the representations of objectivity that they seem—I want to make clear my viewpoint: when the psychoanalyst gets into people's heads and they allow him access to their fantasies, it is apparent to him that all erotic desires are aberrant. Analysts should not legislate (diagnose) on the basis of the engaged anatomy or the positions taken during an act but rather on the basis of what the behaviors mean to the actors.

To bear down, then, on the business of classification and the meaning of the word *diagnosis* is not pedantry; rather, it has broad implications regarding research on etiology, recommendations for treatment, prognostications, questions about the structure of mind, and social issues relating to ethics and laws in dealing with the perversions. If correct, this position undercuts a lot of psychoanalytic and social theory, leaving us without much comfort. But is it not an advantage to remove surety and to replace it by that state of reality testing known as ignorance?

The situation, then, is not hopeless or, at any rate, is not hopeless as long as one admits the problem.

Uses of the Term *Normal*

I think I am in agreement with Freud—which can make one feel good but should never be used to win arguments—that psychoanalysts should know better than to use the word *normal* to describe any piece of behavior, for once the underlying structure of the behavior (its dynamics, fantasies) is determined, *normal* has no meaning. Yet, in discussions on perversion, analysts use that wondrous group of people labeled "the normal" as the fixed point against which all others are measured. That will not do as a description of either a person-as-a-whole or an aspect of a person, such as erotic behavior.

Where is that normal person or aspect? No analyst has ever recorded such a case, met one as a patient, known one in oneself, one's loves, one's relatives, one's friends, one's colleagues. I need not elaborate this point; it is obvious, universally known, and usually denied, especially by psychoanalytic theorists of perversion. Without that guidon—"the normal"—around which analysts wheel their parade, the moralizing hidden in the pseudoscientific jargon would be exposed. For *normal* in psychoanalytic theory usually, if not always, means "virtuous."* (In the same way, for theologians *normal* means "good," "without sin": observing God's natural laws; and for biologists it means "healthy": observing Nature's laws.) Hidden in the phrase "the normal" can be, then, arrogance, defensiveness, cruelty, and dishonesty.

If one feels that development from birth on is not completely controlled by prenatal hard-wiring; if one feels that development is an accomplishment that requires dealing with trauma, frustration, and conflict; if one feels that defense mechanisms are inevitably created in development; if one feels that the family and society at large must thwart the infant/child's desires, then "normal" must give way to "normative,"—that is, to "norms." And norms are not normals; they are arithmetic, statistics. Let us, then, forgo such coercive phrases—discussion killers—as "the normal heterosexual," "in the normal case," "normal sexual arousal," "society's normal standards," and such like-functioning coercions as "natural" (as in "natural tendency"), "healthy" (as in "healthy drives"), "ordinary" (as in "ordinary unperverted desire"), or "genuine" (as in "genuinely erotic").

"Perversion Is Fundamentally Unsatisfying"

This maxim, often repeated in the literature, is supposed to be a scientific statement—that is, a summary of observed, uncontaminated experience. It is not. (Once one is alert to my suggestion that psychoanalysis is a morality procedure, one's skepticism about its objectivity, its scientific stance, increases.) In the first place, outside of their private experience,

* Psychoanalysis is a moral order trying to transform itself into an amoral order—i.e., a science. For instance, the bottom line of analytic treatment—the alleged source of theory—is a moral percept; *thou shalt speak thy mind.* And if failure to do so does not cause friction—e.g., guilt, resistance—there is no analysis.

analysts do not make direct observations on people's erotic doings. Second, even if, like Masters and Johnson, they watched the anatomy quiver, they would not be measuring degrees of pleasure, which is a purely subjective state. Third, *pleasure* is a complex word: one needs to hear from its user what sense of the word is meant in any sentence. (For instance, some women report that clitoral masturbation is, for them, very intense and highly pleasurable locally but not as satisfying as when accompanied by the less focused and intense penis-in-vagina.) Fourth, there is no laboratory or instrumentation for measuring degrees of pleasure. Fifth, patients' reports to their analysts are subject to change at the next telling; the reports may not be reliable. Sixth, what analysts report— for instance, in publications—are not scientific data; they are only hearsay or worse, sometimes not even the truth as the analyst experienced it. Seventh, many of the descriptions given by patients of their erotic pleasures contradict the "perversion is fundamentally unsatisfying" accusation. These people do not make their erotic pleasures sound like descriptions of dribbling faucets, and the gleam in their eyes as they talk gives a sense of truth to their report. (The reader is, however, forewarned by items 1 to 6 above that this last statement, being hearsay, also requires a grain of salt.)

In other words, to use psychoanalytic theory to argue that perversion is erotically unsatisfying has as yet no demonstrated scientific basis (and suggests to my ungenerous mind that we analysts tend to be not only erotically suppressed but also envious).

Eighth, present your evidence that those normals you know have more erotic pleasure than do your filthy perverts.

As a way of arguing, analytic theorists often make use of pseudoquantifications by means of such words as *fundamentally, extremely, primitive, indubitably,* and *certainly.* So suppose one counters the "perversion is fundamentally unsatisfying" remark with "perversion is fundamentally satisfying"? Would you not find that fundamentally unsatisfying?

I believe that until psychoanalysts become less threatened by the pleasures perversions bring the perverse, their theories will be little more than apologia, that old synonym for *rationalization,* which is listed among the defense mechanisms.

Causes and Dynamics

Let me reduce the polemical content of this discussion and turn to the equally pleasurable subject of what starts and what maintains perversion. Such discussions should always take up—or acknowledge the inability to take up—the problem from three viewpoints: biologic, cultural, and psychodynamic (intrapsychic and interpersonal).

Biologic

I shall here only compact the common knowledge: in both gender (reviewed in Stoller 1985b) and erotic aberrations (two different though highly overlapping orders of what has been considered perversion), genetic and other constitutional factors, especially those affecting the brain, are present either as givens (for example, differences in brain organization between females and males owing to prenatal sex hormones) or as abnormal states that disrupt the givens (for example, 17 beta hydroxysteroid dehydrogenase deficiency). In addition, there is growing evidence that what are these days called the paraphilias sometimes have later-in-life biologic origins*—for instance, Kluver-Bucy syndrome (such as traumatic, postoperative, after-herpes encephalitis), epilepsy, postencephalitic Parkinson's disease, or Gilles de la Tourette syndrome (Miller et al. 1986). Still, when one thinks of the endless list of objects to which people, almost always men, become erotically attached—raincoats, dead bodies, shoes, handkerchiefs, amputees—precise biologic explanations are in most cases inconceivable: a nest of cells in the thalamus that drives an erection when one sniffs feces?

We can, nonetheless, accept the sociobiologists' idea that the effects of evolution play their part, that biology maximizes behavior leading to reproductive success and that such an evolutionary process results in anatomic, physiologic, and behavioral differences between the sexes. Perhaps this is one of the anlagen for erotic differences between men and women, such as men's propensity for fetishizing—that fundamental dynamic of perversion—in contrast to the opposite desire in women for

* And it is sensible to assume that certain anatomic areas are constitutionally more pleasure-intensive or subdued in one person than in another; libidinal zonal development contributes to erotic styles.

relationship, intimacy, and constancy. Some speculate that men's greater use of visual stimuli—voyeurism—has such roots and that the great somatic mediator for the differences, from fetal life on, is hormonal differences.

That all makes sense to me, though colleagues in sociobiology and physiology can be as flagrantly philosophic, and thereby as dogmatic, as the most imaginative psychoanalysts. (There is another, purely cultural theory worth noting: in disputing biologic and psychodynamic theories explaining why perversion is so rare in women, a woman once promised me that women will be as perverse as men when women are liberated from our patriarchal society.)

Then there is a second kind of biologic force, formed by external stimuli, for which I invented a term (1979)—*fixing*—as a stopgap, pending future research (by others, certainly not me) to describe precisely what I can only grope for here. "Fixing" is a metaphor drawn from the "fixing" that—for instance, in staining tissues—permanently changes something and stops it from further change. Imprinting in birds and fish is an example. Conditioning of organisms and even cells is another. I believe that some such processes dominate the earliest stages of creating character structure (self, identity) but are a different hard-wiring from that we inherit. Only in time (and a time very different from Kleinian time) does fantasy begin to serve as a method of adaptation/defense. In this way, postnatal hard-wiring induced by the environment is laid on the genetics/constitutional hard-wiring present at birth.

Cultural

I want to stress here—isolated from the great matrix of forces called "culture"—two factors, culture as a source of conscience* and culture as a source of suggestions to people for designing their erotic behaviors.

First, as we know, culture—at large and as it funnels idiosyncratically into the developing child from parents—shapes conscience, and individuals' consciences shape culture. So we find that in different eras and different places, what one group calls erratic another accepts as normal.

---

* After years of rumination, I have come to prefer *conscience* to *superego:* less fancy, fewer syllables, less burden of theory, no less connotations, no less useful in a sentence.

For instance, as a case different from us, among the New Guinea Sambia, an aberrant bachelor is one who does not offer his penis to be sucked by prepubescent boys (Herdt 1981). In this regard, then, one source of our sense of sin comes from cultural norms. Another example: when the medieval church accepted flagellation as a pious act, masochists had a wondrous, more or less guilt-free route to ecstasy that today's church has blocked through its knowledge of perverse masochism.

Second, I want to emphasize that culture proposes perverse erotic games (for example, via television dramas, talk shows, documentaries) for individuals; individuals propose perverse fashions to culture; and culture, on accepting these fashions, encourages (even while disapproving) individuals to try on the practices for erotic pleasure, not just as fashions. We see this process today in sadomasochism, where advertisements for clothes and alcohol exactly depict what, a few years ago, had been practices restricted to the perverse; these advertisements, then, not only encourage us to buy products but also suggest the fun of kinky sex.

Psychodynamic

Recognizing the importance of the first two causes, we can turn to the analyst's strength: how psychodynamic issues contribute to the origins of and/or the precise forms of perverse behaviors. I shall not review the analytic literature on perversions but shall only express the opinion that it is in some ways pretty weak in explaining live, pulsating people. Analysts should stick to what they know about and stop biologizing (for example, death instinct, psychic energy, cathexis) and, granting that biology has its part, stay with what they are competent to study—fantasy. Fantasy, in the form of scripts, memories, images, meanings, and the affects that give fantasies their life. I am not saying that fantasy is everything, only that analysts have access to little except fantasy. Fantasies exist; cathexes do not. When analysts are seduced into philosophizing on biology, they lose their focus on their reality—the clinical.

Let me restrict myself to listing a few of the dynamics that energize erotic pleasure. Example: I have suggested a factor that may help account for men being more perverse than women (in the sense that men, far more than women, practice most of the perverse conditions listed in the classifications, such as fetishism, transvestism, voyeurism, exhibitionism). This factor is the fantasy system I have called "symbiosis anxiety" or "merging anxiety," by which I mean that little boys must perform an act of separation from their mothers not required of little girls; they must establish within themselves a barrier against the earliest stage of wanting to stay as one with their mothers, of not being individuals separate from their mothers, and therefore of not being sure they are fully male: fear of becoming female.* Much of masculinity in all cultures is made up of manifestations of this conflict: emphasis on the phallus, fear of intimacy with women, fear of being humiliated by women, need to humiliate women (such as insulting, locker-room vocabulary), fetishizing women. A few paragraphs back, I mentioned the idea that erotic looking makes evolutionary sense. We could as well use a psychodynamic explanation (they probably synergize each other): that males' greater voyeurism than females' is due to males needing to preserve a distance between their bodies/selves and their mothers. This distance would then be closed by the less intimate (and thereby more fiercely focused) technique of looking.

Another example is this process: "I am humiliated; I discover revenge; I humiliate; I have mastered the past." Think of male pornography, fantasy as script. It is a daydream in which, overtly and covertly, is found an element of humiliation (Stoller 1985a).

These above, then, are two examples of mastery, the generic for the process that, unending from birth on, surmounts the pain of trauma, frustration, conflict, sense of inferiority. And *mastery* is a word that covers beliefs, expectations, desires—fantasies. When using terms such as *mastery, humiliation, childhood trauma, conflict, separation, merging, mother, father, self, defense, ambivalence, excitement, sublimation, feeling, meaning, wish, rage, harm, joy, love, friendship, anxiety,* or any others that stand for experienced subjective states, analysts are referring either to fantasies (beliefs, expectations, memories) or to psychic events

---

* Stern's fine work (1985) is, I think, flawed here. Just because infants are hard-wired to have more reality-focused moments than had been realized, these episodes of alertness—perhaps related to Glover's "ego nuclei," examined in several papers (1956)—are not a sense of self. That individuation process takes many months. Infants have consciousness, which does not mean they as yet know themselves as separate and distinct from mother.

that are made up of and, simultaneously, are responses (desires, affects) to fantasies.

As the years have passed, I have been found by an etiologic factor that did not at first catch my attention: highly unexpected reality experiences (such as trauma) in infancy and childhood, where one sees how the perversion, like the pearl surrounding the grain of sand, grows, by sensual pleasure, out of mastery of otherwise unbearable distress.* I now believe that this idea can be treated as a hypothesis, a testable theory. To the extent tests confirm the hunch, analysts are relieved of some of the problem of choice of neurosis (less at the mercy of filling gaps in knowledge by jargon).

Finding that erotic behavior is partly a response to external events (not just to intrapsychic fantasies) in infancy and childhood does not mean that analysts must abandon Freud's description of the part played by fantasy—intrapsychic elaboration—in development. Freud, properly, gave up the idea that all neurotics (his word, I think, for "everyone") have actually been afflicted by incest, but his doing so need not keep us from looking for other external noxious events. One reason that I like the hypothesis is one of its subhypotheses: in *everyone's* erotic excitement, not just those called perverse, can be found the grain(s) of sand. That metaphor—"grain"—is, in the real world, a powerful (but not necessarily noisy) event/situation in infancy or childhood (which is not to say that erotic development stops at that early time). I am often able to show this by studying people's favorite pornography, which invariably has, overtly or covertly, a humiliating event imbedded in the script (Stoller 1985a).

The trauma hypothesis is no news to most nonpsychoanalytic investigators. By now, it is common knowledge that battered children grow up to be battering parents, that pedophiles were sexually molested boys, that female prostitutes were often used incestuously, and that serial rapists were often victims of forced or exploitive erotic abuse in boyhood.† I

* Or, in the case of primary transsexualism, mother's obsession with preventing distress (Stoller 1968, 1975, 1985b).

† Even "somatization disorder," a piece of what was formerly called "hysteria": "The one childhood experience that clearly distinguished patients with somatization dis-

have studied transvestites who were put into females' clothes as children and severe sadomasochists who were fiercely traumatized by medical procedures in infancy and childhood. But the hypothesis is too simplistic as it stands—for instance, in not explaining all cases in a category or not explaining why what seems (with superficial description) to be the same trauma results in different pathologies in different people. Nor does it suggest exactly how a person lives the process of mastering trauma. Such an investigation requires *very detailed history taking,* which can be well done by means of a psychoanalysis (and nothing else yet invented).

The most visible aspect of this mastery process has been, for me, the dynamics of humiliation. I believe that except for profound traumata striking at the beginning of life, the threat of trauma is not to existence but to self, that developing—and in the small child, not yet stable—sense of identity, including gender identity ("I am a male" followed by "I am a boy"; "I am a female" followed by "I am a girl"). At a rather advanced stage of development—age two or later (Roiphe and Galenson 1981)— these traumatic humiliations are known to us in the forms of castration anxiety and penis envy.

The problem posed to the child is not only to anesthetize a humiliation but, a more brilliant outcome, to transform it into its opposite, an adventure (art, scientific discovery, erotic style, athletic competition, politics): excitement followed by pleasure.

At any rate, there are enough clues at hand that psychoanalysts can relax their clutch on high theory and turn more to demonstrable evidence of externally delivered trauma as one contribution to perversion.

Here is a puzzle with as yet no solution. The literature on the Melanesian people (primarily New Guineans) is without reports of perversions (Herdt 1989). By this, I mean that these people do not think of their fellow tribesmen as having erotic behaviors that are aberrant, and eth-

---

order from patients with primary affective disorders was [sexual] molestation" (Morrison 1989, 240; see also Bryer et al. 1987, and Burgess et al. 1987). And there are a few dozen more references one could cite. A caution: there being so many reports now on the high rate of sexual abuse of children, we could find it as a cause of any pathology. We need, therefore, close examination—analysis can do that—of individuals to sense better when a trauma is precisely linked to a later outcome.

nographers do not present such cases. Herdt recalls no such accounts of primitive people in general, not just Melanesia, nor do I.

And where his experience is definitive, among the Sambia of New Guinea, lengthy and intimate communicating with dozens of natives has not uncovered even a rumor of perverse practices. After listening to him for years and having briefly visited the Sambia, I too have no feeling that, with the exception of one man who is considered aberrant by his fellow tribesmen and homosexually perverse by our standards, there are people with perversions. No desire for cross-dressing (with or without erotic excitement), no erotic fetishism, no consensual sadomasochistic rituals, no men whose preference is rape, no perverse voyeurism, no exhibitionism, no pedophilia, and so on. I do not know how to account for it, and all theories I raise up founder after close examination. Herdt and I wonder, however, now that the tribal cultures are disappearing (as they are infected by Western customs and cargos), will perversions start appearing?

Perversion as Subversion

Calling perversion subversion says no more than that erotic desire in general has a subversive element. Which says no more than that infants must separate and individuate and, in doing so, fight overtly and covertly against the forces that would tame them: first parents, then society. Oedipal conflict is our paradigm. Nonetheless, gross perversion especially exemplifies the perversion/subversion rule: the definition of perversion, in part, contains the idea that the perverse person is acting antisocially. (Think of the contrast between homosexual fellatio being "normal" with the Sambia but "perversion" with most Americans.) The reason is obvious; if one is doing wrong by society's standards, society will crack down, which makes the perverse person not only vigilant but angry. In a state of rebellion. Interested in a spot of revenge.

In view of this, it is not surprising that the pornographers I have been talking with —producers, directors, writers, actors—are in the business because of battles with their parents in childhood; they need the excitement of snubbing their noses (not to say other parts of the anatomy) at society. The "creative" porn people—the nonactors (but not the businessmen)—with whom I talk say they would quit the business if porn were approved by society.

The following interview fragment typifies these dynamics. I am talking with Ron, a former drug runner, now writer of porn scripts, porn actor, and world-class S&M whipmaster.

R: I saw what the face of greed looked like during my years as a drug dealer. It was useful to live as an outlaw. I learned society's assumptions about the difference between legitimate and nonlegitimate business. The difference is one of definition, like the difference between a flower and a weed: a flower is something that you planted, and a weed is something that got there uninvited. That's the definition of criminal enterprise: enterprise that society has voted against. But in terms of business practice, there isn't a lot of difference.

Similarly, from being in the dissenting subculture of S&M, I've learned about the assumptions of the majority culture about its own sexual and social behavior. Voltaire said that he could never understand how two priests could pass in the street with straight faces: I've never understood how two LAPD motorcycle cops could pass in the street with straight faces. I look at those guys in their natty little uniforms and I think, "This is ridiculous. Don't you guys know that you are simply a leather boy's wet dream come to life? Doesn't it feel preposterous to go out on your job dressed that way?" But of course they adopt the attitude that goes with the uniform; so they don't allow themselves to think they might be ridiculous. I can never look at policemen and soldiers and other authority figures, listen to their pronouncements, and watch their frantic struggles to assert dominance over their wretched employees and other victims, without seeing it as a ridiculous dick-measuring contest.

But if people went on this assumption, society would become ungovernable. It's probably necessary for people to take priests and policemen seriously, but if there's anything I can contribute to society, it is a perspective that may help people take those individuals and the hoary myths surrounding them less seriously. See, I think S&M is savagely repressed in every society because it is inherently subversive to make fun of the symbols of authority. That's what people literally do in S&M—make fun of the symbols of authority and the symbolic behavior of domination, not necessarily consciously burlesquing them but using them for recreational purposes. This unsober use of these important talismans is threatening to those whose whole identities are tied up with them. What I really like about S&M in its funny little ant-sized way is how it stands down there at the base of the mighty colossus of social authority and shakes it as hard as it can.

S: Perversion is subversion.

R: Yes. But not all perversion is subversion.

S: Right.

R: But this kind of perversion—perversion that has to do with the mockery of social rituals—is definitely subversion. That's why church and state conspire to crush it. Docs, cops, and padres don't like it, and I can sure understand why. You go to a Janus [S&M organization] party, what costumes do we see? Uniforms; people playing doctor; religious themes [cf. Genet 1966]. I went to a Scorpio party once where there was a topless nun, a woman in a cut-out nun's habit; she had a huge wooden cross she had made, with a dildo on the long end of it. I looked at that and thought, "Now, there is S&M thinking at its most subversive. This is what I like to see."

Morality

It all has to do with morality, that subject acknowledged yet underestimated by analysts.

By my reckoning—to review for a moment—the excitement, erotic or otherwise, that arises in perversion requires two morality elements. First, the person senses that he or she is sinning, harming someone else, and that that someone else is or stands for those from earlier times who deserve to be harmed. The less sin, the less excitement. The second is that of the perverse person versus society. This issue is complicated by the fact that "society" is, among other things, a collection of individuals, many of whom have perversions and all of whom use perverse mechanisms. So when society functions as a conscience by proclaiming its virtue, it protects itself—we are protecting ourselves—from painful self-knowledge.

Let me get slightly personal and thereby illustrate the idea that our private motives color our decisions about theory and practice. That will lead, finally, to my main point about the term *perversion*.

I began over thirty years ago (1955) by not joining colleagues who, in their research on transsexualism, asked me to see an effeminate, cross-dressing homosexual man who enjoyed being chained up. Explaining myself to myself, I said there was nothing to learn from such a person because, as every analytic candidate knew then, the theory was complete, the votes counted, the decisions made. How I have changed! Yet, while moving from distaste to enthusiasm about studying perversions, I still come to each new phase with reluctance.

The latest episode has concerned perverse sadomasochists: that, it had seemed, would be the *last* thing I would ever study. I have been inside that business for five years now. The change from distaste to pleasure has transformed my thinking, theoretic and clinical, because, since I am no longer a covert enemy of my patients/informants, I can let them open themselves up to the search for understanding the origins and dynamics of their erotic practices. And with that flood of new information, I can enjoy giving up previous positions and no longer burn with the fevers of righteousness. This has led to the observations that, as I stated at the beginning of this chapter, erotically aberrant people are as different from one another as everyone is from everyone else and that analysts should no longer even covertly support the cruel positions (claimed to be scientific vis-à-vis aberrant people—that is, minorities) that poison human relations, thereby victimizing de jure and de facto the people who make us uneasy.

This discussion has only approached the central issue. So far, I have suggested no more than (1) that perverse mechanisms, which are present in everyone (everyone is neurotic; so everyone is perverse), and perversions, which are, perhaps, just blown-up versions of perverse mechanisms, are restitutive defenses against earlier, at first unmanageable, pain; and (2) that the name-calling inside our explanations hides professional bias: analysts dislike and fear perversion.

But now, the main point. Though studying the meaning of perversion is worthwhile, what counts for more is the basic question: how much harm does the individual inflict on other living creatures. *Actually* inflict. Not just in imagination, in the theater of erotic behavior (as, for instance, in the case of consensual sadomasochists). "Theater," as McDougall has beautifully emphasized (1985), is a crucial part of the judgment here. For theater takes place on a stage, a construction in the real world or in our mind, and in that staging are placed safety factors allowing people to play out *fantasies* of harm/humiliation/revenge/triumph without actually harming/humiliating/revenging/triumphing over others. Whether a man masturbates into ladies' hats or a woman thrills to the lash marks on her bottom should not make analysts track them down and put them on trial until they confess from the couch their dreadful narcissisms.

For the issue is to define not *perversion* but *evil*. And that issue I— captive of my times—find better studied, as Kernberg (1974a, 1974b, 1977) and Person (1988) have done most creatively, in terms of capacity for not harming another, capacity for intimacy—respect, acceptance, nonfetishizing, affection, friendship, love—the opposite of danger- ousness, of inflicting high, true trauma on others.

Conclusions

Sometimes the best conclusions are questions. Though this essay has scarcely a question mark, they are there, in my mind, at the end of almost every sentence, certainly every paragraph. You—readers—are not the only ones unsure of my ideas. (Of all the things I'm sure about, the surest, the impulse behind this essay, is that psychoanalysis needs all the un- sureness it can muster.)

Here are questions—there are many more—that have been around a long time, that one or another analyst has dealt with in the past, and for which the answers are still tentative:

1. How do nonerotic impulses get transformed into perverse char- acter structure, and how do perverse impulses get transformed into non- erotic character structure (Arlow 1971)?

2. Exactly how in childhood do we take trauma and not only pull its fangs, not only change it to pleasure (as in reaction formation/counter- phobia, for example), but *erotize* it? The process occurs mostly uncon- sciously, probably constantly, and over a period of years. Are there ways analysts could benignly look into children to see these processes at work?

(Child analysis with play techniques is one. Are there some that could be used on children who are not in treatment?)

3. Can we determine, and if so how, when we should speak of perversion rather than perverse mechanisms?

4. Some perversions spring full-blown on the first day they surface; others come up slowly and then stay constant; others persist for years and then die away; others flower, taking on new forms. What is the course—and why—of a particular perversion as the years pass?

5. What forces propel some people to live out their perversions? And what forces prevent some from acting on their fantasies?

6. When is perversion fixation, when is it regression, and when is it neither?

For all the questioning, I want to end declaratively and repeat: we shall not untangle the origins and dynamics of perversion unless we put aside the concept "normal." "Normal" stops exploration; though we need "normal" inside us, as a rudder for our moral codes, we had best know that what we feel is eternal—"normal"—is relative, culture-bound, and subject to change without notice.

References

Arlow, J. A. 1971. "Character Perversion." In *Currents in Psychoanalysis,* ed. I. M. Marcus. New York: International Universities Press.

———. 1978. "A Type of Play Observed in Boys during the Latency Period." In *Separation-Individuation,* ed. J. McDevitt and C. Settlage. New York: International Universities Press.

Bryer, J. B.; Nelson, B. A.; Miller, J. B.; and Krol, P. A. 1987. "Childhood Sexual and Physical Abuse as Factors in Adult Psychiatric Illness." *American Journal of Psychiatry* 144:1426–30.

Burgess, A. W.; Hartman, C. R.; and McCormack, A. 1987. "Abused to Abuser: Antecedents of Socially Deviant Behaviors." *American Journal of Psychiatry* 144:1431–36.

Colby K. M., and Spar, J. E. 1983. *The Fundamental Crisis in Psychiatry.* Springfield: Charles C. Thomas.

Foucault, M. 1970. *The Order of Things.* New York: Vintage Books.

———. 1982–83. Sexual Choice, Sexual Act: An Interview with Michel Foucault." *Salamagundi* 58–59: 10–24.

Genet, J. 1966. *The Balcony.* Rev. ed. Trans. B. Frechtman. New York: Grove Press.

Glover, E. 1956. *On the Early Development of Mind.* New York: International Universities Press.

Goldman, R. 1973. *Principles of Medical Science.* New York: McGraw-Hill.

Herdt, G. H. 1981. *Guardians of the Flutes.* New York: McGraw-Hill.

———. 1989. Personal communication.

Kernberg, O. 1974a. "Barriers to Falling and Remaining in Love." *Journal of the American Psychoanalytic Association* 22:486–511.

———. 1974b. "Mature Love: Prerequisites and Characteristics." *Journal of the American Psychoanalytic Association* 22:743–68.

———. 1977. "Boundaries and Structures in Love Relations." *Journal of the American Psychoanalytic Association* 25:81–114.

McDougall, J. 1985. *Theaters of the Mind.* New York: Basic Books.

Miller, B. L.; Cummings, J. L.; McIntyre, H.; Ebers, G.; and Grode, M. 1986. "Hypersexuality or Altered Sexual Preference Following Brain Injury." *Journal of Neurology, Neurosurgery, and Psychiatry* 49:867–73.

Morrison, J. 1989. "Childhood Sexual Histories of Women with Somatization Disorder." *American Journal of Psychiatry* 146:239–41.

Person, E. S. 1988. *Dreams of Love and Fateful Encounters.* New York: W. W. Norton.

Roiphe, H., and Galenson, E. 1981. *Infantile Origins of Sexual Identity.* New York: International Universities Press.

Stern, D. N. 1985. *The Interpersonal World of the Infant.* New York: Basic Books.

Stoller, R. J. 1968. *Sex and Gender.* New York: Science House.

———. 1975. *Perversion.* New York: Pantheon.

———. 1979. *Sexual Excitement.* New York: Pantheon.

———. 1985a. *Observing the Erotic Imagination.* New Haven: Yale University Press.

———. 1985b. *Presentations of Gender.* New Haven: Yale University Press.

Stoller, R. J., and Geertsma, R. H. 1963. "The Consistency of Psychiatrists' Clinical Judgments." *Journal of Nervous and Mental Disorders* 137:58–66.

Part II

Applications

The Perversions of Everyday Clinical Practice

Chapter Three

Derivative Manifestations of Perversions

Jacob A. Arlow, M.D.

U NDERSTANDING perversions and their derivative manifestations involves primarily a question of method of interpretation.
How do we go about understanding the multiform features of
what have come to be considered perversions or perverse behavior? In
psychoanalytic investigation, problems of method relate inevitably to the
theory of mental functioning and to the nature of the process of patho-
genesis. Take, for example, Freud's first approach to the problem of
perversions in "Three Essays on the Theory of Sexuality" ([1905] 1953).
It was strictly phenomenological. Certain behavior patterns of children
and the manifest activities involved in the sexual perversions seemed
similar, if not identical. Therefore, he concluded, one derived from the
other; a component of the sexual life of the child entered untamed into
the psychosexual constitution of the adult. Why did this happen? The
answer was fixation; the cause of the fixation was an unusually powerful
congenital drive endowment and/or accidental factors, what today we
would call the nature of the primary object relations—that is, too much

gratification or too much frustration. Freud applied the principle of the vicissitudes of the instinctual energy to the phenemona of childhood sexuality and perversions. All this was in keeping with his earlier strictly biophysical approach to mental functioning. It was appealingly simple.

I will not review how and why Freud changed his approach to the issues of perversion. This history is well known. I will, however, note in passing that the theoretical problems posed by such issues as masochism, homosexuality, and fetishism played an important role in Freud's reformulation of his theories of mental functioning (Arlow 1959).

I think it is a fair statement that psychoanalysts today consider many more factors that contribute to the shaping of the individual—dynamic, biological, adaptive, developmental, experiential, and cultural factors. Where they differ is in the relative emphasis they give to one or another of these elements.

For me, the dynamic element in psychoanalysis seems to be the overriding principle because it permits, through the process of compromise formation, the integration of all the other factors noted above. The dynamic interplay of forces in conflict is embedded in the investigative method we use—namely, the psychoanalytic situation. The psychoanalytic situation is geared primarily to elicit a living record of the forces in conflict in the mind. I try to conceptualize the patient's conscious productions in the psychoanalytic situation as derivatives of a fantasy of which the patient is unaware. The patient's unconscious fantasies represent dynamic pressures on the mind, in which the data of perception are more or less selectively perceived, interpreted, and responded to. These unconscious fantasies are few in number, and they articulate attempts to resolve intrapsychic conflicts that reflect the child's early experiences, wishes, and trauma. Although the unconscious fantasies remain unchanged, their derivative expressions are transformed over the years as the child develops and is acculturated. There is a constant mutual interaction between the individual's mental set, as dictated by his persistent unconscious fantasies, and the events of his daily conscious experience. The latter may be misinterpreted or misresponded to in terms of the persistent fantasy. Daily conscious experiences, which include cultural factors, of course, are evocative of unconscious fantasies.

The derivative manifestations of the solutions to unconscious conflicts are protean in nature. They may be pleasant or unpleasant, acceptable or unacceptable, adaptive or maladaptive, enriching, inhibiting, or impoverishing for the individual. They may take the form of character traits, sublimations, dreams, fantasies, masturbation fantasies, symptoms, perversions, and perverse traits. At one time or another, every individual has developed and utilized every one of these possible solutions, including perverse interests, to intrapsychic conflict. We must always keep in mind the fact that any perversion appeared in the mind of the individual as a fantasy before it was acted out.

In fact, in clinical experience, it is often impossible to distinguish perversions and perverse traits from symptomatology and even normal behavior. For example, in most of the cases of moral masochism in men that I have observed, the following patterning of events in the psychodynamics unfolded. After the patients could appreciate how they were using their own consciences to torture themselves, they came to recognize how, through their perversity, they had arranged to suffer at the hands of others. They had maneuvered themselves into positions of being abused, humiliated, and defeated. They had anxiety-provoking dreams and flash fantasies of being assaulted and attacked by men. Freud ([1924] 1961) pointed out that moral masochism consisted of a perversion of true morality, a process in men of regression from true morality to the negative Oedipus complex. Further analysis demonstrated how these traits were derivative expressions of an unconscious fantasy of being beaten, which had appeared in late latency as a conscious sadomasochistic fantasy accompanying masturbation. That fantasy itself was a derivative expression of an unconscious wish to play the woman's role in sexual relations. In this material, how does one distinguish among symptom, perversion, and perverse character trait?

The perverse sexualization of conscience occurs in women as well. Not only do such individuals torture themselves with their consciences, but sometimes they place themselves repeatedly in positions of an unpopular moral, political, or professional nature and thus invite moral criticism from others. In turn, as in the case of the male patients just mentioned, there emerge sadomasochistic fantasies of abuse, humiliation, and sexual subjugation. In some instances the erotization of assault and death is a prominent feature. One patient acted out in great detail the bride-of-death ritual described by Abraham ([1912] 1942). Following this ritual, the patient prepared herself very carefully to welcome the demon lover, death, who represented the oedipal father.

In another woman patient, the erotization of suffering and humiliation was manifest in symptom formation, perverse character trait, and sublimation. A woman of uncontrolled emotionality, she was engaged in constant quarrels with her husband and her father, sometimes, after one of these quarrels, rushing out into the night dressed only in her nightgown. When she was a young woman, she often served as her father's patient, as he demonstrated dental techniques to his students. She had masturbation fantasies concerning being humiliated by being forced to dance nude in front of men and other forms of abuse and humiliation. In a dream I have described elsewhere (Arlow 1953), the patient equated sexual relations with being stabbed with a knife. She woke from the dream with a pain in the exact location where the object in the dream had stabbed her. In her early teens, she had run away from home and contemplated allowing a man in the park to pick her up; instead she had taken a job as a domestic, using the name of the most recent black housekeeper who had worked in her own very affluent home. On another occasion, the patient was lying in bed at night trying to solve some problem connected with decorating her home. She had an idea of how to convert a vase into a lamp, but found herself obsessively concerned with the question: "Whom do I get to drill the hole in the bottom of my vase?" This was followed immediately by the solution of another decorating problem, which involved using some material from her father. She responded to this insight with a burst of excited enthusiasm that had a pattern of orgastic discharge. Thus, a conversion symptom, a perverse character trait, a pattern of perverse or delinquent behavior, and a creative spell all constituted derivative expressions of an unconscious fantasy of masochistic sexual assault.

The case just described illustrates a principle that has important bearing on the topic of our discussion—namely, the relationship between perversions and masturbation. There are two components to the masturbation complex, the pleasurable stimulation of a part of the body and a concomitant fantasy. In the patients we are discussing, the fantasy is of a perverse nature. In the struggle against the perverse wishes, each of the two components of the masturbation complex may undergo independent transformation. The physical activity stimulating part of the body may be given up and may be replaced by substitute motor activities, sometimes of a compulsive nature. Quite independently, the perverse fantasy may be acted out directly or in some disguised derivative form. This latter vicissitude of the struggle embodied in the masturbation fantasy may lead to acting out in the form of juvenile delinquency, as Anna Freud (1949) pointed out. On analysis, many forms of juvenile delinquency can be shown to represent an acting out of derivatives of perverse masturbation fantasies. Acting out of the defensive distortions of the perverse wishes thus brings the individual into conflict with society.

Similarly, there are certain character traits in which the relationship to perversion is at first glance not at all obvious. What is striking about these traits is that they are genetically related to the sexual perversions in that structurally they are reproductions in exquisite detail of the defensive mechanisms that characterize some specific perversion. In the history of the development of these character traits, it is possible to observe how they substituted for or were the equivalent of perverse sexual practices. On the basis of such findings, I have proposed to call such traits examples of character perversion in analogy to the genesis of character neurosis. In the character neurosis, what once had been a symptomatic neurosis is replaced in the course of development by neurotic character traits. In these patients, an original perversion or tendency toward perversion was replaced later in life by an abnormal character trait. Since I have described this condition elsewhere (Arlow 1971), I will give here only a brief summary of the essential features illustrating how perverse tendencies may persist in disguised form in certain character traits.

The first type I referred to was the unrealistic character. These were patients who tended to look away from unpleasant or threatening reality. They acted as if they had not seen what they were confronted with and instead, in the analysis and in life, would fasten their attention on some peripheral, more pleasant subject. On the couch, these patients demonstrated a whole repertory of symptomatic modes of behavior, such as rubbing their eyes or shielding them, in addition to changing the subject when some material ultimately connected with castration anxiety began to appear. Their defense was not to see but to look away. Earlier in life, these patients had shown voyeuristic and fetishistic interests and on occasion indulged in fetishistic practices. To illustrate one detail, one patient for the first few years of his active sexual life found it a necessary condition for his potency that his partner come into bed and get under the covers wearing a full girdle or underpants. Only under the covers could he permit her to be completely nude. He was fascinated by garter belts, was intrigued by see-through clothes, and had a collection of photographs in which the women were revealed but never completely nude. Like the voyeur, such patients are compelled to look but not to see. When confronted with the unavoidable truth of female anatomy, they will have nothing to do with it. The fetishist, in his defensive needs, goes a step further than the voyeur. Not only does he look away in order to deny the unbearable reality of the female genital; he has a compulsive need to fasten his attention onto some reassuring peripheral perception.

The next type, the petty liar, is a variation of the one just mentioned. For some patients, the fetish must have a certain gauzy, filmy quality. Such patients require an item that is neither totally opaque nor fully transparent. They love to look, but they do not want to see what is really there. A defensive shift from passive looking to active showing underlies this pathological character trait of lying. One patient, for example, was a Peeping Tom who complained of the frustrations connected with voyeurism. At the last moment, some item of clothing would obscure his view of the object he was observing at a distance, or a window shade would come down, and so on. He managed never to quite see what he thought he was looking for. Actually, to be free from anxiety he required that something be interposed between him and the truth of the world of anatomy. The object that excited him during masturbation had to be something insubstantial and filmy. His productions during sessions were usually unclear. In his daily dealings he was always telling petty lies. He himself commented on the nebulous, *veil-like* quality of what he had to say, observing once that he never liked to tell "the naked truth." When he was able to deceive people into accepting his fabrications, he felt a sense of mastery. Sometimes, when he succeeded in having people accept his petty lies as real, he almost began to believe them himself. This character disturbance then resembled the structure of certain types of impostors as well as the type of pseudologia fantastica described by Fenichel (1939).

The unconscious import of this kind of behavior may be expressed in the following statement: "If I am successful in preventing others from seeing the truth, then I need not fear that I myself will be confronted with the shocking truth." It is an example of denial by proxy (Wangh 1962).

The third type is the practical joker or hoaxer. Such persons are characterized by the need to inspire panic or anxiety in others, from which they achieve a sense of gratification of aggression and a sense of power. And there is the pleasure of finally exposing the hoax. In these cases, transvestism has been prominent earlier in life. The transvestism represented a defensive denial in fantasy of what they conceived to be the castrated state of the woman. The transvestism represented the patient's acting out the fantasy of being a woman with a phallus. What at first glance appeared frightening—the impression that a woman had no penis—was belied when the true nature of the situation was revealed, when the transvestite lifted his skirt, or now when he reveals the hoax as innocuous. To be sure, other mechanisms come into play in this complex bit of behavior, but one must be mentioned, and that is the identification with the aggressor. As the individual was frightened once by what he saw, he now frightens others by what he shows.

Another form of acting out through a character trait of a perverse fantasy is the petty swindler. Such individuals, by deceptive ingratiation, manage to deprive others of their money. In several patients, I have found this trait to represent acting out of a perverse homosexual fantasy, the type of genesis of homosexuality described by Anna Freud (1950), in which the individual submits to what is called the passive role in homosexual relations but in the process, in fantasy, is castrating the powerful man. A similar case of a swindler was reported by Weissman (1963). I call this type the petty swindler because in my practice I have had no big-time swindlers.

These observations raise the obvious question concerning the relation between perversion and the impostor. I am not in a position to make any generalization about the origin of imposture. The transvestite, the petty liar, and the practical joker may, in some limited sense, be regarded as impostors. In these situations, from analytic observations, we have at least some data relating the manifest behavior or social role with unconscious mental content. This does not enable us to draw conclusions about impostors in general, but it does call attention to the need to investigate the possibility of the role of perverse tendencies in such behavior.

In that connection, a word of warning should be entered concerning the unrealistic character. In those few patients, it was possible to establish a connection between certain modes of dealing with reality and the function that this trait unconsciously served. One cannot and should not conclude that all relations with reality are governed by Lewin's witty and perceptive note of the meaning of reality in the psychoanalytic setting—that is, its equation with the vision of the female genital, with the reality of anatomical differences (Lewin 1948). Specifically, in the case of fetishists, Glover (1933) and Greenacre (1960) have noted some disturbance of the relationship to reality. The exact nature of the disturbance was not detailed. On the couch, several of the patients with fetishistic impulses whom I have described had some mild degree of depersonalization and derealization; that is, things were not completely real (Arlow 1966).

The intimate connection between fantasy and perversion leads directly to the subject of play, theater, and art. Often some person is cast in the role of an observer of the events in the masturbation fantasy. It seems that implicit in most perverse masturbation fantasies is the idea of being observed, as if at some performance. Sometimes the performance is carried out in a solitary manner. The observer is the individual himself. Among the patients described as demonstrating character perversions, most of them played out a voyeuristic, exhibitionistic game with themselves in front of the mirror. They would push their genitals back between their thighs in order to simulate the appearance of the female genital and would then release the pressure on their thighs, permitting their male genital to reappear. The fun of the game derived not from the imitation of the female anatomy but from the reassuring reappearance of the male genital. Some of these men recalled that, as young boys, they played damage games; that is, they would simulate being blind or lame for a period of time and then would reassuringly return to their normal functioning. To be able to end the game at will, whether mirror play or damage play, served not only to reassure against castration anxiety but also to reaffirm the sense of control and autonomy (Arlow 1987). One patient, during childhood, played being a cripple and actually had his mother fashion some form of a crutch out of a broomstick so he could act out his game. As an adult, he would on occasion rent a wheelchair, go to a motel room, and change into women's clothes. Then he would go out, wheel himself about, and be particularly delighted when solicitous individuals offered to help him (Arlow 1971).

In many perversions, such as transvestism, fetishism, exhibitionism, and certain sadomasochistic practices, an audience is almost always implied. Although the subject is trying to prove something to himself, he requires at the same time an audience, seen or unseen, to affirm whatever it is that he is trying to establish.

In some instances, as in a case described by McDougall (1986), the physical setting of the perverse masturbatory activity becomes so complex as to require elaborate stagecraft. Often it seems to be crafted in such a way as to arouse in the imagined or potential observer a sense of heightened anxiety, such as might be evoked by dangerous circus acts or Houdini-type escape performances. One of McDougall's patients staged his perverse masturbation in a way that demonstrated not only remarkable architectural proficiency but extraordinary physical agility in his death-defying act, which also required considerable athleticism. Nonetheless, from time to time you read in the newspapers accounts of some person, dressed in a bizarre outfit and intricately bound, found dead in some extraordinary contraption. A staged form of play ends up as a real-life tragedy.

Finding a partner with a similar or complementary interest is a step that leads from masturbation to game playing. There are many devices of communication, some subtle, some overt, by which one finds a compatible or acquiescent partner. One sadistic patient, a Don Juan type, asked, "Why is it that all the women I meet turn out to be masochists?" It seemed like a fair question, and it directed my attention to how he established relationships with women. Without being aware of it, he pursued a modus operandi by which he tested women and eliminated those who were not masochistic or, more properly stated, nonmasochistic women eliminated themselves. From the very first contact, he would act in a manner that was quietly demeaning and humiliating. One of his more blatant gambits follows: He would call women and say, "I am so-and-so. You don't know me but I know about you. I got your number from a friend who met you at a party and said that you would be fun to take out." If he got by that opening, he would ask for a date. If the woman said, "Yes. When?" he would say, "Tonight." When she replied, "That's very short notice. What about this weekend?" he would answer, "I'm busy. This is the only night I am free." If she agreed to see him, he would set a time to call for her and come an hour or two late. The rest of the scenario I leave to your imagination.

Another patient, at the beginning of a relationship, would tell the woman, "I want you to know that I'm no good for you. I only cause trouble and pain." For certain masochistic women, such a statement constitutes a temptation they can hardly refuse. Once such a liaison has been established, there is a wide range of possible interplay between the partners, from a relatively mild sadomasochistic relationship to an extremely harmful and potentially dangerous engaging in violent sadomasochistic practices. How far either of the partners is willing to go may be explored directly, but more often indirectly, through the use of shared fantasying. Certain agreed-upon scenarios may be acted out or one of the partners may need to have the other partner describe some perverse activity or scene during the act of intercourse. For individuals in such situations who fear that they are not sufficiently imaginative or creative, there is always the possibility of borrowing prefabricated perverse fantasies and images from sex magazines, novels, and, more recently, pornographic videocassettes.

Here a certain cultural factor plays a role in intrapsychic equilibrium. The fact that there is such a thriving industry in sexual videocassettes and that certain sexual perversions have become de rigueur as a theme in literary and stage productions goes far toward easing the guilt many individuals feel about their practices. The change of moral climate is unmistakable. Thus far, however, many, but not all, perversions have come out of the closet. Participating as witnesses to works of art featuring perverse themes amounts to what Hanns Sachs (1942) has called an experience of mutual exculpation. Everybody's guilt is nobody's guilt. The members of the audience exculpate each other, as well as the author of the work of art.

In our age and our country the change in the moral climate was signaled at Berkeley by an outburst of what at the time was considered coprolalia. The free speech movement started its assault on the conventional mores by defiantly shouting the word *fuck*. They succeeded so completely that this word, formerly the principal obscene word of the English language (Stone 1954), has now become commonplace and its special role as the unutterable has been inherited by the vulgar four-letter word for the female genital. Although coprolalia is of itself for the most part a victimless crime, usually more disturbing to the subject than to the individuals around him, its employment by the free speech movement underscores the aggressive and defiant aspects of perversion to which I will refer later.

Because the perverse masturbation fantasy is under conscious control, it affords ample opportunity for variation, invention, and creativity. In the last case, the drive impulses and the creative urge exert a synergistic effect on each other. In fact, several authors have suggested some connection between perversion and creativity. From my clinical experience, I am not in a position to make any judgment on that issue. But, as I have indicated previously (Arlow 1986), I think that in a large measure the rapid tempo of changes in sexual mores leading to freer expression of what had previously been unspoken and unrevealed was heralded in the works of the avant-garde writers and artists.

It is true that such changes represent a historic process, a recurrent phenomenon in the course of human affairs, characterized by alternating periods of suppression or freer expression of the instinctual drives. Nevertheless, it would appear that the harbinger for the current transformation was already apparent in the changing character of aesthetic creations. Both their forms and their content swerved sharply from the traditional modes of expression, and a distinct literature that discarded the customary formulations appeared. Writers began to celebrate the antihero, usually an ignoble character, egocentric and perversely sensual, a stranger to remorse or renunciation, who goes unpunished when he violates the established taboos of society. Perverse themes, even cannibalism and incest, that formerly were hidden under the heavy cloak of taboo or were tied down to a literary tradition demanding tragic resolution have become the subject of lighthearted comic treatment. As a result, what was formerly unthinkable has become not only thinkable but expressible and a prologue to what can become permissible and doable.

Such considerations lend some support to the views advanced by Chas-seguet-Smirgel and Grunberger (1986) that every perversion expresses a rebellion against the authority of the father figure and his values. The link between juvenile delinquency and the acting out of derivatives of per-verse fantasies has been mentioned previously. Like certain classes of juvenile delinquents, there are individuals with perversion or perverse tendencies who flaunt their defiance of conventional morality by the clothes they wear, their hairstyles, and their manner of speech. The uniforms of the sadomasochistic perverts are easily recognizable.

In recent psychoanalytic literature, the psychology of clothes has not received the attention it deserves. The dress one affects is a statement of one's identity and the image one wants to project. This is a very wide and important subject, but I will restrict myself to the topics of transvestism and fetishism as they relate to the subject of dress. In modern Western society, women have wide latitude in dressing in what used to be consid-ered male apparel. Men, on the other hand, are not permitted or rather do not permit themselves an equivalent degree of freedom in this respect. Even to the most casual observer, however, it should be obvious from the new enthusiasm some men are showing for wearing necklaces, bracelets, or earrings, items ordinarily identified with women's mode of dress, that a change is taking place. Preoccupation with hairstyling among men is another indication of this trend, to which we may probably add a tenden-cy for more colorful, stylish, and individually cut clothes. Although it is hard to establish statistically, such decorative enhancement on the part of men seems to arouse in many analysts a suspicion of possible fetishistic import, a tendency toward projecting a bisexual, androgynous image. On the other hand, in our society, women seem to have been enjoying for a much longer time a wider latitude of self-expression of ambiguous or bisexual identity. In women, fetishism as an obligatory perversion is quite rare. Perhaps this may be connected with the fact, as revealed in clinical experience, that women in their mode of dress may flaunt an illusory penis through many forms of self-decoration—men's clothes, massive jewelry, a penchant for extraordinary hats, and the like.

There can be no doubt that cultural factors are of primary importance in these considerations. Although the anatomical distinction between the sexes has remained more or less constant over the years, the economic, social, and political distinctions between the sexes have been blurred enormously. Thus, in our time, the unconscious derivative gratification for women to seem masculine receives social sanction at many levels, part of a rapidly changing political reality. Yet it was not always so one-sided. Although many people are amused by the way women's fashions keep changing from year to year, the fact is that, two hundred years ago, men in the upper middle and upper classes dressed in ways that would be unthinkable today, ways much closer to female attire than is possible now. Gone are the short silk pants, the lace ruffles, shoes with buckles, and powdered wigs. Time has changed all that, and one wonders why. Is it possible that we are now at the beginning of a phase signifying a shift toward male bisexual self-representation? One thing, however, is certain: fetishes and fetishistic equivalents for both men and women have secured for themselves a well-established position in society, as well as in psychotherapy.

I cannot leave the subject of derivatives of perversions without at least mentioning one of its most widespread and important manifestations, namely, pornography. Essentially, pornography is a borrowed perversion. During the course of a clinical psychoanalysis, it is possible to observe how a resort to pornography is the counterpart or equivalent of the urge to practice some perversion. In some patients, one can predict at what point in the treatment or in the session they will introduce the subject of pornography. This was very striking in one of my patients. Anything that occasioned an upsurge in castration anxiety impelled the patient to look for some pornographic gratification. It functioned in a way reminiscent of the addict's resort to his drug, a desperate measure to ensure inner equilibrium. There are, in fact, many ways in which perversions may be compared with addiction, particularly the intensity of the compelling need and the pleasure of gratification.

In the clinical situation, what holds true for pornography also applies to the evocation of perverse practices. To illustrate, a male patient had no real difficulty with his potency. But whenever material or experiences that aroused castration anxiety occurred, he would yield to the temptation to have sexual relations wearing his partner's panties.

Other motives than defense against anxiety are evocative of perverse fantasies or substitute actions for perversions. In both men and women, the oedipal defeat may eventuate in lifelong feelings of inferiority, of narcissistic humiliation, coupled with a wish for revenge in kind (Arlow 1980). A combination of several elements—for example, a sadomasochistic interpretation of the primal scene, a wish to avenge oneself on the parent of the opposite sex, guilt and a fear of punishment from the parent of the same sex—can lead to the organization of a beating or a spanking perversion. One patient, from latency on, would masturbate with fantasies of spanking a woman. On several occasions, he managed to find a sexual partner who agreed to be spanked sexually. The actual practice of spanking was not an obligatory condition for his enjoying sexual intercourse but could be replaced by the patient's having a spanking fantasy. On many occasions, a violent quarrel with the sexual partner just before making love could take the place of actually spanking the partner or fantasying doing so.

Similarly, sadistic fantasies of wreaking vengeance on the unloving parent by emphasizing the elements of sexual subjugation and humiliation may be expressed in specific types of fantasy. In the case of the male, these might be called harem fantasies. They involve ideas, often carried into action, of having many women who are forced to submit sexually to the individual under any kind of condition he may dictate. The wishes of the women are of no concern. She is humiliated and abused. In the woman, such fantasies may be referred to as Circe fantasies. One patient imagined having a group of men at her command. They were totally nude and would have to perform with her unquestioningly at her bidding. These fantasies involve not only the issue of vengeance but the redress of narcissistic injury.

Another subject insufficiently explored here is the role of aggression and hostility in the perversions. This element may play a much larger role in explaining the hostile attitude of society toward perversions than the sexual component alone. In his paper on jealousy, paranoia, and homosexuality, Freud ([1922] 1955) first linked a perversion with aggressive impulses of murderous intensity. In effect, in certain types of homosexuality, the erotic drive is enlisted in order to contain and control murderous impulses toward the rival. While we have been emphasizing the elements that make sexual gratification possible in the face of castration anxiety, we should not overlook the fact that many homosexual relations are characterized by assault and even murder. Similar considerations apply to pedophilia. From my limited experience, I think that pedophilia represents a reaction formation against hostile, murderous impulses toward children. Parents and society at large respond to the sexual molestation of children as abuse, as an assault. It is as if they intuitively recognize the latent hostility expressed in that perversion. Certain forms of homosexuality, pedophilia, and rape may begin as sex and end as murder.

As I conclude this chapter, I am only too aware of its limitations. It is not sufficient to understand the unconscious mental content accompanying the perverse act and its latent unconscious fantasy, or the specific traumatic experiences of childhood that have predisposed to patterns of revenge or the alleviation of fear. Such an approach may suffice for the attenuated derivatives of perverse tendencies, but when it comes to the obligatory perversions—with their persistent, overwhelming compulsion toward action, with the sense of gratification that they and nothing else provide, with the unreasonable risks they entail, and with their all-consuming role in the life of the individual—we are left with too many questions unanswered. We are confronted with the limitations of psychodynamics and a keen awareness of the many things we have yet to learn about this subject.

References

Abraham, K. A. [1912] 1942. "A Complicated Ceremonial Found in Neurotic Women." In *Selected Papers on Psychoanalysis.* London: Hogarth Press.

Arlow, J. A. 1953. "Masturbation and Symptom Formation." *Journal of the American Psychoanalytic Association* 1:45–58.

———. 1959. "The Theory of Drives." In *Readings in Psychoanalytic Psychology,* ed. M. Levitt. New York: Appleton-Century Crofts, 197–212.

———. 1966. "Depersonalization and Derealization." In *Psychoanalysis—A General Psychology: Essays in Honor of Heinz Hartmann,* ed. R. M. Loewenstein et al. New York: International Universities Press, 456–78.

———. 1971. "Character Perversion." In *Currents in Psychoanalysis,* ed. I. M. Marcus. New York: International Universities Press, 317–36.

———. 1980. "The Revenge Motive in the Primal Scene." *Journal of the American Psychoanalytic Association* 28:519–41.

———. 1986. "The Poet as Prophet: A Psychoanalytic Perspective." *Psychoanalytic Quarterly* 55:53–68.

———. 1987. "Trauma, Play and Perversion." *Psychoanalytic Study of the Child* 42:31–44.

Chasseguet-Smirgel, J., and Grunberger, B. 1986. *Freud or Reich: Psychoanalysis and Illusion.* New Haven: Yale University Press.

Fenichel, O. 1939. "The Economics of Pseudologia Fantastica." *Internationale Zeitschrift fur Psychoanalyse* 24:21–32.

Freud, A. 1949. "Certain Types and Stages of Social Maladjustment." In *Searchlights on Delinquency,* ed. K. R. Eissler. New York: International Universities Press, 193–204.

———. 1950. "Clinical Observations on the Treatment of Manifest Male Homosexuality." Paper delivered at the New York Psychoanalytic Society, April 17. Abstract in *Psychoanalytic Quarterly* 20:337–38.

Freud, S. [1905] 1953. "Three Essays on the Theory of Sexuality." In *Standard Edition* 7:125–245.

———. [1922] 1955. "Some Neurotic Mechanisms in Jealousy, Paranoia and Homosexuality." In *Standard Edition* 18:223–32.

———. [1924] 1961. "Economic Problem of Masochism." In *Standard Edition* 19:159–72.

Glover, E. 1933. "The Relation of Perversion Formation to the Development of Reality Sense." *International Journal of Psychoanalysis* 14:486–504.

Greenacre, P. 1960. "Further Notes on Fetishism." In *Emotional Growth.* New York: International Universities Press, 162–81.

Lewin, B. D. 1948. "The Nature of Reality and the Meaning of Nothing with an Addendum on Concentration." *Psychoanalytic Quarterly* 17:524–26.

McDougall, J. 1986. "Identification, Neo-needs and Neo-sexuality." *International Journal of Psychoanalysis* 67, Pt. 1:19–32.

Sachs, H. 1942. *The Creative Unconscious: Studies in the Psychoanalysis of Art.* Cambridge, Mass.: Sci-Art Publishers.

Stone, L. 1954. "On the Principal Obscene Word in the English Language." *International Journal of Psychoanalysis* 35:30–56.

Wangh, M. 1962. "The Evocation of a Proxy." *Psychoanalytic Study of the Child* 17:451–69.

Weissman, P. 1963. "The Effects of Preoedipal Paternal Attitudes on Development." *International Journal of Psychoanalysis* 44:121–31.

Chapter Four

On Sadomasochistic Object Relations

Sheldon Bach, Ph.D.

We need, in love, to practice only this:
letting each other go. For holding on
comes easily; we do not need to learn it.
—Rilke, "Requiem"

I N one of the more philosophical passages of the Marquis de Sade's
The 120 Days of Sodom, the Duke observes with sadness and resig-
nation that people are generally very difficult to comprehend. "Yes,"
replies his friend, "most people are indeed an enigma. And perhaps that
is why it is *easier* every time to fuck a man than to try to understand him."

This aphorism seems especially appropriate for a psychoanalytic exploration of perversions, for it speaks to the regressive nature of perversion and thus to the sadomasochist in each of us. No doubt it is easier to
exploit a person than to relate to him, for relationships require a dialogue, whereas exploitation is often unilateral, requiring only force,
intimidation, or cunning. In this sense psychoanalysis may be viewed as
the opposite of a perversion because in principle it embraces the difficult
task of understanding a person rather than using him, although it can
easily enough become a perversion itself.

I will discuss one of the more ubiquitous perversions of everyday life in
which the individual, rather than using a fetish or fantasy as a prosthesis

to replace a missing part of his ego, uses instead a mode of relating that one of my patients called a "technical" relationship, one that falls under the more general heading of sadomasochistic object relations.

Of course, such sadomasochistic relations may or may not include actual perversions, but they always include sadomasochistic fantasies, which may be conscious or deeply unconscious. They cover a continuum of nosologies from the neurotic through the psychotic, but I believe they are developmentally related to the sexual perversions because, like them, they arise as a defense against and an attempt to repair some traumatic loss that has not been adequately mourned. This loss usually occurs in childhood or adolescence and may take the form of loss of a parent, loss of a parent's love through neglect or abusive treatment, which the child denies, or loss of the self through childhood illness, traumatic disillusionment, or overwhelming castration anxiety. In this view, sadomasochistic relations are seen as a kind of denied or pathological mourning, a repetitive attempt to disclaim the loss or to repair it in fantasy, but an attempt that does not lead to resolution because in some dissociated part of the psyche that loss remains disavowed.

The issue is complex because we are dealing with the interdependence of drive and object relations, for if, as Waelder ([1930] 1976, 72–73) notes, "the act of love . . . comes closest to being a complete and equable solution of the ego's contradictory tasks," then the failure of that act of love, as in a perverse relationship, may be understood as a failure of multiple tasks in many lines of development. Here, I can do no more than touch upon some of these lines, each of which must be given due weight to achieve a theoretically plausible and clinically successful outcome.

From a certain perspective, one might say that a person has a perversion *instead of* a relationship, and to the extent that a relationship is pathologically defective, we may suspect that a perversion or a character perversion exists. But just as perverse drive gratification may be a flight from intimate object relations, so perverse object relations may defend against anxieties about drives.

Regarding the severity of sadomasochistic pathology, a distinction might be made between those cases in which the preoedipal and oedipal struggle with the parents has been over instinct prohibition and those cases in which the struggle has been over recognition of the self. Cases in which the parents condemn the instinctual behavior but recognize the child as a separate entity tend to fall into the range of neurotic perversions, and often enough the instinctual condemnation illuminates rather than eliminates the ego—"Your instincts are terrible but there *is* a you there." Cases of parental nonrecognition or emotional absence, on the other hand, force the child to flee to the sadomasochistic drives in an effort to deny the loss and to buttress a failing sense of self. Let me start with an example of this latter type.

A young man whose chief complaints have been chronic depersonalization and an unbroken series of sadomasochistic relationships with women reported with some astonishment that he was learning to cuddle and fondle his friend's children, something he hadn't known how to do before the analysis. He was astonished that they liked it so much and realized that he had never been cuddled himself and that his own parents were remote and distant. He remembered how afraid he was as a child to ask for anything and how convinced he was that he must do everything for himself.

I noted that he still has ways of doing things for himself when he needs fondling, like masturbating or getting high on drugs.

He said he can't believe that anyone would want to love him, which is why in sex he ties women up and forces them to love him and makes them come even when they don't want to.

There was a long silence, and then he observed in a tone of awe that a strange image had come into his mind of someone lying there screaming . . . being beaten up . . . a memory of crowds coming to watch someone broken on the wheel . . . someone being beaten to death with a stick.

I said that was just like cuddling and fondling, but with a minus sign in front of it.

He answered after a while that the most personal relationship he ever had was when his father came after him with a whip to beat him. "I really had his exclusive attention then, like I never did at any other time. . . . It's just like in my fantasies when I force women to have sex with me and to like it too . . . I suppose you can get to like it if it's the only kind of fondling you've ever known."

In this way we arrived at the beating fantasy, the essential element of the masochistic perversion that Freud ([1919] 1955) described seventy years ago. In that formulation, conflicts around oedipal wishes lead to an anal regression and the punishing and resexualized wish that we have seen: I want my father to beat me as a way of loving me. It is worth noting this patient's report that although his mother and father took good care of him, neither one seemed to derive any real *pleasure* from being with him, nor he from them.

A few months later this young man met someone on the street and became confused about whether it was me or someone who resembled me. He said he could never recognize anybody, couldn't remember names, and didn't understand what motivated people. He plaintively added:

> I really don't know anything about people as human beings. . . . I just have a kind of technical relationship to them. . . . I don't know what you can do to help me. . . . [Go on, I said.] Suppose I expressed sadness and you comforted me and I took that comfort, then how would I get up and leave? I can picture myself begging at the door—please can I stay—I can't go! At home there was nobody with the patience to listen. . . . Nobody sat with me as a kid. . . . And when I grew up in adolescence and someone listened to me sympathetically, I fell in love! . . . if somebody listened sympathetically, that's all it took. [Yes.] I tried to merge with them, to surrender all autonomy, and then it evolved into a contest—I'm controlling you, you're controlling me. [How did that happen?] I would spend long nights with some girl and at some point it came to controlling them, tying them up. . . . Then I could play out the fantasy that she would always be where I wanted her to be and always accessible for what I wanted . . . and the less I knew about her the better, because if I knew who she really was it would make that fantasy impossible. . . . If she lived in the real world she couldn't always be mine. . . . And that must be why I didn't recognize you on the street! . . . You're supposed to be here in your office waiting for me always and not running around West End Avenue.

At this point we were able to do some work on how he ties me up in the transference by maintaining a "technical" rather than personal relationship, keeping himself distant, tantalizing me with half-truths, forcing me to wait on his pleasure, and frustrating my therapeutic efforts. Over the next few years we saw this theme as an expression of oedipal rivalry and aggression, as a defense against homosexual impulses and the wish to be beaten, as a defense against castration anxiety and a means of enhancing his potency, as a way of firming up ego boundaries and reviving a failing sense of self, and as a participation in the primal scene. No one of these perspectives or interpretations magically undid the problem, which was molded into his character and ego pathology, and I continually had to remind myself that in such cases we are attempting no less than to help someone to love, to separate, and to maintain object constancy.

It is worth noting the vicissitudes of this patient's attempts to love. Starting from a situation in which he experiences both parents as unrelated and dead, through some combination of his projected rage and their own failure, he provokes his father into beating him not only as a defense against this rage and a punishment for oedipal wishes but also to keep his father and himself *in love,* to revivify their relationship. In adolescence he falls in love with anyone who listen sympathetically, tries to surrender to them, "and at some point it came to . . . tying them up. . . . Then I could play out the fantasy that she would always be where I wanted her to be and always accessible for what I wanted." The attempt to love has somehow miscarried and become instead an attempt to control, and although the patient is aware that this is only a fantasy, he prefers it to reality.

Because it may not be entirely clear how the attempt to love becomes transformed into a sadistic fantasy that glues both participants together, let us look at the beating fantasy from what appears to be the other side.

A young woman with a disturbed maternal relationship who had also been beaten by her father seemed to be forever in search of some kind of symbiotic experience. As we worked on this she explained:

> It's like when I ask to be blindfolded in sex and tied up. . . . If I'm blindfolded I can imagine that he's tuned in right along with me, whereas in reality you can see how he's *not* with you more than he's with you. . . . The fantasy is, he will take care of you, will feed you, wash your hair, dress you, . . . you can just *be,* it's a fantasy of being perceived in one's essential being. . . . The enigma and the indirectness leave room for the fantasy of being understood. . . . And the other thing about that fantasy is that it can

never be satisfied. . . . You have to keep it in that charged space between people that's never fulfilled. [How do you mean?] I don't feel perceived in the act of consummation the way I do beforehand. . . . Before *it's the apex of power,* it's all charged. . . . They can consummate with any other woman . . . but not with me. . . . I retain my uniqueness because they're still interested, and there must be something special in me to keep them from going where they can be gratified.

With this patient the teasing and castrating behavior was designed to retain a sense of power that consummation would destroy because it would demolish her body-phallus fantasy, make *her* feel castrated and lonely, and make her in reality dependent upon an imperfect object. More concretely, she was trying to re-create a situation in which all her father's attention was focused on her but to prevent a consummation that would feel like the longed-for but humiliating lash of his whip. "If I'm blindfolded I can imagine that he's tuned in right along with me, whereas in reality you can see how he's *not* with you more than he's with you."

It is certainly striking how both these patients insist on their desire not to learn anything real about their partners or the analyst because their fantasies of being "tuned in" or merged with an idealized other become endangered by rage and devaluation if the other person is realistically perceived. But one of them also complains of his *incapacity* to know anything about his partner or anyone else. My clinical impression is that this latter complaint is also to the point and that some of these people cover their deficit in understanding others with a variety of defenses, just as someone who cannot admit he is partially deaf may pretend to understand, may read lips, may claim that nothing is worth hearing, or may become hypervigilant and paranoid. Thus, their deficit in understanding others may be patched over by their technical mode of relating, in much the same way as the pervert uses his fetish to patch over a deficit in the body ego. This mode of relating is both an adaptive way to deal with interpersonal deficit and a defense against the rage and devaluation that would destroy the object entirely.

We should note the instability of the sadomasochistic position, since at one moment the patient is sunk in masochistic surrender to the idealized lover whom she *knows* to be a figment of her imagination, whereas at the next moment she is sadistically manipulating the same lover, willingly exchanging the pleasures of sexual consummation for the pleasure of sexualized power. These oscillations between masochism and sadism and between passivity and activity are typical of such cases, but for the moment I want to emphasize the alternation between reality and its denial in fantasy.

However we may choose to conceptualize this phenomenon in which both the reality and its disavowal remain in conscious awareness, it seems true that in his *experience* the sadomasochist feels himself to be living in two worlds: the fantasy world, where he plays the game of the idealized omnipotent self and object, and the real world, which seems too dangerous to live in. In the fantasied world of the idealized merger, the laws of space, time, and logic, which promote differentiation, are suspended: separation, death, and mourning do not exist.

With my own series of cases, discussion of this "two-world" phenomenon almost always seemed to elicit material about the parents and some strange aspects of *their* relationship to reality. Let me give an example.

A man who was in a state of tormented jealousy and paranoia, which he knew to be unjustified, said: "I know in the real world that my girlfriend has a right to do what she wants to do, but that doesn't matter. . . . There's a different world in which I live, where my feelings really are, and in that world she has no rights." He then remembered a time at school when he was caught breaking the rules and his mother had said: "I'll go tell the teacher what a good boy you are and he'll let you off." He had screamed at her: "Mom, join the real world; they caught me and now I have to pay!" His mother had in fact never joined the real world, but he himself had become a voyager between the two worlds of reality and omnipotent fantasy in order to stay in touch with her.

In 1940 Freud remarked with some wonder at the pervert's ability to both affirm and deny the existence of the maternal phallus and conceptualized this behavior as reflecting a split in the ego. Traditionally, of course, the fetishistic perversion and even the character perversion have been explained as being due to the traumatic sight of the maternal genitalia, but I am not sure if it has been adequately explained why this sight may be traumatic for some and not for others. From an object relations perspective, one may surmise that in some cases the *whole* mother and not only her genitals has been traumatic or, to put it more concretely, that some of those children who find the sight traumatic have discovered not only a horrifying gap in the genital area but also a horrifying gap in relatedness, and that the child's entire psyche has been mobilized to deny and patch over this gap. In certain cases one can regard the frightening genital nothingness as the ultimate body metaphor for a series of developmental losses culminating in the fear that there is *no one there* to love or be loved by and no possibility of finding some libidinal connection behind the screen of technical relatedness. These parents are the sort of people about whom Gertrude Stein once said, "There's no *there* there." Let me give some examples.

A woman with sadomasochistic fantasies, commenting on her mother's presence, said: "You speak to her on the telephone and she's not there. . . . Other people say uh-huh or mm-mmm, or you just know that they're there, but with her you wonder, has she left the telephone? . . . Is she gone? Where has she gone?"

This same question—where has she gone?—became the leitmotif that was repeatedly acted out in the treatment of a man who said about his mother, "She was always absent in my presence." He recounted how his mother had sent him to a doctor as a youngster because he slept too much, but he slept to avoid the emptiness and the pain of her absence. He remembers the doctor asking him questions, but it was a useless experience because it was his mother who should have awakened him by asking him what the matter was or talking to him or being alive or present in his presence. When he was a kid he used to miss her and ask over and over again where she was. Where had she gone? He would read *Playboy* magazine to stimulate himself and keep awake.

He remembered that he sucked his thumb for a long time; the thumb provided a good feeling of connection that he didn't have with his mother—at least he knew where his thumb was! It was like an addiction, and he gave it up only when he turned to masturbation, and that was like an addiction, and then he turned to women, and now with his current woman he is in a state of constant jealousy and driven to ask her where she is going and what she is doing and interrogate her over every detail even though it hurts them both, and when he sees that she is as miserable as he is, then he can stop because it means that she loves him.

We may note again how the attempt to love miscarries, is replaced by fetishistic substitutes, becomes embodied in a merger fantasy that is thwarted, and finally turns to sadomasochism in a tormented attempt to discharge the rage and regain contact through the induction of a mutual sexualized misery: "If I can make you feel as bad as I feel, then I know that you love me and we can retrieve our lost togetherness!" The utter loneliness, misery, and despair of the sadist reaches its apogee in the mad acts of the Marquis de Sade or King Frederick Wilhelm beating his subjects while shouting—"You must love me!"—but sadist and masochist form a couple united in a common enterprise, both seeking in their own ways to complete themselves through the realization of a perfect union.

In this case it seems clear that the sadistic drive is in the service of recapturing the lost object, aggressively punishing it for straying, and maintaining a sexual excitement that will keep both self and object idealized, libidinized, and alive, so that his mother will never again be lost or dead to him and he will never again suffer excruciating pain. In playing this sadomasochistic game, however, he avoids mourning the loss of his mother or renouncing her, which would be necessary in order for the frozen developmental process to resume.

You may wonder why I say that the patient avoids mourning the loss of his mother when I reported that from an early age he was already bemoaning her absence and frantically seeking substitute satisfactions to help him feel alive. In part, of course, this is a retrospective account; he became increasingly aware of the significance of his mother's absence only as analysis progressed. More important, he had split off a part of his psyche so that he could remain close to his mother in her own omnipotent fantasy world, whereas another part of him was strongly connected to reality. Thus, like the pervert who behaves as if he both affirmed and denied the existence of the maternal phallus, he behaved as if he both affirmed and denied the existence of a loving and idealized mother. So long as this dissociation persisted, his mourning could never be complete. Finally, the very defenses that enabled him to survive this cumulative trauma kept him fixated at an anal-sadistic-rapprochement level: he denied his loss by constantly seeking and finding substitute gratifications, he identified with the lost object and became a loser himself, and, most important, he renounced the oedipal struggle by partially identifying with his mother and taking the father for his love object.

Thus his masochism kept him attached to the idealized mother of pain, the mother who was never really there and whose absence was so excruciating, but whom he reactively idealized and was omnipotently attached to in his masochistic fantasies. His sadism, on the other hand, was a denial of his need for her, a manic assertion that he could be omnipotently powerful by himself, but in the end, it became a primitive identification with the aggressive, omnipotent, and androgynous mother of pain.

Most of the time such children appear to be caught in a double bind, because although their sense of effectance is *discouraged* so that they feel no power and no way of having any real impact upon the parent, their sense of omnipotence and guilt is *encouraged* so that they feel responsible for the parent's failure, depression, and rage. One then witnesses a pathetic situation in which the child or adult, even while being physically or mentally abused, feels that he has brought the situation upon himself but is powerless to effect any change.

It is sometimes as early as infancy that the fateful choice to live in pain rather than lose the object may already have begun, a choice that the sadomasochist repeats at each developmental stage. There may be a history of early maternal insensitivity or deprivation resulting in head banging, hair pulling, skin problems, or eating and sleeping disorders, which can be seen as precursors of masochistic adaptations to the unpleasurable maternal dyad (Novick and Novick 1988). In addition, the environment may have conspired with some object loss through the mother's depression, the loss of a caretaker, the birth of a sibling, or a childhood illness, all of which may intensify the sadomasochistic struggle. The conflict achieves heightened impetus in rapprochement, when the basic paradigm of clinging or going-in-search (Herman [1936] 1976) and shadowing or darting away (Mahler 1972) becomes embroiled in the sadomasochistic refusal to resolve the conflict of separation.

This failure to phase-adequately resolve separation has important consequences for subsequent difficulties in handling the heightened sexual fantasies and excitement of the oedipal period and problems around integrating a sexual identity. For sadomasochism is also fueled by the impermissibility of healthy sexual expression, as could be clearly seen in one of my male patients, whose mother had wanted a little girl and had taught him that his phallus and his phallic strivings were unacceptable. He retained these strivings through a combination of drugs, masturbation, and perverse relationships, in which the perversions could be viewed as an idealized or denigrated prescription for what was necessary to complete his sexual identity and sense of self. It may be that one of the reasons we see fewer classical perversions these days is not only that social opportunities have expanded but also that so many of these people now use drugs to help camouflage and patch over the defect in their ego functioning and reality sense.

This defect in reality sense or split in the ego, which is bridged by the fetish or ritual in the classical perversions, is bridged by the mode of relating in sadomasochistic relationships. And just as each fetish or perverse ritual must be unique for the bridge to hold or the patch to fit and function in the perverse act, so one finds a related intolerance for flexible behavior in sadomasochistic relationships. We may presume that this is a reflection of narcissistic intolerance for self-other differentiation as well as an anal omnipotence that declares, "I want what I want when I want it!" But the demand that everything feel just right is reparative as well, because in the childhood of these patients hardly anything felt right for them at all; that is, just as the patient was once a narcissistic extension of the parent, he now makes the partner or the analyst into a narcissistic extension of himself.

We may recall here Stoller's (1988) formulation that "at the center of every erotic fantasy is a childhood trauma which is contained by the fantasy" and which presumably guarantees its uniqueness. I believe this to be true also for sadomasochistic relations, which are, after all, a way of loving. It is the combination of early separation problems with the unique traumata from specific developmental phases that characterizes these relationships. One might say that these patients have to some degree failed to integrate adequately the mother of nurturance and the mother of frustration, or the mother of pleasure and the mother of pain.

Ordinarily, if this integration has been achieved, then under the impetus of the incest taboo and castration threat the child goes in search of a replacement object to love. Going-in-search involves narcissistic affirmation in all phases, but also an acknowledgment of the reality of object failure and loss and the resulting anger that leads to a painful separation. This painful disengagement and symbolic internalization characterize separation and differentiation, whether in rapprochement, in the oedipal phase, in adolescence, or in mourning, which is also a process in which the lost object is separated from by painful detachment and internalized.

It is precisely these painful detachments that the sadomasochist is unable to tolerate because his anger is experienced as an unbearably destructive separation from the object. Thus the masochist says: "Do anything you want to me but don't leave me," and the "anything you want" feels pleasurable because it means that his partner is still with him. The pain of suffering defends against the greater pain of loss.

The sadist turns this around and, in a sort of temper tantrum, plays at destroying the object in order to achieve pleasure, but it is only a false game because in the complicity of the perversions, the object is seldom destroyed or even harmed, while the pleasure of gratification through discharge only temporarily overcomes the pain of separation. Even in those rare instances where the object is destroyed, the identification with the lost object is often so extreme that suicidal thoughts and reunion-in-death fantasies predominate, as Schwartz and I have shown in our study of the Marquis de Sade (Bach and Schwartz 1972). So if the masochist says, "Do anything you want to me but don't leave me," the sadist proclaims, "I can do anything I want to you and you'll still always be there!"

Thus the sadist denies his object needs by overvaluing the importance of his drive discharge, whereas the masochist denies his drive needs by overemphasizing the importance of his object attachments. Since the sadist and the masochist are often the same person at different times or in different topographic states, sadomasochism may be viewed as a pathological oscillation between overvaluation of the drives and overvaluation of the object. In both masochism and sadism, however, holding onto the object typically wins out over letting go because at the stage of incomplete separation where the sadomasochist is fixated, letting go means losing not only the object but also a part of oneself.

It is in order to avoid this loss that the sadomasochist flees from the real world of dependency to the world of his fantasies, where he can play the false game of the idealized self and object. I call it a false game because, as we have seen, it takes place in that split-off world of perversion that is acknowledged as both real and unreal at the same time (Freud [1940] 1964; Steingart 1983). But whereas the child's game is in the service of discriminating reality, uses the transitional object as a help in letting go, and is on the developmental line toward independence and creativity, the sadomasochist's game is in the service of confounding reality, uses the fetish as a help in holding on, and is on the regressive line toward merger and stereotypy. The child's game involves *playing,* whereas the pervert's game involves *play-acting.*

It is also a false game because it requires the suppression of real emotionality, especially anger, and the substitution of a "technical relationship"—that is, a withdrawal of cathexes so that one is dealing with part-objects or self-objects in a world of one's own creation. In this world of dehumanized part-objects, which is typified by pornographic literature, a regressive anal economy prevails: all objects are interchangeable, and one can scarcely be distinguished from the other; the most horrifying sadistic and masochistic fantasies have no real consequence, and *nothing is ever permanently lost* (Bach and Schwartz 1972).

Unfortunately, in our real psychic economy, if nothing is ever permanently lost, then nothing can ever by truly gained. For the price the sadomasochist pays by denying castration, loss, and death is to remain forever frozen into a lifeless stereotype, which he is doomed to repeat. Where no loss, mourning, or renunciation is possible, then no progression is possible from one set of ambivalent life conflicts to another.

This fantasy of part-objects manipulated without loss unfolds in a world that the sadomasochist has split off or dissociated, in an altered state of consciousness characterized by extreme sexual excitement, sharply diminished reflective self-awareness, and a diminished sense that his acts are his own and under voluntary control. While in this altered state he feels as if hypnotized or in an *erotic haze,* and under its spell events take on a hyperreal and hallucinatory quality that makes them seem larger and more compelling than reality itself. What I call the erotic haze serves to deny that reality is not in accord with fantasy, just as my patient had herself blindfolded in order not to notice that her lover was really *not* in tune with her.

Variations on this denial range from closing one's eyes in sex or on the analytic couch to a characterological preference for the vague, the amorphous, and the ambiguous (Lewin 1948; Arlow 1971).

But in this state one also finds hyperrealistic imagery, images that in their hallucinatory clarity seem to deny that the object was lost and to proclaim instead, "No! It's not that she's gone! On the contrary, I see her more clearly and brilliantly than ever!" This is particularly striking in the works of de Sade, where the memory of his dead mother is transformed into that of a ravaged whoremonger whose image, in a moment of passion, becomes once again more glorious, bright, and beautiful than it was in life, a veritable resurrection of the dead imago. One recalls here the many visually concretized denials of loss in fantasy, from the luminescence of dead souls and the incandescence of the wake to the brightness of fetishistic perceptions and the screen memory (Greenacre 1968).

While the sense of voluntary action and reflective self-awareness *decreases* during the sadomasochistic act, the sense of aliveness *increases,* so that the patient feels he is being lived by his instincts or his id. The fascination of this regressive state is known to many, but it is especially attractive to people who feel chronically alienated, anxious, or depressed. In some cases sadomasochistic sexualization defends against a profound libidinal deadness in the patient traceable to a defective libidinization in the early mother-child matrix (see, for example, *Perfume* by Patrick Suskind). In other cases we can see how the idealization of the drives is used as a defense against the intimacy of object relations and the fear of loss, because to the sadomasochist the danger of losing his objects momentarily outweighs the fear of his drives.

Sooner or later, however, he begins to fear the loss of boundaries and becomes anxious and guilty about his omnipotent sexual and destructive fantasies. Many patients do not have the capacity to move easily from this fantasy world to the real world and to feel relaxed in both spaces: they cannot, as it were, get them together. It is important for the treatment to help such patients integrate these dissociated states of consciousness. But although it is essential that this split-off area be brought into the transference, analyzing it is no small task since it is precisely at this point of diminished reality testing and reflective self-awareness that the therapeutic alliance tends to break down.

In the area of the split these patients appear concrete, tend to view the world in stark either-or fluctuation, seem unable to comprehend ambivalence, and may have difficulty in appreciating that a single reality can be understood in different ways by different people. Since this appreciation of multiple perspectives is a basic prerequisite for transference interpretation, these patients have often been regarded as unanalyzable, oppositional, or, in another sense, "perverse."

The problems these patients have in differentiating and separating from their objects is reflected endopsychically in their inability to differentiate and separate from their own point of view or to take perspective on their own thought processes and thus to develop reflective self-awareness. I have discussed these problems elsewhere (Bach 1985, 1988) and hope to return to them again.

In some ways it might not be misleading to compare sadomasochistic alternations and ambivalence to that of a person with pathological mourning, someone who frantically oscillates between believing that the love object is dead and believing that it is still alive, but who does so in such a way that true mourning never becomes possible. Thus, instead of mourning we find a split in the ego, and instead of separation through painful detachment and symbolic internalizations, we find repeated attempts at reunion with the mother of pain through the false game of the idealized self and object.

For although, as Freud ([1919] 1955) noted, sadomasochistic object relations are inextricably linked to beating fantasies, in many cases interpretation of the beating fantasies alone may not produce therapeutic success. I am suggesting that a more regressive fantasy of union with the omnipotent self and object must be analyzed before an enduring change can take place. The working through of this fantasy requires dealing with that split-off area of omnipotent objects that is defended by pseudoemotionality and a frozen aggression that prevents separation and mourning from taking place. Once separation and mourning have been facilitated, the patient is enabled to take up again the developmental line of dependence-independence that had been blocked and replaced by sadomasochistic oscillations.

Another way of putting this is that these patients get better as they learn to be in a transference relationship that is not sadomasochistic. This is more complex than it may seem, however, because in the transference they do everything possible to subtly provoke either sadistic or masochistic reactions that are difficult for the analyst to discern, to understand, and to control.

One sometimes sees in consultation cases in which the sadomasochistic transference has been interpreted seemingly to no avail, or in which it has been jointly acted out in ongoing squabbles about who is going to control whom until both parties to the analysis have reached a state of mutual exasperation and exhaustion. Sometimes confrontational interpretations simply repeat the beating fantasy in another form, so that the patient is secretly gratified while being beaten with interpretations. This is but one situation in which the treatment itself can become a kind of perversion. To a certain extent, of course, incidents like this must be re-created before they can be understood, but the hope is that they will not be repeated indefinitely in the transference as in life.

In certain cases the analyst may not have fully appreciated that the patient's mental organization is in some respects still at a primitive level, and that one cannot explicate the transference, which is a metaphor, to a patient whose mind cannot embrace the cognitive flexibility of metaphors. What this means in practice is that such a patient will confuse or confabulate what should be transferential and symbolic issues into *real* issues of love or death, and will struggle with the analyst as if the analyst were *in fact* trying to rape or kill him.

If certain of these patients are persistently confronted with the analyst's reality before a reliable autonomy has developed, then two perversions of treatment may ensue. In the first, the patient becomes acquiescent and agrees, but does not develop a genuine sense of self, and a prolonged pseudoanalysis results. In the second, the patient disagrees and eventually either leaves or conforms, but he becomes internally isolated, suspicious, and schizoid. He learns, in short, to keep his thoughts to himself and renews his conviction that there is no one in the world he can really trust and nothing to believe in.

Because the person with sadomasochistic tendencies has never learned to trust his objects, he can never feel truly at home in the world. One of my patients constantly compared his life experience to that of a character in Hemingway who says, "When you're born they put you into the game and they tell you the rules and the first time they catch you off base they kill you." In the world of the sadomasochist there is no margin for error, no compassion, and no forgiveness. It is consequently very difficult to help these patients learn to love, to separate, and to mourn.

It seems that the sadomasochist interposes an impersonal or technical relationship between his desire and his object. This alienates him both from himself and from the object of his desire (Khan 1979), in the interest of denying his dependence upon objects that have failed him in the past. This denial takes the form of manic or grandiose assertions of exceptionality, perfection, and omnipotence, the game of the idealized self and object, which includes denial of separation and sexual identity, denial of loss and castration, and denial of helplessness and depression. The masochist's longed-for surrender to an idealized other or the sadist's merger with the omnipotent self-object is the ultimate way of avoiding the ambivalence conflict between dependence and independence. One might say that in searching to avoid a real dependence upon an actual fallible object, the sadomasochist substitutes a fantasied dependence upon an idealized infallible object.

In this way, much like those political terrorists exiled from their homeland, the sadomasochist spends his days in fantasies of recapturing a lost Paradise that never in fact existed, while at the same time refusing to compromise by living in the real world that might actually be possible.

References

Arlow, J. 1971. "Character Perversion." In *Currents in Psychoanalysis,* ed. I. Marcus. New York: International Universities Press.

Bach, S. 1985. *Narcissistic States and the Therapeutic Process.* New York: Aronson.

———. 1988. "On Being Heard: Attunement and the Growth of Psychic Structure." Edmund Weil Memorial Lecture, Institute for Psychoanalytic Training and Research.

Bach, S., and Schwartz, L. 1972. "A Dream of the Marquis de Sade." *Journal of the American Psychoanalytic Association* 20:3.

Freud, S. [1919] 1955. "A Child Is Being Beaten: A Contribution to the Study of Sexual Perversions." In *Standard Edition* 17:175–204.

————. [1940] 1964. "Splitting of the Ego in the Process of Defense." In *Standard Edition* 23:275–78.

Greenacre, P. 1968. "Perversions: General Considerations Regarding Their Genetic and Dynamic Background." In *Psychoanalytic Study of the Child* 23:47–62.

Hermann, I. [1936] 1976. "Clinging—Going-in-Search: A Contrasting Pair of Instincts and Their Relation to Sadism and Masochism." *Psychoanalytic Quarterly* 45:1.

Khan, M. 1979. *Alienation in Perversions*. New York: International Universities Press.

Lewin, B. 1948. "The Nature of Reality and the Meaning of Nothing, with an Addendum on Concentration." *Psychoanalytic Quarterly* 17:524–26.

Mahler, M. S. 1972. "Rapprochement Subphase of the Separation-Individuation Phase." *Psychoanalytic Quarterly* 41:487–506.

Novick, K. K., and Novick, J. 1987. "The Essence of Masochism." *Psychoanalytic Study of the Child* 42:353–84.

Steingart, I. 1983. *Pathological Play in Borderline and Narcissistic Personalities*. New York: S. P. Scientific Books.

Stoller, R. 1988. Panel on Sadomasochism in the Perversions. American Psychoanalytic Association, December.

Waelder, R. [1930] 1976. "The Principle of Multiple Function: Observations on Overdetermination." In *Psychoanalysis: Observation, Theory, Application*, ed. S. Guttman. New York: International Universities Press.

Chapter Five

Perversion in Fantasy and Furtive Enactments

Helen C. Meyers, M.D.

She is on her way home. A group of disreputable men pull her into a doorway. At knife point, the leader orders her to undress, kneel in front of him, and perform fellatio and oral-anal acts on him. At the same time, he tells his fellows to introduce a variety of objects into her bodily orifices while calling her derogatory names. In great distress, she pleads with him to stop, but he continues. Slowly, to her great humiliation, she realizes that she has become uncontrollably excited; he knows it and taunts her with it. She now begs him to continue more violently, inventing new humiliations, asking him to whip her and brand her as his property. At the point of maximum humiliation and imagined pain she has an orgasm. Everything stops.

THIS is the repetitive masturbation fantasy of a highly functioning woman patient with an obsessive-compulsive character structure. A successful lawyer, she is married and has children and many friends. She is somewhat inhibited sexually but enjoys intercourse with her husband and has intermittent orgasms. She has no perverse fantasies during intercourse. There is no overt perverse behavior, and there has been no extramarital affair.

This is just one example of a "perversion" encountered in the everyday clinical life of an average American analyst. It is not one of the dramatic, flamboyant perversions we read about in literature and in the news, but one of the more ordinary, sometimes subtle manifestations and derivatives that patients frequently present in analysis, the perverse fantasies and furtive enactments that I will address in this chapter: (1) conscious fantasies and furtive enactments that exist prior to analysis and are subsequently revealed to the analyst, (2) perverse fantasies that develop during analysis, and (3) transference enactments.

Unconscious Fantasies, Perverse Conscious Fantasies, and Perverse Action

The relation of conscious perverse fantasies—fantasies that enhance or are obligatory for excitement and orgasm—to perverse action has attracted interest and controversy in psychoanalysis. Some authors see these fantasies and acts on a continuum, as merely a matter of degree. Others see them as sharply differentiated. Those who see a continuum usually stress the similarity in psychodynamics, regarding differences in psychic structure as less important. Those who place perverse action in a category of its own emphasize the difference in psychic structure and relegate the similarity in dynamic content to a lesser role. Arlow (1971), for example, suggests that conscious perverse fantasy, perverse act, and character perversion can and often do occur in the same patient, in that all are based on a similar unconscious fantasy. This unconscious fantasy involves castration anxiety and the denial of the female genital. Coen (1985), on the other hand, definitely separates masturbation fantasies, which he does not consider perverse (and which he claims belong to the realm of higher-level neurotic and nonneurotic character), from perverse activity. He further divides perverse action into "higher-level-type perversions," with predominantly oedipal conflict, and "lower-level perversions," which he postulates as occurring in more severe character pathology with a disturbance in internal object relations. McDougall

(1972) makes qualitative distinctions among neurotic, psychotic, and what she considers a specifically perverse psychic structure. This "perverse structure," as she calls it, is a clinical concept that includes conscious erotization of defenses, compulsive sexuality, and an impoverished fantasy life. As she puts it, "The erotic expression of the sexual deviant is an essential feature of his psychic stability, and much of his life revolves around it." She differentiates this perverse structure from the occasional perverse symptom that may occur in ordinary neurotics with various personality structures, such as a hysteric with occasional homosexual acting out, or an obsessive compulsive with previous phases of fetishism or anal erotic experiments. Masturbation fantasies, the prerogative of everyone, are different still. In fact, McDougall objects to the notion of "perverse fantasy" altogether. She asserts that there is only perverse behavior since she argues that all fantasy, by definition, is about the objectionable and unobtainable. I believe, however, that she may not differentiate sufficiently between unconscious fantasy, where I agree that the term *perverse* loses its meaning, and conscious fantasies, which clearly can be "perverse."

I am among those who do not like the term *perverse* when it is misused in a judgmental way. To slightly misquote the Roman writer Terence (100 B.C.), "I am a woman—nothing human is alien to me." But as a technical or descriptive term, the concept of a conscious "perverse fantasy" can be useful. I agree in that respect with Stoller, who also believes that the term *perversion,* when defined by the purpose, function, and meaning of the behavior, is useful. I do not fully agree with him, however, that hostility, though an admittedly important ingredient, is the sine qua non of perversion. Stoller (1975) specifically differentiates deviant behavior from perverse behavior on the criterion of hostility: in fact, he has defined perversion as the "erotic form of hatred."

In my opinion, fantasy is qualitatively as well as quantitatively different from action and behavior. Certainly conflicts that cannot be contained in fantasy may spill over into overt action. For instance, a phobia is preceded by a fantasy that may contain the anxiety until an external situation intrudes to make it no longer sufficient, or until the anxiety is so high that the conflict must be externalized to an external object or situation, which can then be avoided defensively. And like symptoms, perversions also always involve unconscious fantasy as well as the conscious fantasy scenario that is acted out. But something must be added or be missing for fantasy to become action.

In my experience, most perverse masturbation fantasies, though they may be associated with character disorders, such as obsessive-compulsive, hysteric, narcissistic, masochistic or other character trait perversions (Arlow 1971), do not turn into perverse behavior. In fact, they seem to owe some of their sexual excitement to or derive permission for the excitement from precisely the fact that they exist only in fantasy; they will not be realized and will not expose the fantasizer to reality danger. Indeed, these fantasies often occur in rather inhibited, controlled characters, patients who would be most disturbed by and in actuality avoid any "unusual" sexual act or real pain or humiliation.

What, then, is involved in this action differential in perversion? Some analytic theorists have associated a tendency to perverse action with a superego distortion; the superego itself condones or demands the perverse act, perhaps because of the internalization of parental perverse ideation or character, or because of corruption, seduction, or permissiveness by parents. Others have associated this tendency to perverse action with extra intensity of the drives, including the aggressive drive, leading to ego weakness, which they view as being due to defensive splitting. This splitting, then, permits the gratification in action of a partial or partly acceptable instinct, while repressing the larger, more unacceptable part. The escaped part also serves as an expression of and condensation with the repressed part, as well as a defense against it (Sachs [1923] 1986).

In more current developmental conceptualizations, such factors might be put in terms of defective early mother-child object relations, leading to problems in identification and in the formation of self- and object-representations in the superego and ego. Consequently, there is a need for a concrete, erotized object or action to replace the missing secure internal self and object. This would certainly seem to apply to lower-level perversions.

These conceptualizations of superego distortion, ego weakness owing to inner pressure, inadequate internal structure, and need for external concretization help me understand perverse action as opposed to mere fantasy, but do not fully satisfy me. A promising addition, though probably no final answer, is the concept of impairment in the development of the cognitive ego function of fantasizing. (Fantasy as an ego function has been discussed by Person [1989] and Sarnoff [1975] particularly in relation to latency.) Along analogous lines, McDougall (1972) describes impairment in the capacity to symbolize based on inadequate early mother-child relations. It appears to me that this capacity or function might enable the higher-level neurotic to use rich conscious fantasy to deal with and contain conflict, while those with impaired fantasy function are unable to do so. Their conscious fantasies and scenarios are too narrow, rigid, and stereotyped. The compromise solution needs to be acted out concretely.

Furtive Enactments

Following these thoughts further, I am led to propose the clinical concept of "furtive enactments." I refer here to such clinical phenomena as the exciting, furtive, yet compulsory glancing at others' genitals in inappropriate situations, where associations reveal that these genitals are perceived as if they were disembodied objects; or the furtive watching in the mirror of oneself and one's partner entwined in intercourse, with associated fantasies of being either partner or both, as if to establish that there is no difference between them; or the furtive anal self-stimulation during intercourse, with a sense of being both male and female at the same time.

Perverse furtive enactments have not been explored much in the psychoanalytic literature nor have they been well conceptualized. I suggest that they may be thought of as halfway between perversion in fantasy and perverse behavior: not just fantasy yet not quite fully perverse acts. They may be conceptualized as compromises that, on the one hand, are unable to be contained in fantasy (because of instinctual intensity, superego distortion, or problems in fantasizing ability) yet, on the other hand, are not quite able to be expressed in perversion as such (because of the ego's reality functions, superego inhibition, or inhibition of action potential). The result is episodic, small, furtive acts. This conceptualization may be related to McDougall's (1986) concept of theater or Arlow's (1986) characterization of perversion as play or play acting—not quite real, yet quite serious. Fantasy, furtive enactments, and perverse acts might then be thought of as representing quite different stages of such theater.

In this same halfway zone of furtive enactments, to my mind, is the use of kinky pornographic magazines and movies: not able to use one's own fantasy, one needs an external object such as a magazine or movie for excitement. Yet it still is in fantasy only, even though someone else's fantasy. This fantasy must, of course, correspond to one's own potential fantasy. At the same time, it does involve furtive voyeuristic enactment, although again not "real" but only with images. Conversely, it involves the producer's, writer's, or actor's perverse fantasy plus a kind of enactment. This is not a direct act, however, since it is contained not in fantasy but by the screen or printed page.

Perhaps even more intriguing than the overtly erotic perverse movies are the more indirectly perverse. These are often intentionally sadistic movies such as *Clockwork Orange,* in which violence is raised to a fever pitch of pleasurable excitement. In a showing of this film I attended, I heard a member of the audience whisper with breathless excitement, "Violence is beautiful!" In another film I saw recently, a supposedly beautiful, gentle, and loving mother, in order to regain her father's love and obtain a socially desirable marriage, coolly and slowly poisoned her four equally beautiful and loving children who more or less passively submitted to this. A perversion indeed of mother love! This is a cruel movie, strangely fascinating and exciting to the audience, who seemed to identify with excited horror with the sadistic grandmother, the sadomasochistic mother, and the masochistically submitting children.

The Phenomenon of Perversion

Before I present some clinical examples, let me pose one more question: What is it that truly defines what we call perversion? What is unique about it? Some people, of course, say there is nothing unique, that it is defined only by social moral conventions. Others say that it is not only a disorder of a sexual nature but a dimension of the human psyche in general, a temptation in the mind common to us all. In this view, there is a latent perverse core in everyone that tends to emerge at times of social upheaval. The cruelties and the perverse cabarets of Nazi Germany and the appearance of the Marquis de Sade around the time of the French Revolution (Chasseguet-Smirgel 1983) are well-known examples. Some define a sexual act as perverse simply and only when it is *not* between consenting adults and if it hurts someone or dehumanizes the partner.

Descriptively, perversion involves an *obligatory* and *unusual* (often painful, humiliating, dehumanized, or "unnatural") fantasy, scenario, act, or object that is necessary for sexual excitement and gratification. Such fantasies or actions may then also lead to derivative nonsexual character trait disorders or transference manifestations that may serve other purposes besides sexual excitement and pleasure, such as revenge, mastery, or rescue of a sense of self or self-esteem.

Freud, in "Three Essays on the Theory of Sexuality" ([1905] 1953) originally defined perversion as the negative of neurosis (actually the "positive" of neurosis): the direct expression of a libidinal component instinct. He modified his views in his discussion of masochistic perverse sexual fantasies in "A Child Is Being Beaten" ([1919] 1955), in which he stressed the defensive regression from the Oedipus complex to anality because of anxiety and guilt over oedipal sexual and aggressive wishes. He thus introduced into the conceptualization of perversion the role of oedipal conflict and castration anxiety, of guilt and aggression (expanded in late 1922), and of defensive regression to earlier libidinal stages, particularly the anal stage with its component instincts of sadism and masochism. With this he had laid the groundwork for Sachs's ([1923] 1986) conflict explanation and our later conceptualization of perversion as a compromise formation, like any symptom or character. This concept currently is particularly relevant to our understanding and increasing awareness of female perversion (Richards 1989).

Having said that perversion is a compromise formation, we have said something true and clinically useful. But what have we really said about the specialness of perversion? Perhaps we come closer to saying something unique if we are more specific about what this compromise solution is about. The most common view is that it involves the characterologic or ritualized denial of castration and of the female genital (Arlow 1971) acted out through the regressive revival of the fantasy of a maternal or female phallus by way of substitution of a fetish, or by cross-dressing, or by voyeurism (looking for the hidden penis). The perverse symptom is then seen as a regressive adaptation of the ego to secure gratification without destroying the object or endangering the self (Bach, chap. 4, this volume). Such perversions, when partial or transient in latency or adolescence, might then lead to derivatives in the form of certain adult character perversions, as suggested by Arlow (1971), where the need to deny sexual reality is expressed in character traits of the "unrealistic character," petty thefts, or a tendency toward playing practical jokes or hoaxes. But again I must assert that this explanation, while certainly describing psychodynamics that may be virtually always present, still fails fully to delineate the specialness of perversion. Castration anxiety, after all, can and often is defended against by other compromise solutions. Why then do these patients use the particular solution of perversion? Furthermore, anxieties other than oedipal castration fears may also be defended against by the perversions. These fears include disintegration, annihilation, or separation anxieties, or fear of loss of self or of self-definition. These latter fears are, of course, more prominent in lower-level psychic organizations.

It is perhaps the perverse patient's particular partial distortion of reality, the "special manner in which," as Freud ([1927] 1955) put it in relation to fetishism, "they yield to reality" that is unique to perversion? Both Arlow (1986) and McDougall (1986) have referred to it as a form of theater, an illusory solution, not a delusion, as in psychosis. The perverse act, McDougall suggests, is like a stage play or a dream, where object relations are dominated by defenses of disavowal, false splitting, projection, regression of instinct, and manic defenses. Arlow, Bach, and others relate this reality distortion to the need to deny the female genital and its attendant castration anxiety. McDougall (1972) sees it more in terms of denial of the difference between the sexes and of the primal scene, by which she refers to the whole sexual relationship between male and female. The secret fantasy is that the "parents' genitals do not complete each other," behind which lie deeper terrors of separation and identity. The primal scene is then reinvented and "new sexualities" are created (1984). In fantasy there is recovery of the lost object and defiant punishment of the object. Chasseguet-Smirgel (1978) sees in this subversion of reality the need to deny the difference between generations as well as the difference between the sexes, thus eliminating the infantile narcissistic wound of the little boy's inadequacy to fill mother's organ. The "bedrock of reality" being created by the differences between sexes and generations, according to Chasseguet-Smirgel (1983), the destruction of this order creates a new anal universe, where all particles are the same. Male equals female; child equals parent. Greenacre (1968) also talks of haziness and denial of the perception of reality in perversion. Of course, a partially distorted view of reality as such hardly is unique to perversion; indeed it is the hallmark of all neuroses.

What about *preoedipal* factors in the genesis of perversion? While many authors seem to agree that the crucial mobilizing factor for future perversion arises in the oedipal conflict, many (particularly McDougall 1984; Greenacre 1968; Coen 1985) also stress the role of early disturbance in the mother-child relationship—the infrastructure of impaired object relations—in shaping the oedipal solution in perversion, particularly in the so-called lower-level-type perversion (Coen 1985). Impaired early object relations as such can, of course, also lead to other solutions, such as borderline, psychotic, and psychosomatic disorders. Greenacre indicts early impaired object relations in the formation of perversion, but adds that there is a specifically determined weakness in the body and self-image. This is due to actual trauma leading to increased aggression and castration anxiety, wherein the sexual drives are distorted in the interest of bolstering the body image for narcissistic rather than object libidinal purposes. The fetish both defends against and represents the trauma, a disembodied substitute for a missing body part. The fetish, therefore, goes beyond the transitional object, which is used only for anxiety reduction. Valenstein (1974) even suggests that the fetish or ritualistic behavior may actually re-create some aspects of the original trauma, turning passive into active. Goldberg (1975) takes the narcissistic purpose of perversion a step further. He sees perverse behaviors as sexual displays of missing self-structure or erotized substitutes for structure deficiency.

Or finally is it the amount of *aggression* that is unique to perversion? From Freud on, all authors have agreed on the essential role of aggression in perversion. Chasseguet-Smirgel (1983), for example, argues that perversion is inevitably sadistic in its destruction of order and values. Greenacre (1968) sees sadomasochism in all perversion, and Arlow (1971) talks of the control of aggression in perversion. And Stoller (1975), of course, considers hostility as central in this "erotic form of hatred."

So there we have it: compromise formation; oedipal conflict with castration anxiety and regression; impaired early object relations and erotized narcissistic trauma, with annihilation anxiety, humiliation, and attempt at mastery; denial of sexual reality; substitutive conscious and unconscious fantasy but often impoverished fantasy function; and aggression with risk and revenge. These are some of the ingredients that taken all together, in varying proportions, form the uniqueness of perversion. Perversion is that unique sexual expression that is both a derailment from its original purpose in aim, object, zone, or form, a "turning away from the ordinary course" (Arlow), and also a creative new solution, "new sexualities" (McDougall 1984).

Clinical Illustrations

Having discussed the theory of perversion in fantasy in relation to perversion in action, the border concept of furtive enactments, and the unique ingredients of perversion per se, I would now like to present clinical material that will expand upon my theoretical discussion. In these examples, I will return to the categories differentiated at the beginning of this chapter: (1) perverse fantasies brought to the analysis, (2) perverse fantasies developed during analysis, (3) furtive enactments brought to analysis, and (4) perverse transference enactments.

Perverse Fantasy Brought to Analysis

The reader will recall the masturbation fantasy with which this chapter opens—the woman who fantasized about being sexually abused. This is a fairly frequent and typical fantasy occurring in women patients with classic oedipal dynamics, often, as in our example, patients with high-level neurotic obsessive-compulsive characters with mild masochistic features, a harsh superego, guilt over oedipal desires and aggression, and regression to the anal sadomasochistic phase. This is very much related to Freud's classic description in "A Child Is Being Beaten" ([1919] 1955). The superego in our case is assuaged in the fantasy both by the initial coercion and by the final beating, pain, and humiliation, thus permitting sexual gratification. It is also a good example of perversion in fantasy with no overt perversion in a patient with a neurotic character structure. Typical is the well-developed capacity for fantasy, well-delineated ego with predominantly inhibitory high-level defenses, good reality perception, good internal and external object relations, and a well-functioning though rather punitive superego. These features allowed and led to fantasy but inhibited perverse action. Indeed, this woman patient is actually fastidious and sensitive, something of a princess, and would not tolerate the slightest pain, discomfort, or humiliation in actuality.

In her background was a reasonably happy childhood with reasonably good parenting. There was, however, an adored and adoring father and a somewhat competitive, domineering mother, which intensified the patient's oedipal desires for her father and increased her guilt and anger toward her mother on both oedipal and preoedipal grounds. The patient's aggression stemmed from her early dyadic battles with mother, as well as from the patient's oedipal competition. The harshness of the superego, then, came from the internalized punitive mother representation, further endowed with the patient's own intense projected aggression. This projected anger probably also accounted for the violent conception of the primal scene. There was no evidence for some of the other uses of masochism, such as the maintenance of object relations or self-delineation, except for the narcissistic function of masochism of maintaining control over the scenario of her fantasy suffering, particularly in the later part of the fantasy. Why this fantasy was obligatory for masturbatory satisfaction but absent in orgastic intercourse with her husband is open for speculation.

It is interesting to note that similar masochistic masturbation fantasies sometimes develop only after such a patient has been in treatment for a while. This phenomenon is apparently due to the fact that such patients may previously have been too inhibited even to masturbate and certainly too inhibited to let themselves fantasize consciously.

Perverse Fantasy Developed during Analysis

An interesting perverse fantasy developed during an analysis (supervised by the author) of a patient with a predominantly narcissistic personality disorder. The patient, a woman artist, developed the fantasy of performing oral and anal sex on her female analyst in a particular stylized manner. This fantasy was used only during intercourse with her husband. At first sporadic, it became obligatory for orgasm for three months and then disappeared. There had been no previous homosexual fantasy or activity. Intercourse with her husband (and other men before him) had always been exciting and orgastic without fantasy. Although professionally successful and superficially friendly, the patient had somewhat shallow internal object relations; her external object relations tended to be sexualized.

An only child, raised in a household without a father (there had been an early divorce), the patient had a submissive relationship with her narcissistic and depriving but demanding mother. The patient had difficulty with the capacity to depend in the analysis. As the defective early mother-child relationship and trauma to the self-image emerged in the transference, the above sexual fantasy appeared as an apparent sexualization of a pathologic narcissistic configuration in an attempt to substitute this new erotized object relationship with the "mother" analyst in fantasy for the missing self-structure. As this was further worked through, especially in its oral dependent and anal hostile aspects, and with the emergence of a more real object relatedness to the analyst, the fantasy disappeared. Two years later, when higher-level oedipal conflicts emerged for the first time, the same fantasy reappeared briefly, but this time with the analyst representing the missing oedipal father in the transference.

Furtive Enactment Brought to Analysis

A furtive enactment by a male patient consisted of anal self-stimulation during intercourse with his wife, without her knowledge. This man, a rather successful journalist, had a neurotic obsessive-compulsive character structure with predominantly oedipal pathology (both positive and negative) with anal regression. The furtive enactments were not obligatory but greatly enhanced his pleasure. The conscious fantasy with this activity was one of being in complete control and self-sufficient. The unconscious underlying fantasy was that of being penetrated by father and simultaneously penetrating mother, thus being and having both father and mother at the same time.

The background to this complex fantasy included some problems in identification. The patient both identified with and wanted to possess his beautiful, literate mother as well as his successful, overpowering father. The need to deny the double castration threat of mother's vagina and submission to father led to this furtive perverse enactment, with both his finger and his wife's genital experienced as disembodied, serving as quasi fetishes. Hostility was manifested in this dehumanization of his wife's body, as well as in an easily aroused rage at women in general. This enactment could also be viewed in McDougall's terms, as the fantasized obliteration of the difference between the sexes and the denial of the primal scene, with the patient becoming his own new version of the primal scene. He had, however, a well-developed superego, good ego strength and functions, and good internal object relations. The perversion thus remained as furtive enactments and never became a full perversion.

Perverse Transference Enactment

Here I refer to a particular kind of transference, one we might call a derivative perverse transference enactment. This is akin to the derivative character perversion. There is a characteristic sadomasochistic transference that is frequently observed, particularly in male patients. These patients have a mixture of obsessive-compulsive character with sadomasochistic features, predominantly oedipal pathology, severe castration anxiety, and regression to anality. Their superego is harsh in places and permissive in others. Their rage and guilt is turned masochistically upon themselves, but the rage slips out sadistically toward the object.

I remember one such patient who also fit Arlow's description of character perversion (1971). In his adolescence he had been an occasional voyeur and a flasher. In adulthood, he was evasive about reality ("unrealistic character") and given to sadistic practical jokes. In the transference, evidencing more than a negative therapeutic reaction, he took sadistic pleasure in subverting interpretations, worked hard to undermine the analytic work, and became pleasurably excited when he so succeeded in defeating the analyst, even when it was to his own detriment. One time, for example, he came to a session with evident excited triumph to report that his first party, which he had been able to arrange only as the result of much analytic work, had failed utterly: not one guest had shown up! These sadomasochistic transference enactments may be subtle or not so subtle, furtive or overt, but certainly are "turned away from the intended course" of analysis. And if getting pleasure and excitement out of hostility is perversion, these sadomasochistic transference phenomena assuredly are perverse.

In summary, I have concerned myself here not with the dramatic perversions described in literature and reported in the news but with the perversions of everyday clinical life: perverse fantasies and furtive enactments. To do this, it was necessary first to conceptually define and dynamically formulate the phenomenon of perversion as such, including a review of the relevant literature, and then to delineate my own understanding of the uniqueness of the perverse phenomenon. I then differentiated perverse fantasy from perverse action and speculated upon the complex question of what makes for action rather than containment in fantasy. I then introduced and described my own concept of perverse furtive enactments, a border concept halfway between perverse fantasy and actions. This is a clinical phenomenon often observed but not previously explored in the psychoanalytic literature. Finally, I presented and discussed a number of clinical examples of perverse fantasies and furtive enactments, illustrating the ubiquity and diversity of these phenomena and the crucial necessity to recognize and understand them in clinical practice.

References

Arlow, J. 1971. "Character Perversion." In *Currents in Psychoanalysis,* ed. I. M. Marcus. New York: International Universities Press, 317–36.

———. 1986. "Discussion of Papers by McDougall and Glasser on Identification and Perversion." *International Journal of Psychoanalysis* 67:245–50.

———. 1987. "Trauma, Play and Perversion." *Psychoanalytic Study of the Child* 42:31–44.

Bak, R. C. 1968. "The Phallic Woman: The Ubiquitous Fantasy in Perversions." *Psychoanalytic Study of the Child* 23:15–36.

Chasseguet-Smirgel, J. 1974. "Perversion, Idealization and Sublimation." *International Journal of Psychoanalysis* 55:349–58.

_____. 1978. "Reflections on the Connection between Perversion and Sadism." *International Journal of Psychoanalysis* 59:27–36.

_____. 1981. "Loss of Reality in Perversions, Especially Fetishism." *Journal of the American Psychoanalytic Association* 29:511–34.

_____. 1983. "Perversion and the Universal Law." *International Review of Psychoanalysis* 10:293–302.

Coen, S. 1985. "Perversion as a Solution to Intrapsychic Conflict." *Journal of the American Psychoanalytic Association* 33:17–57.

Compton, A. 1986. "Neglected Classics: Hans Sachs' "On the Genesis of Perversion: Introduction and Discussion." *Psychoanalytic Quarterly* 55:474–76, 489–92.

de Sade, A. D. [1785–95] 1967. *Ouevres completes*. Paris: Cercle du Livres Precieux.

Freud, S. [1905] 1953. "Three Essays on the Theory of Sexuality." In *Standard Edition* 7:125–245.

_____. [1919] 1955. "A Child Is Being Beaten." In *Standard Edition* 17:175–204.

_____. [1927] 1955. "Fetishism." In *Standard Edition* 21:149–57.

Goldberg, A. 1975. "A Fresh Look at Perverse Behavior." *International Journal of Psychoanalysis* 56:335–42.

Greenacre, P. 1968. "Perversion: Genetic and Dynamic Background." *Psychoanalytic Study of the Child* 23:47–62.

McDougall, J. 1972. "Primal Scene and Sexual Perversion." *International Journal of Psychoanalysis* 53:371–84.

_____. 1984. "Neosexualities: Reflections on the Role of Perversions in the Psychic Economy." Reported on in *Bulletin of the Association for Psychoanalytic Medicine* 24:24–29.

_____. 1986. "Identifications, Neoneeds and Neosexuality. *International Journal of Psychoanalysis* 67:19–32.

Person, E. 1989. Personal communication.

Richards, A. 1989. "Female Fetishism and Female Perversion: A Case of Female Foot or Boot Fetishism by Hermine Hug-Hellmuth Reconsidered." Paper presented at the meeting of the National Psychological Association for Psychoanalysis, New York.

Sachs, H. [1923] 1986. "On the Genesis of Perversion." *Psychoanalytic Quarterly* 55:477–88.

Sarnoff, C. 1975. "Narcissism, Adolescent Masturbation Fantasies and the Search for Reality." In *Masturbation from Infancy to Senescence,* ed. L. Marcus and J. Francis. New York: International Universities Press.

———. 1988. "Adolescent Masochism." In *Masochism: Current Psychoanalytic Perspectives,* ed. R. Glick and D. Meyers. Hillsdale, N.J.: Analytic Press.

Stoller, R. 1975. *Perversion: The Erotic Form of Hatred.* New York: Pantheon.

Valenstein, A. 1974. "The Role of Early Experience." *Sexual Deviation: Psychoanalytic Insights,* ed. M. Ostow. New York: Quadrangle.

Chapter Six

A Case History of a Man Who Made Obscene Telephone Calls and Practiced Frotteurism

Wayne A. Myers, M.D.

I N this chapter, I will describe the case of a man who practiced two separate perverse acts in his sexual life. One was frotteurism: he would rub up against women on a crowded subway train until he experienced an orgasm. The second involved making obscene phone calls to women. While conversing with them or breathing heavily, the patient would masturbate to orgasm.

These perversions have been described infrequently in the literature (Harris 1957; Nadler 1968; Stoller 1975; Almansi 1979; Shengold 1982; Silverman 1982a, 1982b; Richards 1989), and their psychodynamic underpinnings have not been fully elucidated. The material to follow will endeavor to redress this gap in our knowledge and understanding.

Clinical Material

Mr. A came for analysis at the urging of his wife, who was frightened by the physical abuse he inflicted upon her when he had been drinking too much alcohol. When he was not drinking, he behaved in a detached manner similar to his father, who had also been a periodic drinker and wife abuser. In his work life, the patient was a hardworking, successful, middle-level executive for a major multinational corporation. He was highly thought of by his superiors because of his painstaking attention to the details of his job and was clearly a man marked for advancement in his company.

The patient had never felt secure in his masculinity. During adolescence and young adulthood, he masturbated with fantasies of older women seducing him. In these autoerotic sagas, the females were always available and would become immediately aroused without any effort on his part. In addition, after once having seen a pornographic film depicting lesbian sex, he would occasionally fantasize about two women making love to each other. These fantasies were very exciting to him and he masturbated a good deal during this period in his life.

When he first had intercourse, in his early twenties, he experienced some problems with erectile impotence. This symptom recurred when he married and found that his wife was not a virgin. The problem cleared up rather quickly, and the sex life of the couple improved. This was especially true for Mr. A's wife, who experienced considerable pleasure in their infrequent relations. The patient, however, found it hard to relax sexually and was primarily concerned with pleasing his wife. Prior to beginning treatment, Mr. A had had two transient affairs. With neither of the women, however, was there any real emotional involvement.

Mr. A was the third of five children of a lower-middle-class Catholic family. He had worked since the age of ten and continued to do so through college. Mr. A reported only one close relationship in his life, with a boy in his scout troop during adolescence. There was some transient mutual masturbatory play with this boy, which the patient instigated, but no other evidence of overt homosexual activities in his life. As an adult, he had occasional fleeting thoughts of being forced to submit to other men in oral and anal homosexual play, but these ideas were repugnant to him and were not accompanied by feelings of sexual excitation.

The patient reported feeling rather distant from his parents and siblings. Though he denied harboring angry feelings toward family members, he said he always rejected their overtures of friendship, feeling that it was necessary to stay at arm's length from them.

In discussing his wife, he frequently complained about her housekeeping and about her own heavy dependence on alcohol. The aura that pervaded his discussions of all these people was one of disappointment and a touch of bitterness, as if they had all hurt him in some rather profound way and his aloofness was a way of getting even with them.

The only person he seemed to love unreservedly was his three-year-old son. He was very protective of the youngster and always fearful that some harm would befall him. On the one or two occasions when his son had seen him inebriated, Mr. A felt enormously guilty and ashamed of himself. After the second such occurrence, he vowed that he would never let it happen again.

As the analysis proceeded, the patient's occasional bouts of drinking began to be restricted to weekend and vacation separations from the analyst. When I attempted to link this to his feelings about being apart from me, he denied this. Instead, he connected his drinking to his long-standing fears of "defectiveness." He revealed that he had been blind in one eye since birth and had a minimal spinal deformity. Both of these physical limitations made him feel "unmanly." The inchoate rage and underlying depression aroused by this perception of himself as "imperfect" intensified during weekends and vacations, as these were typically times when "real men," like his older brother, engaged in sports, at which he felt inadequate.

Toward the middle of the first year of the treatment, the patient expressed anger one day at his son's obsessional rituals around going to sleep, which interfered with the time Mr. A and his wife had for sexual activities. This was the first negative feeling he had expressed toward the boy. In associating to it, he recalled having spent the first four years of his own life in the parental bedroom. His younger brother was born when the patient was aged four, and the new arrival led to his expulsion to another room, where he shared a bed with his older brother.

Mr. A was embarrassed to reveal that as a child he too had had a number of rituals associated with going to sleep. Most of them seemed related to his attempts to control his mother and to keep her near him, thus ensuring that the intimate contact with her he had felt prior to his exclusion from the parental bedroom had not been broken. In this setting, he disclosed his tendency to make late-night obscene phone calls to women when his wife was away or was too intoxicated to interact with him.

In these calls he usually pretended to be taking a survey of female attitudes on a variety of subjects. If the women answered his initial questions and remained on the phone, he quickly steered the inquiries to matters concerning their sexual practices and desires. The longer he could keep a woman on the phone in such a call, the more aroused he would become. As he at the same time masturbated to orgasm, he would verbalize aloud his desire to "eat" the woman until he had "sucked her dry" or to "fuck" her into "oblivion."

A pair of dreams late in the first year of treatment helped elucidate some of the dynamics behind the patient's telephone calls. In one dream, a man and a woman are married in a double-ring ceremony. In his associations to this dream, he thought first of descriptions of his parents' wedding and then of the recent marriage of his younger brother.

The two rings in the dream also brought his most recent obscene phone call to mind, inasmuch as the woman to whom he had spoken had answered the phone after two rings. The patient acknowledged having made the call shortly after the wedding party, where he had had too much to drink. He had been irritated by his mother's apparent indifference to him during the festivities, as if she preferred the younger brother, who was getting married.

In a second dream, which occurred shortly before the summer vacation break, he had started to "ring up" a familiar number on the telephone. He then tripped over the phone wire, and the cord became tightly entwined around his wife's terry cloth bathrobe. For a moment, he was uncertain as to whether she was in the robe, and he feared that he might have harmed her. At that juncture, he awoke feeling a combination of anger, anxiety, and sadness.

In his associations to this second dream, he was embarrassed to acknowledge that the familiar telephone number seemed similar to mine or perhaps to his parents' number. His wife's robe was like one his mother had worn when he was a child. In his mind, the telephone line represented an umbilical cord connecting him with his mother, his wife, and me. He realized that my upcoming vacation intensified his need to be "connected" to someone who could offer "sustenance" to him in periods of need.

Thus the wish to "suck dry" the women he was calling could be seen as expressing his desire to obtain the nourishment from the mother that he originally felt deprived of after the birth of his younger brother and more recently at this brother's wedding. Hence at one level, the call constituted an undoing of the trauma involved in the birth of the younger sibling and the concomitant expulsion from the parental bedroom.

The patient's rage toward the indifferent mother, the absent or intoxicated wife, and the vacationing analyst was expressed in the murderous strangling of the wife-mother robe with the phone wire in the dream. It was also seen in his verbalization of his wish to "fuck" the woman into "oblivion" in his calls. Anxiety over the murderous intensity of his rage and the separation from the needed object that he feared would ensue was responsible for his awakening from the dream.

As the affects aroused by this dream began to be worked through in the months following my return from the summer vacation, the patient stopped his drinking and desisted from physically abusing his wife. He further realized that he had been angry at her not having been a virgin when they married, inasmuch as this called to mind his having to share his mother with his father, as well as with his younger brother.

The idea of sharing the mother with the father resonated with Mr. A's irritation about having to share me with my other patients. If I was unable to change an appointment with him when he called, there were moments when he could barely contain his rage on the telephone. In the office, however, he was more temperate in his expressions of anger.

When we began to look at this behavioral difference, we came to realize that another function of the telephone calls was to distance the ambivalently perceived love object from his rage. In so doing, the patient was also protected from the anxiety that would have been aroused (as in the telephone–terry cloth robe dream) by the loss of the object from an acting out of his murderous feelings.

Late in the second year of treatment, Mr. A began to express curiosity as to what I might be doing with my female patients during sessions.

When questioned about this, his associations quickly turned to speculations about his wife's interactions with her previous lovers and then to thoughts about his parents' sexual activities in the bedroom during the years he had shared the room with them.

He was infuriated about the idea of having been exposed to the intimacies of his parents. It was as if this bespoke their indifference to his feelings or even to his very existence. He had no direct visual memories of their sexual acts, but he was certain that he had heard them making love on a number of occasions. Once their heavy breathing had awakened him from sleep, and he recalled that when he had cried out his father became infuriated with him, presumably for interrupting the couple's lovemaking.

On recalling this particular incident, Mr. A suggested that perhaps his own breathing on the phone with women was a means of reenacting the situation to which he had been exposed by his parents. The turning of the original passive experience into an active one could be seen as an attempt to achieve a belated sense of mastery over the early traumatic situations.

This mechanism of turning passive into active, an identification with the aggressor, was also a major part of the other perverse sexual practice he revealed to me at this time, the act of frotteurism. In this ritual, he would ride the subway home from work during the evening rush hour. If he spotted a woman alone standing with her back to him, he would inch his way along the crowded car until he was stationed right behind her. Then he would let the crush of the people on the subway car carry him and his erect penis against her buttocks. He would not move at first, in order to allay any fear or anger the woman might feel at the presence of his penis against her buttocks. Then, when he felt more secure in her lack of verbal response, he would press closer to her and begin to move his penis against her gluteal region until he had an orgasm.

Occasionally a woman would scream out or would attempt to hit him, and he would pretend that she was imagining the assault on her. This tactic inevitably worked in the crowded subway cars, as most of the passengers were essentially disinterested in the machinations of their fellow travelers.

In analyzing Mr. A's frotteurism, a number of important determinants came to light. One of the most interesting features he mentioned was his feeling that these acts invariably occurred when he was in a "trancelike" state, which he characterized as being akin to "sleepwalking."

These "altered states" had first occurred during his late teens or early twenties, usually when he was under the influence of alcohol or marijuana. He recalled a number of such episodes as having occurred in conjunction with his masturbation. In these instances, he felt that he had been especially "keyed up," which translated roughly into being angry. On the half dozen occasions in which he reported these experiences during his treatment, they seemed to occur at times when he was angry with his wife, his mother, or me. At such moments, we were perceived as being either disappointing or depriving objects.

In describing specific episodes, Mr. A noted that not only the women he rubbed up against but the other passengers as well were all passive participants in the scenarios he was enacting or imposing upon them. The sexual acts with the women had a "dreamlike" quality, which once more recalled the primal scene experiences of his childhood. The female victims of his sexual aggression were seen as being especially passive and helpless, as he had felt himself to be in the early bedroom scenes.

In addition, when he came to recognize the hostility inherent in his acts of frottage, he realized that the trance or dreamlike nature of these episodes also served to protect the women from the consequences of his rage. Even though he could "kill people or have sex with them in dreams, no one really gets hurt. After all, they're only dreams." The layers of clothing interposed between the patient and his victim also served to protect the woman from the instrument of his rage, the "dangerous" phallus.

During the third year of the treatment, following a dream in which I anally penetrated him, Mr. A came to see that the frotteurism contained homosexual elements as well. The dream occurred shortly after the Christmas holiday break, during which time he had missed me and the analytic sessions very much. He expressed the feeling on returning of being "left out" and then related the dream mentioned above.

His associations went back to the period of his expulsion from the parental bedroom after the younger brother was born. He also thought of having to share a bed with his older brother at that time and had a vague, uncertain recollection of some sort of anal homosexual play initiated by the brother. Although he was embarrassed to reveal this material to me, he thought that he had enjoyed the experiences and had seen them as helping him through the traumatic period after the displacement by the younger brother, when he could no longer "see" or know what the parents were doing and was "blind" to their nocturnal activities.

I suggested to him that he had never before spoken of "seeing" the parents making love. I speculated as to whether he meant that he had perceived the expulsion from the bedroom as a kind of castration as well as a separation. I further wondered if this idea had been organized in his mind under a memory of not being able to "see," which related to his awareness of his blind eye and to his feelings of being "defective."

The anal play with the brother reenacted the primal scene machinations of the parents. In addition, the sensation of the brother's erect penis next to or within his anus served to bolster his own flagging sense of masculinity by incorporating the other sibling's manliness through having incorporated his organ. At some level, however, Mr. A felt victimized by the older brother's "night games," the sports he was not manly enough to participate in actively, just as he had felt victimized by the parents' "sporting around" in the bedroom. In repeating this process of victimization first with his friend in the scout troop and later with the women on the subway, he once more turned passive into active via the medium of his identification with the aggressor.

Toward the end of the third year of treatment, the patient reported that he had not engaged in any acts of frottage for several months. His relationship with his wife had gotten better, and though she still drank occasionally, he no longer did. He was still devoted to his son, and he and his wife decided to have another child.

In this setting, the patient was offered an excellent job in another city. Although he was reluctant to leave the analysis, he felt that he had to accept the promotion, and we terminated shortly before summer break. In a follow-up visit some eighteen months later, Mr. A reported making no further obscene phone calls or performing any acts of frottage since he had left the analysis.

Review of the Literature and Discussion

Harris (1957) described phobic avoidance of the telephone as a manifestation of castration anxiety. In one of his three cases, the act of telephoning was found to be highly erotic, after the initial anxiety state had been ameliorated. To the three men he described, the human voice on the telephone had a fetishistic (female phallus) valence.

In a psychiatric report in a state medical journal, Nadler (1968) described three young men whom he saw in court evaluations or in brief psychotherapy who made obscene telephone calls. He essentially likened these patients to exhibitionists, who show off their penises in order to alleviate their prominent feelings of castration anxiety. In two of the cases, where the author had some material on the family history, the mothers were seen as overly controlling and the fathers as detached and uncommunicative. Although this type of family constellation is hardly unique, I would like to note here that it is consistent with the family milieu in which my patient was reared.

All three individuals described by Nadler had prominent difficulties in self-esteem regulation and were dependent on the responses of others to bolster their sense of self-worth. In addition, the three men had a considerable amount of rage toward women. In the author's opinion, the aggressive, exhibitionistic tone taken by the patients toward the women they contacted in their calls represented an attempt to neutralize the destructive power of women in general and of their overly controlling mothers in particular. Again, this is quite similar to what I observed in my patient's case.

The three patients mentioned by Nadler seemed considerably more disturbed than my patient, though the rage against the nonnurturing mother which he describes was similar to my patient's feelings. In Nadler's cases there was an almost overpowering need to make the calls, which was of much greater intensity than the feelings described by my patient. The inability to control the obsessive-compulsive thoughts and impulses was an important issue for the three individuals mentioned by Nadler.

What is of special interest in this article with respect to my patient is that one of the men was also noted to indulge occasionally in acts of frottage on the subway. Unfortunately, little detail is given about this practice. It may be that the linkage of these two practices is not uncommon and that analysts should be on the lookout for it in patients who mention one of these behaviors and not the other.

Almansi (1979) described the analysis of a businessman in his mid-thirties who frequently masturbated while voyeuristically peeping at women through windows. He also often telephoned women he did not know and attempted to draw them into conversation about their reactions to cunnilingus and to big penises. If he succeeded in doing so, he would become sexually excited and would ejaculate. If the woman at the other end of the telephone seemed older and implied that she had younger lovers, the patient would become very aroused. This "old mistress fantasy" had both oedipal and oral connotations for him.

As a child, the patient saw his mother (who was also a voyeur) masturbate while listening to conversations on a party-line telephone. The mother also frequently exhibited her naked body to the patient during his teenage years. Prominent themes in the analysis centered about an early intestinal illness and recurrent observation of the primal scene between the ages of two and three and a half, when he slept in his parents' bedroom.

Almansi saw the scopophilia as serving to ward off prominent oedipal castration anxiety. The telephoning was additionally seen as a way of both exciting women and keeping them at a safe distance. He linked early object loss (feelings of abandonment by the mother) and hostility toward the mother as an ungratifying object to the patient's scopophilic perversion. Many of the factors mentioned in this case were of importance in my patient's history as well.

Shengold (1982) mentioned two patients who had been considerably overstimulated by their mothers during childhood. One was a heterosexual young man whose impulse to telephone women he knew and engage them in suggestive, rather than obscene, calls arose out of a need to ward off frightening anal masturbatory urges. When he made the calls, his anxiety would ease and he felt reassured about himself as a man. By this maneuver, he turned passive into active, thus warding off the homosexual impulses he felt and the attendant castration anxiety. Shengold further observed that in playing the role of a female flirt on the telephone with the women he called, he was enacting that which he was attempting to escape from. The telephone link to the women was analogous to the enema tubes his mother had prodded into his anus as a child. Thus the perversion revealed further attempts to turn passive into active in order to triumph belatedly over the early maternal domination.

A second patient briefly mentioned by Shengold was a homosexual man who was ashamed to reveal a sexually arousing call from his lover during which he masturbated to orgasm. In speaking of this to the analyst, that patient likened the telephone call to an incestuous contact with a parent. This man, too, had been overstimulated by his mother's exhibitionism. Thus in both instances, the turning of passive into active was a prominent part of the perverse scenarios, as with my patient.

Silverman (1982a) related sounds coming from an unseen source to the voice of conscience. He also noted the general use of the telephone to elicit reassurance and approval from the person called or from the operator as a means of relieving superego anxieties. In a second publication, Silverman (1982b) described the utilization of the telephone by a nine-year-old boy as a defense against castration anxiety. The patient was frightened by the emergence of positive and negative oedipal wishes in the transference and used the telephone as a means of controlling his excitement, anxiety, and guilt. As something that could be touched and handled, the telephone readily replaced the genitals for the discharge of masturbatory impulses. For the patient, it represented his own, the paternal, and the maternal genitals. Although his transference enactment could not be called a perversion, the patient's telephoning people during sessions shared many of the same features found in cases of adult obscene callers, such as the overriding need to turn passive into active.

Richards (1989), in an article on a telephone perversion in a young woman, related her frequent calls to an organizing fantasy of phallic intrusiveness on the part of her mother. Richards sees her patient's fantasy as a means of turning passive viewing into active exhibitionism in an effort to undo a number of early traumata.

Despite the limited number of case reports in the literature, obscene telephone calls do not appear to be uncommon. In Nadler's article cited earlier, he notes that some sixteen thousand obscene phone calls were reported in a nine-month period in 1966 in New York State. As for frotteurism, I am certain that a multitude of female subway riders would attest to the frequency of the practice on the crowded cars of such cities as New York and Chicago. Given their frequency, it seems reasonable to subsume these two acts under the rubric of the perversions of everyday life.

In this regard, the *Diagnostic and Statistical Manual* (3rd ed., rev.) defines frotteurism (302.89) as a disorder of "recurrent, intense, sexual urges and sexually arousing fantasies, of at least six months' duration, involving touching and rubbing against a nonconsenting person. It is the touching . . . that is sexually exciting. . . . The person with frotteurism usually commits frottage in crowded places, such as . . . public transportation vehicles, from which he can more easily escape arrest. . . . While doing this he usually fantasizes an exclusive, caring relationship with the victim." This definition is consistent with the facts of my patient's case.

Moving on now to Stoller's definitions of a perversion (1975), we find that both of Mr. A's practices meet all his definitional criteria for such acts. First, there was conscious erotic excitement inherent in both acts. Second, there was a desire to harm the object. This is most clearly evident in the dream involving the strangling of the wife's (mother's) robe with the telephone cord. Although the underlying rage toward the object was well defended against, as in the trancelike depersonalized states in which the acts of frotteurism occurred, the motivation of revenge against the early objects was quite clear.

The connection between anger and the trancelike states also occurred earlier in the patient's life, in his early masturbatory experiences. I have previously reported episodes of erectile impotence connected with excessive rage toward disappointing objects as concomitants of periods of depersonalization (Myers 1977). Like Mr. A, the patients I described were subject to early, chronic primal scene exposure. These early traumata frequently predisposed these individuals to having inordinately large increments of anger toward females (see Myers 1973, 1979), which the states of depersonalization served to ward off.

Returning to Stoller's criteria of a perversion, in addition to the conscious erotic excitement and the desire to harm the object present in Mr. A's practices, a degree of triumph over the originally traumatogenic early objects occurred in each perverse enactment, as well as a fantasied re-enactment of the factors subsumed in the genesis of the perverse acts. A few examples suffice to give support to Stoller's viewpoint. Let me first note the undoing of the expulsion from the parental bedroom seen in the reconnection to the early mother via the telephone call–umbilical cord linkage. The active mastery Mr. A achieved in his perverse acts over the objects involved in the passively experienced primal scene and homosexual traumata of his childhood also qualifies in this regard. Finally, the perverse acts described above involve a degree of sexually arousing risk and also achieve a vengeful dehumanization of the object. This quality, the dehumanization of the object, again actively attempts to overcome the passive traumata experienced at the hands of the indifferent parents of the primal scene and the homosexual aggressor brother of the post–primal scene expulsion period.

In essence, then, my material and the case reports of Nadler (1968), Almansi (1979), Shengold (1982), Silverman (1982b), and Richards (1989) provide further substantiation for Stoller's (1975) views on the importance of aggression toward the early traumatogenic object(s) in the genesis of perverse acts. The patient's masturbatory fantasies of omniavailable women and of lesbian sex (see Person 1986) serve as compensations for his massive feelings of insecurity vis-à-vis women. Both fantasies also serve to defend against the immense aggression directed toward females. In the first (the omniavailable woman), the woman's compliance negates the need for anger, and in the second (lesbian sex), the replacement of the patient by a second woman removes him from the possibility of being the aggressor.

Although we might think of Mr. A's acts and those of the other patients cited as being rather extreme, there are probably more common variants of these actions that are not generally thought of as perversions. A common example is the individual who has been spurned by a lover and then persists in telephoning the loved one and hanging up when he or she answers. This behavior is not dissimilar in certain respects to Mr. A's. Many of the criteria delineated by Stoller and detailed in this chapter are present in this instance as well, in particular the hostility to the lost lover and the sense of vengeance and triumph in causing the person pain.

A second example of ordinary behavior that can be likened to an obscene telephone call involves groups of construction workers shouting obscenities at women walking on the street. In such instances, under the guise of a group exhibition of machismo spirit, hostile and obscene taunts are directed at women in order to neutralize their threatening sexuality. By virtue of the homosexual bolstering of masculinity seen in such situations, a degree of triumph over and humiliation of the female sexual object is achieved. In addition, a collective type of depersonalization occurs in which the perception by the individuals of the intense aggression they are demonstrating in such situations is warded off by the pseudosexuality they are also exhibiting.

Similarly, with respect to the act of frotteurism, a number of normal correlates or precursors can be found. So-called harmless practices such as the male masturbatory act of "humping" the bed or the male pubertal foreplay practice of "dryhumping" a female bear considerable resemblance to the perverse act of frotteurism. In the former ("humping the bed"), the dehumanization of the woman Stoller (1975) speaks of is clearly evident. In the latter ("dryhumping" a female), the massive insecurity of the male vis-à-vis the female in general and in particular vis-à-vis the act of intercourse (with its implicit need for physical closeness to the woman) is demonstrated.

My point here is simply to underscore the idea that we should not regard the more extreme variants as mere "freakish" aberrations. Rather, we should realize that the seeds of such perverse scenarios lie within us all.

References

Almansi, R. 1979. "Scopophilia and Object Loss." *Psychoanalytic Quarterly* 48:601–19.

Harris, H. I. 1957. "Telephone Anxiety." *Journal of the American Psychoanalytical Association* 5:342–47.

Myers, W. A. 1973. "Split Self-representation and the Primal Scene." *Psychoanalytic Quarterly* 42:525–38.

———. 1977. "Impotence, Frigidity and Depersonalization." *International Journal of Psychoanalytic Psychotherapy* 6:199–226.

———. 1979. "Clinical Consequences of Chronic Primal Scene Exposure." *Psychoanalytic Quarterly* 48:1–26.

Nadler, R. P. 1968. "Approaches to Psychodynamics of Obscene Telephone Calls." *New York State Journal of Medicine,* Feb. 15, 521–26.

Person, E. S. 1986. "The Omni-available Woman and Lesbian Sex: Two Fantasy Themes and Their Relationship to the Male Developmental Experience." In *The Psychology of Men,* ed. by G. I. Fogel, F. M. Lane, and R. S. Liebert. New York: Basic Books.

Richards, A. K. 1989. "A Romance with Pain: A Telephone Perversion in a Woman?" *International Journal of Psychoanalysis* 70:153–64.

Shengold, L. 1982. "The Symbol of Telephoning." *Journal of the American Psychoanalytic Association* 30:461–70.

Silverman, M. 1982a. "The Voice of Conscience and the Sounds of the Analytic Hour." *Psychoanalytic Quarterly* 51:196–217.

———. 1982b. "A Nine Year-Old's Use of the Telephone: Symbolism in Statu Nascendi." *Psychoanalytic Quarterly* 51:598–611.

Stoller, R. J. 1975. *Perversion: The Erotic Form of Hatred.* New York: Pantheon.

Part III
Wider Applications
Women, Couples, and Psychoanalysts

Chapter Seven

Women Masquerading as Women

Louise J. Kaplan, Ph.D.

HE perversions have been distinguished from neuroses, character disorders, and psychoses, and have been given a new label "paraphilia," deviant sexual attraction, in the *Diagnostic and Statistical Manual* (3rd ed., rev.). But this is not how matters evolve in the psychoanalysis of a perversion. Most people do not come into treatment wanting to analyze their perversion; they are happy with it and want to talk at first about other symptoms. Moreover, a perverse enactment of some sort is present in every analysis, even in that of patients who are predominantly neurotic. A perversion has always grown up *alongside* a neurosis, in every man or woman, and in the context of a certain level and type of character formation.

In a perverse enactment, one perversion—usually in the case of a male perversion, fetishism, or sadomasochism—appears as a dominant theme, but embedded in the script are elements from the other perversions—transvestism, voyeurism, exhibitionism—if not as immediately observable enactments, then as whispered hints, fleeting shadows, secondary props, background tonalities. The same is true for the female perversions. Each reveals one or more facets of the perverse strategy, but in every perversion the same overall strategy is at work. It is best from an analytic point of view, therefore, to think of the perversions not as separate, neatly defined clinical entities but as differing facets of some larger, more encompassing perverse strategy.

In this chapter I shall examine the motif of gender masquerades (transvestism, homeovestism, impersonation) because that facet of the perverse strategy illuminates the issues of gender-role identity that are present in every perverse script. My thesis is that perversions, insofar as they derive a great deal of their emotional force from social gender stereotypes, are as much pathologies of gender-role identity as pathologies of sexuality. There is always a subtle collaboration between the individual unconscious with its infantile gender attributions and the structure of the social order with its primitive notions of masculinity and femininity. Ironically, therefore, socially normalized gender stereotypes are the crucibles of perversion.

Perversions and Gender Stereotypes

The male transvestite uses the cover of an infantile ideal of masculinity in order to both conceal and reveal forbidden and shameful feminine wishes. In the analogous female perversions an infantile ideal of femininity would be used as the disguise for forbidden and shameful masculine wishes. Transvestism is extremely rare in females, but other perversions—what I will refer to later as impersonations or masquerades of femininity—are more common than we recognize. In the female perversions there is an emphasis of preoedipal ideals of femininity over the more flexible identifications and resolutions of the oedipal phase. Since all male perversions emphasize preoedipal over oedipal masculine identifications, they could be regarded similarly as impersonations or masquerades of masculinity.

By suggesting that female perversions are different from male perversions, I am not consenting to the idea that the minds of males and those of females function according to different psychological processes, nor to any mythology that males and females acquire different mental disorders.

The perverse strategy is the same for both males and females. It is only one factor in the strategy—the differing gender stereotypes that are given expression in the perversion—that distinguishes the male and female perversions.

Over the course of the century, the diagnostic categories into which the perversions have been slotted have shifted here and there. But two factors have remained constant. First, the medical profession at the end of the twentieth century is still preoccupied with boxing aberrant sexual behaviors into lists and categories. Second, except for sexual masochism wherein the ratio is approximately twenty males to one female, less than 1 percent of the cases cited as sexual perversion occurs among females.

Upon hearing these statistics, some people, usually males, are offended at the suggestion that females might somehow have an edge on males. They insist that I have been taken in by statistics, which as we know always lie. Others, usually females, are happy with this evidence of their moral superiority, and they admonish me for questioning the assumption that females are less perverse than males. No sooner are questions raised about these odd statistics than an array of stock responses is marshaled to explain them away. Among the standard responses is a listing of all the exceptions to the rule: women who have the same perversions as males, women who participate in the male perversions by "submitting unwillingly" to the deviant sexual demands of men. A more carefully considered response, but one that assigns an inordinate weight to biological factors, is that males are androgen-testosterone driven and therefore possessed by the urgencies of enabling and maintaining erections, whereas females, because of their estrogen restraints, genital inwardness, and delicacy of human-relatedness, are less inclined toward perverse acting out as a solution to their sexual and moral dilemmas. In this argument, the premise is that the statistics on perversion are yet another proof of all the differences between males and females that we like to attribute to biology and anatomical destiny.

Still another reason offered for the unbalanced sex ratios in perversion is that men must have erections to perform sexually and therefore cannot hide their genital anxieties and inadequacies, whereas women can fake sexual arousal and orgasm, obviating the need for fetishes and such to prove their sexual adequacy. Indeed, that argument continues, women do not have to employ prostitutes to get beaten and dominated; men will gladly do it for nothing. Another response, based on the mistaken assumption that the perversions are erotic adventures, "kinky sex" undertaken in the spirit of sexual liberation, is that women would be as perverse as men if they were granted greater sexual freedom.

Although there is a grain of truth in each of these standard responses, they all miss the crucial point of *the perverse strategy*. What makes a perversion a perversion is a mental strategy that employs some social gender stereotypes of masculinity and femininity in a manner that deceives the onlooker about the unconscious meanings of the behaviors she or he is observing. Were we to think about perversions solely in terms of manifest behaviors without penetrating below the surface and analyzing the motives and affects that give meaning to those behaviors, we could simply conclude that the male perversions are quests for forbidden sexual pleasures and nothing more.

The Perverse Strategy

Let me state at the outset that the *essential* ingredient in perversion is not the kinky sex that is immediately evoked by the word *perversion*. A perversion is a central preoccupation of a person's life, an act of desperation performed by a person who has no other choices and would otherwise be overwhelmed by unbearable anxiety or severe depression or psychosis. The male perversions use some manifest form of kinky sex to prevail over these other devastating emotional states. The kinky sex, however, is the lie held up to keep the devils at bay. Sexual behaviors per se, kinky or otherwise, are not the key to the female perversions since females use other sorts of behaviors—one could say other sorts of deceptions—to keep the devils at bay.

Certain facets of the perverse strategy are common to all psychological symptoms. For example, like other symptoms, the perverse strategy allows one or two forbidden wishes to become conscious, but in order to keep other, more dangerous or shameful wishes and desires unconscious.

One of the features that distinguishes a perversion from other psychological symptoms is the fact that the strategy is expressed in a performance, an enactment, rather than in the more covert mental compromises seen in the analysis of a neurotic symptom or character disorder. In a perversion there is always an extensive enactment and always a fantasized or real audience.

Another feature that distinguishes perversion from other psychological symptoms is the special way that guilt and anxiety are written into the perverse script. For example, the preoccupation in a perversion is very different from the preoccupation in an obsessive-compulsive disorder, such as making money or constantly tidying up, activities that entail a consciousness of anxiety but serve to mollify moral anxiety—guilt. The preoccupation in a perversion regulates what would otherwise be massive anxiety reactions, but leaves the person more consciously at odds with the moral order though nevertheless haunted by a pervasive apprehension of doom and unconscious moral anxiety—guilt.

The perverse strategy allows a part, a *relatively* harmless detail, to be used to symbolize an entire narrative of the traumatic childhood events that led to the perversion. For example, in fetishism, the perversion that exemplifies the perverse strategy, an object like a leather boot or lace garter belt or blue velvet bathrobe is employed by a man with the conscious motive of enhancing sexual excitement and erection. That simple detail, however—the boot, the bathrobe—is a complex symbol that reveals and yet conceals all the forbidden and dangerous wishes, all the losses, abandonments, anxieties, and terrors of childhood. While on the surface the sole function of a fetish object is to enable sexual performance, the perverse strategy *is* to focus attention on sexual performance with its manifestly wholesome motive of male virility so that this larger history of desire and punishment can be kept secret and unconscious.

The manifest behavior in a female perversion will, of course, be different according to the gender ideal the female is striving to achieve—which may, but often does not, include the manifest aim of sexual excitement and performance. Women whose lives are dominated by a perverse performance do have a sexual life, sometimes an extensive and varied one, sometimes a limited kinky one, sometimes a totally impoverished one. As I shall be demonstrating, this sexual life, whatever it is, will figure in her perversion. But the perversion itself is meant to deceive as to the forbidden, shameful, and frightening elements in that sexual life.

According to most official definitions, past and present, the manifest aim of the perverse behavior—sexual excitement and sexual performance—has been taken as the qualifying mark of a perversion, rather than the perverse strategy that conceals the underlying more dangerous and humiliating desires. Analysts have missed noticing the female perversions because they have been looking for them in the wrong place; they were led astray by the official definitions. To qualify as a legitimate and official perversion, or as the latest label has it, a paraphilia, the aim of the act *must* be sexual excitement and sexual performance. Since the perverse strategy *is* to divert attention away from latent forbidden or shameful desires, then it should not be surprising if the official definitions, which also keep the focus on manifest, conscious aims, simply mirror the perverse strategy itself.

The perverse strategy has been at work even in the psychoanalytic theory of perversion. I say "even" because the methods and fundamental ideals of psychoanalysis could have provided an antidote to the prevailing sexological and behaviorist approach to perversion.

Freud was alert to the perverse elements in his male patients' sexual attitudes, their misperceptions and disavowals of the female genitals, their quests for virility, their quiet and noisy desperations about sexual performance, the various fetishistic devices they employed to attain erection and orgasm. But contrary to his stated ideals about the psychoanalytic approach to human behavior, Freud accepted for his definition of perversion a behavioristic criterion based on a male gender stereotype of virility. As for females, behaviors and traits that fit into some gender stereotype of femininity were considered normal—passivity, submission, purity, cleanliness, caretaking. Every behavior that went counter to these stereotypes—aggression, domination, sexual virility, the refusal to submit to a man's sexual advances, even a desire for sexual and economic equality—was considered abnormal, a neurotic outcome of a woman's so-called masculinity complex, her penis envy. It was generally assumed that perversion was a male activity. Perversions in females remained a mystery. Moreover, no one seemed very intrigued by this mystery and the issue was never pursued.

The theory of psychoanalysis had in it, latent or manifest, every principle of motivation needed to appreciate the nature of female perversion. As time went on, the latent principles for understanding the female perversions were gradually elaborated but still not put into practice. Even today, as the extent of the clinical and theoretical neglect of perversions in females has become apparent, the tendency is to cast about for female fetishists, transvestites, sadomasochists, exhibitionists, rather than to plumb the depths of the fetishistic strategy that has for so long kept the female perversions hidden from view.

Officially, psychoanalytic explorations of the perversions began in 1905 with Freud's understanding that the sexual aberrations are the persistence into adult life of elements of infantile sexuality at the expense of adult genitality and his aphorism that the neuroses are the negative of the perversions ([1905] 1953, 165). In his later paper on beating fantasies ([1919] 1955) Freud demonstrated that perverse symptoms, like neurotic symptoms, are regressive maneuvers in response to the Oedipus complex.

Taking Freud's paper as his cue, Sachs stressed the ego's role in the creation of a perversion. His central point was that the ideation representing a component drive "is allowed admission into the ego as a wishful pleasure aim, in order to obtain its support in repression" of the rest of infantile sexuality but "particularly against the Oedipus complex" (1923, 488). The infantile components are worked over and refracted through the oedipal lens and thus given the capacity for a normal libidinal cathexis of an object. Not until the oedipal phase—when the sexual and generational differences are the psychological issues that demand resolution—do infantile sexual components acquire the psychological wherewithal to be expressed through genital aims and objects. Gillespie, along with many others, emphasized the role of the superego: "The choice by the ego of the particular piece of infantile sexuality is dictated to an important extent by the ego's judgment of what will please, or at least pass relatively unchallenged by, parental imagos, eventually internalized, i.e., by superego formations. The attempt to please the superego is especially obvious in masochism, but it operates in other perversions as well" (1956, 309). Lowenstein then underscored Freud's view that masochism in males represented a flight from feminine wishes toward the father. In the masochistic ritual, which Lowenstein dubbed "seduction of the aggressor," the sexual partner is induced to enact a scenario of threat, punishment, rejection, or other humiliation. The aim of the perverse enactment is to undo the childhood rebuff or castration threat "through a simulated repetition," which in the adult succeeds in permitting a "veiled incestuous gratification" (1957, 202). More recently, McDougall (1972) elaborated the relevance and complexity of preoedipal and oedipal interactions in a perverse interpretation of the primal scene. Kernberg (1984) advanced our appreciation of the contributions of narcissism and aggression to the cognitive, affective, and defensive aspects of perversion. Certainly, as Kernberg and many others have stressed, a central element in the perverse strategy is the attempt to contain and regulate a primitive hostile aggression, a vengeful hatred in response to the deprivations and traumata of childhood.

Adding to these emendations of Freud's original understandings of the sexual aberrations, I have emphasized considerations of the repetition compulsion (Kaplan 1990). The sadomasochistic motifs that are so much an integral part of most perverse enactments are also no less a manifest content that disguises other latent unconscious fantasies. As in Lowenstein's "seduction of the aggressor," what looks like a seeking for pleasure in pain or humiliation is a ritualized reenactment of an infantile trauma, a repetitive cycle of losing love and finding love, of castration and restitution, of abandonment and reunion, of death and resurrection. To a greater or lesser extent, all perverse scenarios are *fort da* games played out with penises and vaginas.

Each of these principles of symptom formation, derived from different phases of the history of psychoanalysis, applies equally to females and males. What I am stressing here is another central feature in the latent content of a perversion—the preoedipal feminine and masculine identifications that are regressive outcomes of the resolution of the Oedipus complex. Whatever else is enlisted in support of a perverse enactment, the perversion itself is a disorder of gender identity. Arlow, in his discussion of identifications in perversions, stated the principle this way: "The striking feature [of the perversions] is to be found in the identifications that the perverse activities articulate. . . . No matter what other factors pertain, perversions constitute problems of gender identity, of male-female differentiation. . . . The evidence indicates that, in the development of perversions, the identifications effected during the oedipal phase are decisive" (1986, 248–49).

It is the regressive outcomes of the Oedipus complex, the regressions to preoedipal gender ideals that are responses to primal scene mortification and castration anxiety, that find expression in a perversion. As one prevalent outcome of the male Oedipus complex, a little boy preserves his penis by giving up his love for his mother, repudiating his femininity, and accentuating certain ideals of masculine virtue—bravery, risk taking, assertiveness, rebellion, domination, virility—ideals that are confirmed and insisted upon by the social order as attainments of a normal masculinity. As an outcome of her Oedipus complex, a little girl might seek to alleviate her genital anxieties and assuage her narcissistic mortifications by accentuating certain ideals of feminine virtue—cleanliness, purity, kindness, concern for others, submission. This is one typical solution that female children adopt in a retreat from oedipal anxieties and humiliations. But when the social order colludes with these infantile ideals of femininity by insisting on innocence and submission as the way of achieving a normal adult feminine sexuality, then females will learn very early on to disguise their intellectual powers as "feminine intuition" and to compromise their active sexual desires into flirtatiousness and a teasing sexual unavailability.

In a male perversion an infantile ego ideal of sexual prowess has been enlisted to repress, yet give expression to, latent forbidden or shameful desires. The ego admits a defensive phallic-narcissistic exaggeration of masculinity into consciousness because it is pleasing to the ego ideal and will pass relatively unchallenged by parental imagos, as they have been internalized in superego formations. The manifest perverse scenarios of males put the focus on sexual excitement and genital orgasm in order to lend expression to a number of other latent wishes, among them those entailing feminine strivings. Macho genital prowess and the impersonation of fantasized idealized males are hiding places for the man's humiliating feminine strivings.

Female Perversions

In the female perversions, we would expect to find certain impersonations of fantasized idealized females as hiding places for a woman's forbidden masculine strivings. As I stated earlier I have selected the masquerade motif, for that motif illuminates the collaboration between infantile gender ideals and social gender stereotypes, which I believe is present in all perversions.

Female Transvestism

Transvestism is extremely rare in females and when it is a symptom, two of the features characteristic of male transvestism are either absent or play relatively inconsequential roles—namely, the accompanying sexual excitement and the fascination with clothing of the opposite sex. Moreover, although she has no desire to pass permanently as a male, the female transvestite, unlike her male counterpart, is more comfortable with her bisexuality and will often admit her desire to play the role of a man in an erotic relationship with a woman. But in its latent content, female transvestism does resemble the male perversion in one striking regard. The male transvestite is expressing his identification with the castrated mother while simultaneously repudiating his feminine longings with the fantasy "under this dress there is a penis." The female transvestite is expressing an infantile ideal of masculinity, a regressive identification that in females also represents a repudiation of forbidden and denigrated *feminine* longings.

After illustrating this feature of female transvestism through the life of Vita Sackville-West, a woman who hid her feminine longings in a masquerade of masculinity, I shall turn my attention to other perversions, more typical of females; homeovestism (a perversion also found in males), female impersonation, and the masquerade of womanliness, which is a character perversion—a perversion of everyday life.

When, in the early years of our century, Vita Sackville-West strode along Piccadilly and sat at the cafés of the Palais Royale masquerading as a young man, no one recognized her as the well-bred wife of the diplomat Harold Nicolson. In her pose as Julian, the lover of her adorable Violet, Vita enjoyed fantasizing what people would think if they knew that the boy with the *voyou* appearance was "the silent and rather scornful woman they had perhaps met at a dinner-party or a dance." Part of Vita's satisfaction was her ability to put one over: "I never appreciated anything so much as living like that with my tongue perpetually in my cheek, and in defiance of every policeman I passed" (Nicolson, 1973, 116).

Vita was brought up at Knole, a palatial country mansion said to contain as many staircases as there are weeks in the year and 365 rooms (Glendinning 1983). A slave-master mentality was integral to her aristocratic breeding. She grew up with a conviction that in human relationships there are only two possible positions, one of rapacious domination and another of docile submission.

Her female lovers were quick to intuit what it was in Vita that so entranced them. Violet scribbled a note on a scrap of paper: "The upper half of your face is so pure and grave—almost childlike. And the lower half is so domineering, sensual, almost brutal—it is the most absurd contrast, and extraordinarily symbolical of your Dr. Jekyll and Mr. Hyde personality" (Nicolson 1973, 34–35). Vita recognized the truth of her lover's words and knew that Jekyll and Hyde referred to the feminine and masculine sides of her personality. Although she claimed that she was too weak to struggle against this duality, Dr. Jekyll got very short shrift in her scheme of gender. Aside from her enduring affection for her husband and her sporadic flashes of tender concern for the welfare of her many lovers, Vita rarely exhibited her feminine side. She fully embraced the harsh, domineering Mr. Hyde persona while effectively preventing anyone, including herself and her two sons, from recognizing the caring, nurturing, conventional Dr. Jekyll.

Virginia Woolf was another lover who appreciated the complicated desires of her fabulous Vita. In *Orlando* (1928), the novel that Vita's son Nigel would call "the longest and most charming love letter in literature," Vita is granted one boyhood and manhood after another, tossed gaily from one sex to the other, costumed as a sexually avid Elizabethan youth and as a sexually experienced duke in the service of King James, and later transformed into a ravishing woman whose form combines "the strength of a man and a woman's grace" (86) and who is the female ambassador to Turkey given permission to dress in those oriental coats and trousers that "can be worn indifferently by either sex." Later, when Orlando is transposed to eighteenth-century England, her early mornings are devoted to lounging about her library in a "China robe of ambiguous gender" (140), her late mornings to gardening in heavy knee breeches, her middays to attending luncheons in flowered taffeta, her afternoons to visiting court sessions in a lawyer's gown and wig, and her evenings to junketing about the streets and alleyways of London dressed as a dashing nobleman in search of masculine excitements (141).

In actual life, Sackville-West could not be as expansive as Woolf's generous wish-fulfilling gift allowed her to be. After her passionate and tumultuous affair with Violet, Vita never again dressed as Julian. She retired to the countryside and adopted permanently the traditional Kentish garb—man-tailored rough shirt, big pocketed leather jacket, sturdy whipcord jodhpurs tucked into knee-high heavy workman's boots.

In her autobiographical confessions, which her son Nigel published as the introduction to his portrait of his parents' marriage, Vita makes evident her conflicted feelings about her mother who, perhaps mercifully, was frequently off on the Continent visiting her lover. "Mother used to hurt my feelings and say she couldn't bear to look at me because I was so ugly" (Nicolson 1973, 4). "Although the most incomprehensible she is certainly the most charming, person on earth, whom I adore" (6). Little Vita was determined to be hardy and brave, "as like a boy as possible"— and not just any boy, but a boy who enjoyed dominating the playmates who would obey his commands and tormenting the unlucky ones who would not, "stuffing their nostrils with putty and beating a little boy with stinging nettles" (5).

I agree with Stoller that a female transvestite, like any other overtly masculine woman, has "a lifelong daydream with the theme that if she were a man rather than a woman, she could undo the past and find a loving mother inside some female erotic partner" (Stoller 1985, 154). Perhaps a few of these mothers and daughters were present in Vita Sackville-West's sexual relationships with women. Did Vita yearn to find a loving mother in her female sexual partners? Did she always fantasize that if she were a man, then her mother might love her? From the time she was a little girl, she knew that because she was a female she could never inherit the stately home with 365 rooms; though she was an only child, Knole would have to go to the nearest male heir. Did she always wish to one day get the phallic trophy that would have been the sign of a mother's true love? Neither her own confessions nor Virginia Woolf's love letter (which restores Vita to Knole) gives us decisive answers to those questions. We do know that Vita learned very early to conceal her femininity, which she equated with a loathsome vulnerability, in the costumes and attitudes of a Don Juan who gloried in the sexual seduction of married women. There is certainly something perverse in Vita's desperation to find her feminine identity in a caricature of male virility, her equation of nurturance and surrender with a susceptibility to debasement, her division of the world into phallic and castrated beings.

Homeovestism

Not too long ago the Canadian psychoanalyst George Zavitzianos (1971, 1972, 1977) challenged some cherished ideas about transvestism. He was struck by an offbeat feature of the perverse scenarios of two of his patients, one male, the other female. After grappling for some years with the psychological meaning of what he was observing, Zavitzianos realized that he might be dealing with a previously unrecognized form of perversion. He hazarded that one might call this rather perverse perversion, *homeovestism,* or dressing up in the clothes of a same-sexed person. He claimed that previous reports of male fetishism and transvestism by Freud ([1927] 1961), Bak (1953), Gillespie (1940), and many others were actually cases of homeovestism. To put Zavitzianos's diagnostic distinctions briefly: fetishism represents a denial or warding off of a primary identification with the castrated mother; transvestism represents a wish to strengthen the identification with the castrated mother and simultaneously to repudiate that wish; homeovestism represents an identification with the idealized phallic parent of the same sex in order to overcome an unconscious identification with the castrated mother (1977, 492–93).

Although I do not concur entirely with Zavitzianos's distinctions, they have some merit. Certainly, his quirky notion of a perversion called homeovestism provides an important clue to the fundamental principle underlying the female (and male) perversions. Obviously, not everyone who dresses in the clothes of his or her own sex should be thought of as a homeovestite. But we can guarantee missing the point of a perverse scenario if we take for granted that a "normal-looking" outside is a sign that nothing perverse is going on underneath.

Zavitzianos's several accounts of homeovestism concentrate on his female patient Lillian, who in everyday life dressed as the castrated, unlovable woman she felt herself to be. Her homeovestism was expressed in driven, impulsive acts of dressing up as the valued and valuable phallic woman she wished to be. When we first encounter Lillian, it is apparent that dressing up in women's clothes is the comparatively benign man- ifestation of a far more serious disturbance:

> Lillian, a 20-year-old psychopath of the impostor type, was cruel with animals and children, masturbated little boys (but not girls), lied and was sexually promiscuous. The most characteristic feature of her delinquent behavior was kleptomania. She used to steal various things: books, money, clothing, stockings, costume jewelry and anything which could enhance her appearance as a woman. She also spent all her money to buy such articles. Lillian had a tendency to imitate the manners of women she envied and admired, and also tended to dress like them. Most of these women were married or pregnant. She found it particularly exciting to steal from them. (1972, 472)

Each of the details in this dramatic introduction to Lillian's person- ality makes some sense in the context of her early family relationships. Lillian's mother made no secret of her disappointment at not having given birth to a boy. She could not bear to handle Lillian any more than was absolutely necessary; consequently the baby was rarely touched, ca- ressed, or cuddled. To compensate for these deprivations, the mother, a woman with a perverse and psychopathic character structure, would mas- turbate Lillian. It was the one source of mutual pleasure in this highly ambivalent mother-infant relationship. Lillian slept in the parental bed- room until a baby brother came along to displace her when she was three years old.

The mother during her pregnancy had been hopeful and therefore more patient and loving with her daughter. Lillian's participation in her mother's pregnancy was the high point of her childhood. But as soon as the son was born, Lillian's mother became totally preoccupied with his care, and Lillian now had no mother at all. She reacted to the sight of her brother's penis and of her mother's resumed menstrual flow with an intense anxiety about the possible destruction of her own excited genitals. Her severe castration reactions were compounded by unmanageable an- nihilation and separation anxieties. She tried to console herself by wear- ing her mother's dresses, stuffing the front with a pillow. In that way she recaptured the days when she felt like a valued child united with her marvelously exciting pregnant mother.

Although her early childhood was very troubled, her distress and humiliation worsened as she approached adolescence and became aware that her body was growing unambiguously into that of an "ordinary" woman. Her attacks of kleptomania and homeovestism coincided with the monthly onsets of menstruation. The only way Lillian could overcome sensations of body disintegration and experiences of loss and abandonment was to steal women's clothing to wear. When Lillian wore beautiful, elegant, and expensive dresses, she felt like a valued child from a different family—important and rich. On a less conscious level, the sensation of having her body inside these glorious clothes gratified her lifelong wish to be back inside the belly of her loving mother. In that way she could be reunited with her phallic mother and then reborn with the magnificent body part that had made her brother so valuable to her mother.

Lillian was promiscuously heterosexual. During these escapades, Lillian did not feel compelled to wear stolen female clothing and jewelry as a means of achieving sexual arousal. Rather, the presence of her lover's actual erect penis was enough to reassure her that she was a good, adored, and valued little-girl-with-a-penis. By grabbing and pulling at her lover's penis, performing fellatio, making it erect, and bringing it to orgasm, or by simply looking at it in a state of erection, Lillian imagined she was taking the penis inside her and making it her own. In her extensive, rigidly ritualized heterosexuality, Lillian was one of those women who believe that the anatomical penis is a magical phallus that can repair a castration. In her homeovestism, which Zavitzianos concluded was "closer to imposture than to sexual perversion" (1977, 494), Lillian dressed in the clothing of a powerful woman, the phallic mother of her childhood, in order to overcome annihilation, separation, and castration anxieties of an order of severity that was tantamount to the mutilation anxiety that characterizes the perversions.

Female Impersonation

Olympia, the *Raunch* centerfold striptease artist and go-go dancer interviewed by Stoller (1985), protested that she and women like her are not aptly described by the label "exhibitionist." I think she was right in insisting on this diagnostic refinement and right to think of herself as a female impersonator. Because she was convinced that she lacked natural femininity, Olympia decided long ago that the best she could do was dress up as a woman. Before she discovered her calling, Olympia was always uncomfortable in her body. She explained that she was able to appear to be more feminine than the average woman only because she had been extremely devoted to her craft, which depends on a conscientious study of feminine movements and styles of dress.

Olympia seemed aware of the split images of herself. "I always thought I had the grace of a truck driver, but I discovered that it's not a matter of gracefulness, it's a matter of knowing how to do things by studying. For example, I could show you two ways of sitting on the floor, one graceful like an accomplished dancer and one like a clod." Olympia described her body as a container or at best a tool for accomplishing her craft—turning men on. "Without the container, I could totally disperse and be in a billion places all over the universe at the same time" (81).

The only way women like Olympia can come to life or feel confident that they exist is through impersonations of femininity. They are as dominated by their rigid gender impersonations as are the men they captivate and serve. They know they are lost, says Stoller, "so they are vulnerable to those who promise them a connection. They are not just willing to serve as fetishes; they have no other options" (84).

The Masquerade of Womanliness

In "Womanliness as a Masquerade," Joan Riviere (1929) described a gender-identity solution that became available to women when they were given permission to pursue the callings that had been previously limited to males. Now they were going to have to find a way to express their masculine ambitions and still be considered feminine women. Said Riviere, "Of all the women engaged in professional work today, it would be hard to say whether the greater number are more feminine than masculine in their mode of life and character. In university life, in scientific professions and in business, one constantly meets women who seem to fulfill every criterion of complete feminine development" (304).

Who are these marvels of "complete feminine development"? They are the legion of professional intellectual women who not only are wives, mothers, and excellent housekeepers but also maintain an active social life and participate in the cultural life of their community; they are women whose dress and hairstyle, whether or not they wear pants and bob their hair, are impeccably and unmistakably feminine. Moreover, they have excellent sexual relationships with their husbands, including frequent sexual performance and orgasm.

Riviere's patient, whom I shall call Janet, had every outward sign of "complete feminine development." But one symptom gave away the masquerade. Although Janet was a highly respected, well-paid, immensely successful lecturer, each of her grand performances would be followed by a severe anxiety attack. Sometimes she would be apprehensive all night, unable to sleep and imagining all the inappropriate things she might have said or done. Gradually, because of the increasing severity of her postlecture anxiety reactions, Janet became obsessed by a need for reassurance. She finally developed a symptom that replaced the terrible anxiety but left her wondering about the solution's driven and repetitive character. Immediately after completing her speech or lecture, she would seek the attention and compliments of a fatherly-type man who had witnessed her performance. Janet needed to hear in so many words how impressive, knowledgeable, and well spoken she had been. With those reassurances behind her, she would quickly move on to a more important matter. Scarcely skipping a beat, she would transform herself into a hip-wriggling, eyelash-batting seductress. What she needed now was some sign from the man that she was sexually attractive. In contrast to the magisterial, impersonal style with which she had commanded her audience, there would suddenly appear at the back of the auditorium a flirtatious girl, a silly chatterbox, a pure and simple coquette.

Until Janet recognized the incongruity between her intellectual power and her ridiculous postlecture flirtations, the womanliness that was so much a part of her character had effectively masked the gender conflicts that were generating her anxiety reactions. It was Riviere's thesis that her patient used her womanliness as a mask both to hide the possession of masculinity, which her patient had interpreted as a castration of the father, and to avert reprisals if she was found to possess it—"much as a thief will turn out his pockets and ask to be searched to prove he has not

[got] the stolen goods" (305). Riviere also carefully specified that there was no sharp distinction between "genuine womanliness" and a masquerade. She implied that whenever womanliness is used as a device to avoid anxiety, it has the quality of a masquerade (305–06). Using Riviere's paper as the template for my own analytic cases of women who have found it necessary to hide their masculine ambitions behind a masquerade of womanliness, I have constructed a composite narrative about the mental life of a Janet.

There is something fetishistic about a narrative such as this that both conceals and reveals the various Janets that it represents. Let us say that "Janet" was born to a mother who had already given birth to two daughters and this time was longing for a son. When Janet was born, however, her mother looked at her lively, alert baby girl and decided that she would do nicely for the son she did not have. The mother, all unconsciously, elected Janet to fulfill her own frustrated "masculine" ambitions. Consequently, Janet had been unusually close to her mother during the first two and a half years of life and was protected by this special relationship from the customary disappointments, frustrations, and humiliations of separation-individuation.

From birth Janet had been alert, lively, and curious—and also unusually aggressive, persistent, and determined to get what she wanted when she wanted it. Undoubtedly, Janet's temperament influenced her mother to invest in this daughter the ambitions she had long ago renounced in herself. Indeed, those very qualities of determination and persistence that made Janet so special to her mother also made Janet's eventual fall from grace, her banishment from the Garden of Eden, particularly insupportable and mortifying. Janet's closeness to her mother had not prevented her from becoming a separate self with a clear-cut identity apart from her mother, but she never quite gave up the fantasy that her mother was an extension of her own self, a possession that belonged to her and to no one else. So when she had to come to terms with the presence of her father in her mother's life and to recognize that she was prohibited from and incapable of possessing her mother the way her father did, she could not accept that inevitable defeat with grace or equanimity.

The unconscious bargain struck between Janet and her mother—that

Janet would fulfill what was unfulfilled in the mother—played a considerable role in the intensity and violent content of the unconscious fantasies that expressed Janet's reaction to the mortifications of the primal scene. Until then she had protected herself by accentuating a phallic position in relation to the mother, an attitude that the mother encouraged for reasons of her own. With the onset of primal scene mortification, however, and the consequent crumbling of Janet's phallic defense, all the earlier deprivations, frustrations, and humiliations of infancy were reawakened and with them the hostile aggression and rage that had been kept in abeyance by the fantasy of being mother's "everything." The commonplace childhood fantasy of stealing the phallus that the father had mistakenly given to the wicked, undeserving mother could temporarily assuage Janet's humiliation and temper her rage. As the possessor of that magical phallus, she would rectify the mortifications of the primal scene trauma and triumph over both parents. But Janet's fantasy of stealing the father's phallus was more violent than the commonplace versions, making the retaliations she feared more terrible than the usual ones. Unconsciously, her theft was the equivalent of a violent and ruthless destruction of everything that stood in the way of her childhood wishes. What better vengeance against the betraying mother than to penetrate and devour her mother's insides, to chew up all the leftover babies and the penis—the glorious phallus given to the mother by the father. Then, for good measure, she lopped off her father's phallus so that he would lose his power over her mother. In short, she destroyed every part of her parents that they had and she did not have, especially those genital parts that made the mother desire the father and the father desire the mother.

In Janet's three-year-old mind, where the distinction between sadistic fantasies and actual crimes is always ambiguous, she has vengefully destroyed the envied and hated parents' genitals and, in a triumph of wish fulfillment, has appropriated the father's phallus for herself. Since a phallus is not a penis but an imaginary and detachable part, it can be destroyed several times in several ways and still be appropriated. But if the phallus has been given to the mother and now little Janet has stolen it for herself, then the mother is the one who will devise a punishment suitable to the crime. One day the mother, by now transformed into a crazed witch-mother in a reflection of Janet's own envy and rage, will destroy her daughter's body, devour her insides, mutilate her beautiful face, carve up her sexual organs so that she cannot bear children, or, should she dare to have children, eat them.

Here is the dilemma for a little girl who does not want to relinquish her ambitions and is determined to show off her talents, but is terrified because she feels that she is exhibiting stolen goods. How can she atone for her savage crimes against the mother without relinquishing the glorious stolen phallus? Clever Janet found a way and it worked until she became an eminent scientist and renowned lecturer who had to show her stolen trophies to the world.

Janet did not give up the paternal powers she had stolen from her mother, nor did she hide her ambitions and talents as so many other little girls do in order to assuage the gods. No, she would keep her stolen powers but fool the authorities by putting her determination, persistence, intellect, ambition, to work for her mother. By placating her mother's imagined rage in this way, Janet was the perfect self-sacrificing daughter and also the powerful and majestic son her mother had been wishing for.

In a moment I will show how this solution worked out for Janet and how it influenced her character, her gender identity, and the symptoms she developed when she became a lecturer. But first let us look at the social world that gave plausibility to Janet's solution to her childhood dilemmas. Her infantile way of reconciling her masculine and feminine strivings coincided with the way the masculine strivings of women were dealt with in the early decades of the twentieth century and, sadly, still are at the end of the century. The social order was having to reconcile to the emancipated woman, the woman who was demanding that she be treated on an equal footing with men. It was all too evident that the ideal of the passive, submissive woman who stayed at home and cared for children and polished furniture was not appealing to every woman. Quite a few were rebelling against that ideal of femininity, and very soon there would be more and more of these troublesome types. It was imperative that the social order devise an accommodation, a way of placating the feminists who were marching through the streets proclaiming that they were the equal of men and could do anything men could do. The accommodation of the day corresponded to Janet's infantile solutions to her gender dilemmas. Women were permitted, even encouraged, to aspire to the "masculine" occupations, professions, and callings. There was a price, however. If a woman did not also prove that she was a proper feminine type—submissive, innocent, helpless, powerless—she would be suspected of being a virago, of having stolen her talents and gifts, and of emasculating the men who were entitled to own these trophies of power. It was in this sort of social climate that Janet's infantile fantasy life could flourish and find expression. By the time she was an adolescent, the infantile fantasy of gaining permission to keep her stolen phallic trophies by paying the price of masquerading as a "castrated" female was already an entrenched aspect of Janet's character structure, and all she had to do was look around to the conventions in her society to see if she could make that infantile fantasy work in the grown-up world.

When Janet became a famous lecturer, she became aware first of her need to placate the father figures in her audience. Her determination to surpass her father contributed to Janet's anxiety and to the neurotic elements of her character structure. It was her unconscious strategy for appeasing the mother that gave form and direction to her masquerade, her character perversion, if you will.

The coup de grace was little Janet's strategy of putting her stolen phallus to work in the service of her mother. She would act like a protecting father to her mother. In that way she would give back to the mother what she had stolen from her and still retain the fantasy that she was a bigger daddy than her own father.

After she started school, Janet took pride in reading aloud to her mother. It was not long before she was able to solve many mental and physical problems that were beyond her charming, frivolous, and intellectually inhibited mother. As an adolescent, Janet helped her repair the broken toaster, the stereo, the television set. She alone could find her scatterbrained mother's missing eyeglasses and keys. The proud mother, whose own narcissism was gratified by having a daughter who was as competent and masterful as a son might have been, was delighted to acknowledge Janet's superiority over her. She bragged to her friends about her brilliant and beautiful daughter—the valedictorian, the summa cum laude, the college professor, the world-famous lecturer, the potential Nobel Prize winner.

When Janet arrived at womanhood, she continued to use what she unconsciously imagined she had stolen and put it in the service of women less fortunate than herself. She was extremely self-sacrificing and completely devoted to women who needed her assistance—her students, her two older sisters, her less talented female colleagues. All she required in return was gratitude and a recognition that she was superior to them. In one way or another, the women she assisted had to make tribute to her superior know-how. So long as they recognized that she and she alone had the phallic power, she would protect them and give to them unstintingly.

But Janet paid a heavy price for this scheme. There seemed to be no limits to her need to placate and make reparation to the helpless "feminine" women in her life. She could never do enough for her mother. She would give up a precious evening with her husband and children to help a friend in crisis. She would neglect her own writing to rewrite a student's mediocre thesis. After a strenuous day of rescuing vulnerable female students, she would drive fifty miles to help her sick sister care for her children and then drive home to make dinner for her own family. The strain of all this was exhausting. Janet suffered occasionally from excruciating backaches, which she cheerily minimized. As Riviere pointed out about her patient, the device of placation and reparation "was worked to death, and sometimes it almost worked her to death."

The securely established, tenured male professors at the university where Janet taught were impressed with the way she tempered her intellectual brilliance with a proper submission to their authority, and they referred to her as a saint. Her younger male colleagues, who were unconsciously threatened by the number of papers and books she wrote, would joke about the "Big Momma," who didn't have to be taken seriously anyway. But a few of her equally brilliant and self-sufficient female colleagues saw through the masquerade and knew that with all her saintly ways and just feminist causes, Janet was merely another "Big Daddy" in disguise.

At the end of a seemingly endless day of placation, the still undaunted Janet was ready and willing for sex. As much as she needed to play "Big Daddy" to all the helpless women in her life, she also desperately needed to assure herself of her femininity by having sexual intercourse as frequently as possible. It was imperative that she get more sexual pleasure than those inferior feminine women like her mother. She was determined also not to be outdone by her husband. (She was a technical virgin before marrying him and had sought to avoid the humiliation and pain of defloration by having her hymen stretched by her gynecologist.) She always wanted sex more than her husband did, and it was crucial that he not have an orgasm before she did. She was as afraid of impotence as any man. In bed, as in her postlecture masquerade, she played the role of a subservient woman, but under the screen of that impeccable femininity, she orchestrated the sexual scenario, essentially robbing her husband of his active masculinity. Her performance was efficient. She took care of her husband's sexual needs as expertly as she managed their household and their social life. She brought to the marital chamber all her practical know-how and managerial skills, making absolutely certain that everything came off without a hitch. She performed fellatio with alacrity and was an inventive bed partner, more than willing to dress in whatever clothes and assume whatever position her undemanding, overwhelmed, and rather passive husband might require. Although he never asked for very much (and might have been relieved with less), Janet would do everything necessary to make sure her husband had an erect penis to give her. She used her womanly arts almost as a man would use a fetish, more as a device to avoid anxiety than as a means of obtaining sexual pleasure.

Reading this account of Janet's life, no one would doubt that her solution to her gender conflicts was far less tormenting and troubling than the solutions of a Lillian or an Olympia. Except for the occasional backaches and the bouts of fatigue that resulted from the do-or-die intensity of her daily reparations, Janet's postlecture symptom was the one aspect of the situation that was consciously painful to her. That strategy was eminently successful in that it alleviated Janet's postlecture anxiety at the same time that it covered over what her conscience would not allow her to remember, the rage and disappointment and mortification that had to remain "forgotten." But all psychological symptoms work in this way—phobias, paranoid suspicions, jealous rage, obsessional ideas, compulsive rituals, hysterical paralysis. Janet's postlecture scenario, like any symptom, was a screen for an entire childhood history. It was the trace of a complicated narrative of deprivations, losses, defeats, clever tactics, unsuccessful self-deceptions, the fantasied triumphant usurpation of the phallic powers of the adult generation. Why then am I likening Janet's masquerade to a perversion?

Janet's perverse strategy represented a stage in the formation of a typical neurosis rather than a full-fledged perversion. Nevertheless, in certain crucial respects, the strategies that expressed and concealed her fantasy of the stolen phallus had the characteristics of what analysts are more used to labeling as a perversion. For Janet, the common childhood fantasy of usurping the phallic powers that belonged to the parents became a furtive enactment of everyday life; her masquerade of womanliness was a full-time occupation; her symptom was an attempt to reconcile a rigidly dichotomized view of maleness and femaleness; and she was trying to regulate massive castration anxiety. Moreover, her script was repetitive and stereotyped. Every time she spoke in public her postlecture scenario had to be enacted and reenacted without variation. And when she was not lecturing, each day was an elaborate juggling act of keeping her masculine wishes in some sort of balance with her femininity. Her preoccupation with reparation and placation indicated that this most womanly of women, who managed to present herself to the world as the epitome of a successful adult woman, still interpreted masculinity and femininity on the infantile level of "phallic" and "castrated." Her castration anxiety—her anxiety that her own genitals would be mutilated in retaliation for her childhood fantasies—was sufficiently severe to indicate that it gathered some of its force from the more primitive anxieties of annihilation and separation, tantamount to the mutilation anxiety that characterizes the perversions.

Janet's psychic bargain was exhausting, but it had worked efficiently in that it left exposed only a remnant of what it was all about. Janet's postlecture impersonation of femininity alleviated her anxiety by appealing to an ego ideal of normal femininity and by appeasing her superego, which then gave permission to appropriate and keep the phallic trophy she had stolen. Like Janet, many a contemporary woman experiences her intellectual and sexual powers as a stolen phallic trophy. They exhibit their talents and succeed in their ambitions, but are always finding some way to appease for having won. The talents are real and they belong to the women, but they are always edgy that something terrible will happen unless they placate the gods.

Janet's limited postlecture masquerade—"reassure me that I am entitled to keep the golden phallus and then reassure me that I am really only a castrated woman"—expressed succinctly the fuller masquerade of womanliness that constituted an entire way of life devoted to a socially normal but unsuccessful resolution of her feminine and masculine identifications. Janet had disguised her masculine ambitions under a masochistic submissiveness that represented an infantile ideal of femininity. As she put on her mask of self-demeaning femininity, no one would be the wiser, least of all herself.

References

Arlow, J. A. 1986. Discussion of papers by Dr. McDougall and Dr. Glasser. Panel on Identification in the Perversions. *International Journal of Psychoanalysis* 67:245–50.

Bak, R. C. 1953. "Fetishism." *Journal of the American Psychoanalytic Association* 1:285–98.

Freud, S. [1905] 1953. "Three Essays on the Theory of Sexuality." In *Standard Edition* 7:125–245.

———. [1919] 1955. "A Child Is Being Beaten—A Contribution to the Study of the Origin of Sexual Perversion." In *Standard Edition* 17:175–204.

———. [1927] 1961. "Fetishism." In *Standard Edition* 21:152–57.

Gillespie, W. W. 1940. "A Contribution to the Study of Fetishism." *International Journal of Psychoanalysis* 21:401–15.

———. 1956. "The General Theory of Sexual Perversion." *International Journal of Psychoanalysis* 37:396–403.

Glendinning, V. 1983. *Vita.* New York: Knopf.

Kaplan, L. J. 1990. *Female Perversions: The Temptations of Emma Bovary.* New York: Doubleday.

Kernberg, O. 1984. *Severe Personality Disorders.* New Haven: Yale University Press.

Lowenstein, R. 1957. "A Contribution to the Psychoanalytic Theory of Masochism." *Journal of the American Psychoanalytic Association* 5:197–234.

McDougall, J. 1972. "Primal Scene and Sexual Perversion." *International Journal of Psychoanalysis* 53:371–84.

Nicolson, N. 1973. *Portrait of a Marriage.* New York: Atheneum.

Riviere, J. 1929. "Womanliness as a Masquerade." *International Journal of Psychoanalysis* 10:303–13.

Sachs, H. 1923. "On the Genesis of Perversion." *Psychoanalytic Quarterly* 50:477–88. Translated by R. B. Goldberg with a discussion by A. Compton, 489–92.

Stoller, R. 1985. *Observing the Erotic Imagination.* New Haven: Yale University Press.

Wolff, V. 1928. *Orlando.* New York: Harcourt, Brace.

Zavitzianos, G. 1971. "Fetishism and Exhibitionism in the Female and Their Relationship to Psychopathy and Kleptomania." *International Journal of Psychoanalysis* 52:297–305.

_____. 1972. "Homeovestism: Perverse Form of Behaviour Involving the Wearing of Clothes of the Same Sex." *International Journal of Psychoanalysis* 53:471–77.

_____. 1977. "The Object in Fetishism. Homeovestism and Transvestism." *International Journal of Psychoanalysis* 58:487–95.

Chapter Eight

Aggression and Love in the Relationship of the Couple

Otto F. Kernberg, M.D.

T HE basic objective of this chapter is to illustrate the indissoluble nature of the interaction of libido and aggression, of love and hatred, in determining the emotional relationship of the sexual couple. In previous work (1988c) I suggested that sadomasochism, an ingredient of infantile sexuality, is an essential part of sexual functioning in love relations and of sexual excitement, and that sexual excitement, in turn, is a basic affect, a fundamental constituent of libido, which I see as a hierarchically supraordinate drive. I also explored how love and aggression codetermine the capacity for sexual excitement, and how sexual excitement incorporates aggression in the service of love. I defined clinical perversions as conflictually determined syndromes, characterized by a specific restriction of the normal range of sexual experience, including its perverse elements: here, one particular perverse component monopolizes the sexual field (Kernberg 1988a). I defined perversity as the recruitment of love in the service of aggression, the consequence of a

This chapter is a modified version of a paper appearing in the *Journal of the American Psychoanalytic Association* (in press).

predominance of hatred over love; its essential expression is the break-down of boundaries that normally protect the love relationship (Kernberg 1985). These proposals form the background for what follows.

Here I examine the interplay of love and aggression at the level of a couple's emotional relationship rather than at the level of their sexual interaction. The effect of the couple's interaction at the level of their ego ideal, the mutual activation of superego functions in both partners, and the interplay between love and aggression at the boundary between their jointly established value systems and cultural conventionality would complete this outline, but exceeds the limits of this presentation.

Because I want to present a comprehensive view of the emotional dynamics of the couple, I shall have to refrain from a full discussion of the clinical observations underlying these proposals, which may result in their sounding too categorical.

Falling in Love

The capacity to fall in love is a basic pillar of the relationship of the couple. It implies the capacity to link idealization with eroticism and, implicitly, the potential for establishing an object relationship in depth. A man and a woman who discover their attraction and longing for each other, who are able to establish a full sexual relationship that carries with it emotional intimacy and a sense of fulfillment of their ideals in the closeness with the loved other, are expressing the capacity to link unconsciously not only eroticism and tenderness, sexuality and the ego ideal, but also to recruit aggression in the service of love. Each couple in a fulfilling love relationship defies the ever-present envy and resentment of the excluded others and the distrustfully regulating agencies of the conventional culture in which they live. The romantic myth of the lovers who find each other in a hostile crowd expresses in mythological form an unconscious reality for both partners. There may be some cultures that highlight romanticism and others that rigorously attempt to deny it, but as an emotional reality it is revealed in the art and literature throughout historical times (Bergmann 1987).

The unconscious dynamics involved in the couple's defiance include overcoming oedipal prohibitions against sexual involvement with a loved and idealized object of the other sex. The man is engaged in an unconscious search for the ideal mother and a woman who will both replicate his relationship with mother and permit him to overcome it in a relationship where sex and tenderness may finally come together; the woman is searching for a man who will unconsciously represent the oedipal father and permit her to reencounter her vaginal genitality by helping her to open herself sexually to him. Behind this oedipal father, a woman's lover represents the preoedipal mother as well, satisfying her dependency needs while expressing tolerance of sexual intimacy with a symbolic oedipal object. For both man and woman, the love relationship represents daring to identify with the oedipal couple and overcoming it at the same time.

Another major dynamic is the couple's defiant rupture of the submission to the unconsciously homosexual groups of latency and early adolescence (Braunschweig and Fain 1971): the men defy the anally tinged devaluation of sexuality and the defensive depreciation of women of latency and early adolescent groups as a defense against profound dependent longings and oedipal prohibitions; the women overcome the latency and adolescent group's fear of male aggression, their collusion in denying the longing for sexual intimacy, and the defensive idealization of partially desexualized men as a shared group ideal.

A man and a woman may have known each other from childhood, may have constituted a couple in the minds of everybody who knows them; they may marry, and not really be a couple. Or they may become one secretly, sooner or later: at bottom, many if not most marriages are several marriages, and some only consolidate as a couple long after they have faded from the attention of their social group.

If the couple can incorporate their polymorphous perverse fantasies and wishes into their sexual relationship, discover and uncover the sadomasochistic core of sexual excitement in their intimacy, their defiance of conventional cultural mores may become a conscious element of their pleasure. In the process, a full incorporation of their body eroticism may enrich each partner's openness to the aesthetic dimension of culture and art and the experience of nature. Their joint stripping away of the sexual taboos of childhood may cement their emotional, cultural, and social life as a couple as well.

Love and the Stable Couple

With sexual intimacy comes further emotional intimacy, and with emotional intimacy, the unavoidable ambivalence of oedipal and preoedipal relations. We might say, to put it in a highly condensed and simplified way, that the man's ambivalence toward the exciting and frustrating mother from early childhood on and his deep suspicion of the teasing and withholding nature of mother's sexuality become issues interfering with his erotic attachment, idealization, and dependency on the woman he loves. His unconscious oedipal guilt, his sense of inferiority to the idealized oedipal mother may result in sexual inhibition with or intolerance of a woman who becomes sexually free and is no longer a little girl-woman toward whom he may feel reassuringly protective. This development may perpetuate the dichotomy between erotized and desexualized idealized relations to women typical of early male adolescence. Under more pathological circumstances, particularly in cases of narcissistic pathology, the unconscious envy of mother and the need to take revenge against her may bring about a catastrophic unconscious devaluation of the woman as the longed-for sexual object, with consequent estrangement and abandonment.

In the case of a woman who did not have an early satisfactory relationship with a mother who tolerated the little girl's sexuality, the unconscious experience of a hostile and rejecting mother who interfered with her early development of bodily sensuality and, later on, with her positive relationship to father may result in exaggerated unconscious guilt about sexual intimacy in conjunction with commitment in depth to a relationship with a man. Under these circumstances, the little girl's normal shift in object from mother to father is unconsciously distorted, and the relationship with men becomes a sadomasochistic one. Under circumstances even more severe, a narcissistic personality structure evolves and may be expressed in intense unconscious envy of men, leading to a defensive devaluation of the men who love her, to emotional distancing, and perhaps to a narcissistically determined promiscuity that parallels the corresponding one in narcissistic men. The experience of an unavailable, sadistic, sexually rejecting, and/or seductive and teasing oedipal father will exacerbate these early conflicts and their effects on a woman's love life.

Granted the frequency of severe unconscious oedipal guilt and of narcissistic defenses derived from both oedipal and preoedipal sources, the question is, what factors are responsible for creating and maintaining a successful relation between a man and a woman? Two standard and superficial answers are, first, that it is society's mores that protect the structure of marriage and that, insofar as cultural and social structures now seem to be disintegrating, the institution of marriage is in danger; and second, that "mature" love implies friendship and comradeship, which gradually replace the passionate intensity of initially romantic love and ensure the continuity of the couple's life together.

From a psychoanalytic viewpoint, the longing to become a couple that would fulfill the deep unconscious needs for a loving identification with paternity and maternity in a sexual relationship are as important as the aggressive forces that tend to undermine the couple. What destroys passionate attachment and may appear to be a sense of imprisonment and "sexual boredom" is actually the activation of aggression, which threatens the delicate equilibrium between sadomasochism and love in a couple's sexual excitement and in their emotional relationship.

But more specific dynamics come into play as emotional intimacy develops. The unconscious wish to repair the dominant pathogenic relationships from the past and the temptation to repeat them in terms of unfulfilled aggressive and revengeful needs determine their reenactment with the loved partner. By means of projective identification, each partner tends to induce in the other the characteristics of the past oedipal and/or preoedipal object with whom they experienced conflicts around aggression. If such conflicts were severe, this includes the possibility of reenacting primitive, fantastically combined mother-father images that carry little resemblance to the actual characteristics of the parental objects.

Unconsciously, an equilibrium is established by means of which the partners complement each other's dominant pathogenic object relation from the past, and this tends to cement the relationship in new, unpredictable ways. Descriptively, we find the many small, "crazy" ways in which couples interact in their intimacy, their "private madness" (to use André Green's term [1986]), which can be both frustrating and exciting because it occurs in the context of a relationship that, at a different level, may well have proven to be the most exciting and satisfactory and fulfilling one that both partners could have dreamed of. From an observer's position, the couple enacts a strange scenario, completely different from their ordinary interactions, a scenario, however, that has been enacted repeatedly in the past. This "union in madness" ordinarily tends to be disrupted by the more normal and gratifying aspects of the couple's relationship in the sexual, emotional, intellectual, and cultural realms. In fact, a normal capacity for discontinuity in their relationship plays a central role in maintaining it.

Discontinuities

This capacity for discontinuity, as it has been described by Braunschweig and Fain (1971, 1985), has its ultimate roots in the discontinuity of the relationship between mother and infant. According to Braunschweig and Fain, when a mother becomes unavailable to her baby because she has returned to her husband as a sexual partner, the baby eventually becomes aware of this fact. Ideally, a woman can alternate her two roles and move easily from being a tender, subtly erotic, affectionate mother to her baby to being an erotically adult, sexual partner to her husband. And her child unconsciously identifies with her in both roles. Thus, the discontinuity is played out in both mother and infant: in mother, whose materna' functions are discontinuous, disrupted by her return to her sexual partner, thus triggering the earliest sources of frustration and longing in the infant, but also, through identification with mother, in the infant's and child's capacity for discontinuity in his or her intimate relations. According to Braunschweig and Fain, the infant's autoeroticism derives from the sequence of narcissistic gratification and subsequent frustration of his or her sensuous fusion with mother: masturbation reflects an object relationship before it becomes a defense against it.

The capacity for discontinuity is played out by men in their relationships with women: separating from women after sexual gratification reflects an assertion of autonomy (basically, a normal narcissistic reaction to mother's withdrawal) and is typically misinterpreted in the—mostly female—cultural cliché that men have less capacity than women for establishing a dependent relationship. In women, this discontinuity is normally activated in the involvement with their infants, including the erotic dimension of that involvement, which leads to the man's frequent sense of being abandoned: once again, in the cultural cliché—this time a male one—of the incompatibility between maternal functions and heterosexual eroticism in women.

The differences in capacity for discontinuities in men and women also show in their discontinuities regarding love relations, as Francesco Alberoni (1987) has pointed out: women usually discontinue their sexual relations with a man they no longer love and establish a radical discontinuity between an old love relationship and a new one. Men, usually, are able to maintain a sexual relationship with a woman even if their emotional commitment has by now been invested elsewhere; that is, they have a greater capacity for discontinuity between emotional and erotic investments and for a continuity of erotic investments in a woman, in reality and in fantasy, over many years even in the absence of an ongoing relationship in reality with her.

Men's discontinuity between erotic and tender attitudes toward women is reflected in the "Madonna–prostitute" dissociation, their most typical oedipal defense against the unconsciously never-abandoned, forbidden, and desired sexual relationship with mother. But beyond that dissociation, profound preoedipal conflicts with mother tend to reemerge in undiluted ways in men's relationships with women, interfering with their capacity to commit themselves in depth to a woman. For women, having already shifted their commitment from mother to father in early childhood, the problem is not that of the incapacity to commit themselves in depth to a dependent relationship on a man; rather, it is a matter of how to tolerate their own sexual freedom in that relationship. In contrast to men's assertion of their phallic genitality from early childhood on, in the context of the unconscious erotization of the mother-infant relationship, women have to rediscover their original vaginal sexuality, unconsciously inhibited in the mother-daughter relationship. Throughout time, one might say that men and women have to learn what the other comes prepared with in establishing the love relationship: for men, to achieve a commitment in depth, and for women, sexual freedom. Obviously, there are significant exceptions to this rule, such as narcissistic pathology in women and severe types of castration anxiety of any origin in men.

But discontinuity in the love relation is also fostered by the mutual projection of superego functions; the projection onto the sexual partner of the sadistic aspects of the infantile superego may lead to masochistic submission and unrealistic, sadomasochistic distortions in their relationship, but also to a rebellion against the projected superego, precisely by means of the temporary separations that characterize normal discontinuities in the love relationship. By violently rejecting or attacking the guilt-inspiring object, both partners may achieve a temporary freedom from a projected sadistic superego. That relief, paradoxically, may permit love to reemerge.

Complementarity, Collusion, and Twinship

My hypothesis would explain why some couples may have a deep and stable relationship in spite or because of the aggression and violence enacted in their love life. If we group nonorganic psychopathology roughly into neurotic, borderline, narcissistic, and psychotic levels, partners coming from different levels of pathology may establish varying degrees of equilibria that stabilize their relationship while permitting them to enact their world of madness contained by protective discontinuities. For example, a neurotic man with an obsessive personality married to a borderline woman may unconsciously admire her freedom for violent aggressive outbursts, whereas she, on the other hand, may be protected from the real and feared consequences of her aggressive behavior by the discontinuity achieved by the splitting processes that she imposes as the most natural way of relating within the marital relationship. And her obsessive husband may be reassured by the self-containing nature of aggression that he unconsciously fears in himself. But the relationship of another couple with a similar structure may be destroyed because of the intolerance of the obsessive man toward the inconsistency of the woman, and the intolerance of the borderline woman of the persecutory nature, as she experiences it, of the man's rational persistence and continuity.

Throughout many years of living together, a couple's intimacy may be strengthened or destroyed by certain types of unconscious scenarios. I am referring to unconscious scenarios enacted throughout time that differ from the periodic enactment of ordinary, dissociated past unconscious object relations in that, unconsciously, a specific feared and desired scenario is gradually brought into action by the cumulative effects of dissociative behaviors. These scenarios may become highly destructive in reality, sometimes simply because they trigger circular reactions that engulf the couple's love life beyond their intentions and capability to contain them. I am referring here, above all, to the enactment of oedipal scenarios linked to the invasion of the couple by excluded third parties as a major disruptive force, and to various imaginary twinship relations enacted by the couple as a destructive centripetal force. Let us first explore these latter relations.

Narcissistic conflicts show not only in unconscious envy, devaluation, spoiling, and separation but also in the unconscious desire to complete oneself by means of the loved partner, who is treated as an imaginary twin. Didier Anzieu (1986), in developing further Bion's (1967) work, has described the nconscious selection of the love object as a homosexual and/or heterosexual completion of the self—a homosexual completion in the sense that the heterosexual partner is treated as a mirror image of the self. Anything in the partner that does not correspond to that complementing schema is not tolerated. If the intolerance includes the other's sexuality, it may lead to extremely severe cases of sexual inhibition. Behind the intolerance of the sexuality of the other lies the narcissistic envy of the other sex. In contrast, when the selection of the other is as a heterosexual twin, the unconscious fantasy of completion by being both sexes in one may act as a powerful cement. Bela Grunberger (1979) first pointed to the unconscious narcissistic fantasies of being both sexes in one.

It is a frequent observation that, after many years of living together, partners begin to resemble each other, and one marvels at how two such similar persons found each other. The narcissistic gratification in this twinship relationship, the combination, we might say, of object love and narcissistic gratification protects the couple against the activation of destructive aggression. Under less ideal circumstances, such twinship relations may evolve into what Anzieu (1986) has called a "skin" to the relationship of the couple, a demand for complete and continuous intimacy that seems at first an intimacy of love, but eventually becomes an intimacy of hatred. "Do you still love me?" as a constantly repeated question that reflects the need for maintaining the common skin of the couple is the counterpart of the assertion, "You always treat me like that!" indicating the shift of the quality of the relationship under the skin from love to persecution. Only the opinion of the other really counts in protecting one's safety and sanity, and that opinion may turn from what is at first a continuous stream of love to a continuous stream of hatred.

Unconsciously enacted long-range scenarios may reflect wish-fulfilling fantasies, the enactment of unconscious guilt, the desperate search for a different ending to a feared and endlessly repeated traumatic situation, and an unwillingly, unwittingly triggered chain reaction that destroys the internal sequence of the scenario. For example: a woman with a hysterical personality structure, an oedipal fixation to an idealized father, and profound prohibitions against sexual involvement with him is married to a man with a narcissistic personality structure and intense unconscious resentment of women. He selected her as a desirable heterosexual twin whom he unconsciously expected to be totally under his control as a support for his narcissism. Her sexual inhibition frustrates his narcissism and triggers him to seek extramarital satisfaction, while her disappointment in the oedipal father triggers first ineffectual masochistic submission to her husband and a masochistic, and for the same reason, sexually gratifying love affair with a forbidden and socially dangerous man later. Her abandonment of her husband brings about his awareness of his dreaded dependency on her, denied by his previous treatment of her as a slave, while her now fully awakened sexual response in a threatening but unconsciously permitted relationship (because of its nonmarital nature) brings about her acceptance of her own genital sexuality, and husband and wife reencounter each other with a better understanding of their mutual needs.

Now, it is true that both underwent psychoanalysis and without treatment probably would not have been able to reconstruct their relationship. He unconsciously needed to provoke her to become the rejecting mother, thus justifying retrospectively, so to speak, his devaluation of her and his search for a new idealized woman; she unconsciously needed to reconfirm the unavailability and disloyalty of father and to pay the price of a socially dangerous situation as a precondition for responding sexually to a man not her husband. Thus, rather than simple discontinuity, this example illustrates a progressive path to the destruction of the relationship based upon the mutual unconscious enactment of a dominant conflictual relationship from the past.

Triangulations

Direct and reverse triangulations, which I have described in earlier work (1988b), constitute the most frequent and typical of unconscious scenarios that may, at worst, destroy the couple or, at best, reinforce their intimacy and stability. Direct triangulation refers to the unconscious fantasy of an excluded third party, an idealized member of the subject's sex—the dreaded rival replicating the oedipal parental rival. Every man and every woman in their intimate sexual relationship unconsciously or consciously fears the presence of somebody who would be more satisfactory to their sexual partner, and this dreaded third party is the origin of insecurity in sexual intimacy and of jealousy as an alarm signal protecting the couple's integrity.

Reverse triangulation refers to the compensating, revengeful fantasy of involvement with a person other than one's partner, an idealized member of the other sex who stands for the desired oedipal object and consolidates a triangular relationship in which the subject is courted by two members of the other sex, instead of having to compete with the oedipal rival of the same sex for the idealized oedipal object of the other sex. I propose that, given these two universal fantasies, there are in fantasy potentially always six persons in bed together: the couple, their respective unconscious oedipal rivals, and their respective unconscious oedipal ideals. This formulation arises from a context having to do with unconscious fantasies based on oedipal object relations and identifications; Freud's comment to Fliess, "I am accustoming myself to the idea of regarding every sexual act as a process in which four persons are involved. We shall have a lot to discuss about that" (1954, 289, letter 113), was made in the context of discussing the existence of bisexuality.

One form that aggression related to oedipal conflicts takes frequently in clinical practice and in daily life is the unconscious collusion of both partners to find, in reality, a third person who represents a condensed ideal of one partner and a rival of the other. The implication is that in marital infidelity, short-term and long-term triangular relationships more often than not reflect unconscious collusions between the couple, the temptation to enact what is most dreaded and desired. Homosexual as well as heterosexual dynamics enter the picture because the unconscious rival is also a sexually desired object in the negative oedipal conflict: the victim of the other's infidelity often identifies unconsciously with the betraying partner in the sexual fantasies about the partner's relationship with the jealously hated rival. When severe narcissistic pathology in one or both members of the couple precludes their capacity for normal jealousy—the capacity for jealousy implies a certain achievement or tolerance of oedipal rivalry—such triangulations easily become enacted.

But then a couple able to maintain its sexual intimacy, to protect its boundaries against invasion by third parties, is not only maintaining its obvious, conventional boundary but also reasserting, in its struggle against rivals, its unconscious gratification of the fantasy of the excluded third party, an oedipal triumph and a subtle oedipal rebellion at the same time. Fantasies about excluded third parties are typical components of normal sexual relations. The counterpart of sexual intimacy that permits the enjoyment of polymorphous perverse sexuality is the enjoyment of secret sexual fantasies that express, in a sublimated fashion, aggression toward the loved object. Sexual intimacy thus presents us with one more discontinuity: discontinuity between sexual encounters in which both partners are completely absorbed in and identified with each other, and sexual encounters in which secret fantasied scenarios are enacted, thus carrying into their relationship the unresolved ambivalences of the oedipal situation.

The perennial questions, What do women want? What do men want? may be answered by saying that men want a woman in multiple roles—as mother, as little baby girl, as twin sister, and, above all, an adult sexual woman. Women, because of their fateful shift from the primary object, want men in fatherly roles but also in motherly roles, a little baby boy, a twin brother, and an adult sexual man. And at a different level, both men and women may wish to enact a homosexual relationship or to reverse the sex roles in an ultimate search for overcoming the boundaries between the sexes that unavoidably limit narcissistic gratification in sexual intimacy: both long for a complete fusion with the loved object with oedipal and preoedipal implications that can never be fulfilled.

Perversity and Boundaries

Basically, the experience of the boundaries between the sexes can be overcome only under extreme conditions in which the symbolic destruction of the other as a person permits the use of his or her sexual organs as mechanical devices without emotional involvement. Sadistic murder is the extreme but logical consequence of an effort to definitely penetrate another person to the very essence of his or her existence and to erase all sense of being excluded from that essence. Under less extreme circumstances, the dimension of perversity—the recruitment of love in the service of aggression—transforms the depth of sexual intimacy into the mechanization of sex that derives from the radical devaluation of the personality of the other, an observation first made by Fairbairn (1954).

Perversity in the sexual encounter may be illustrated with the typical developments of couples engaged in group sex for whom, after six months to a year of consistent participation in multiple polymorphous perverse activities, their capacity for all sexual intimacy and, for that matter, for all intimacy typically ends (Bartell 1971; Kernberg, 1980). Here, the oedipal structure tends to become dismantled, in marked contrast to the opposite, stabilizing effects on a couple of a maintained triangular love relationship in reality in which an equilibrium is reached that permits acting out nonintegrated aggression by splitting in the relationship with two objects, and acting out unconscious guilt over the oedipal triumph by maintaining a love relationship that is less than fully satisfactory.

In the emotional relationship of the couple, a corresponding perversity may be observed in long-standing sadomasochistic relationships wherein one of the partners enacts the functions of the perfectionistic and cruel superego, thereby gratifying his or her own sadistic tendencies through self-righteous indignation, while the sexual partner masochistically expiates his or her guilt derived from oedipal and, more frequently, preoedipal sources.

Or perhaps, such a perverse equilibrium no longer involves superego-sanctioned expression of aggression but the enactment of more primitive sadomasochistic scenarios, with life-threatening types of aggression and primitive idealization of a powerful and cruel object without moral dimension. One partner, for example, may agree to sterilization as symbolic castration or even to actual mutilation or self-mutilation. Primitive dissociative mechanisms may protect perversity within a stable equilibrium of the couple that reaches an extraordinary intimacy dominated by aggression.

The circular reaction created by rageful outbursts of one partner, a response of righteous indignation and identification with primitive superego functions on the part of the other partner, masochistic submission of the first perpetrator followed by his or her renewed angry outbursts or by an immediate reinforcement of rage as a secondary defense against unconscious guilt may all escalate until this dissociated primitive object relation acquires a fixed quality, and ordinary discontinuity of the relationship may no longer contain it. Ethel Person (1988) has described a typical situation in which one partner has an extramarital relationship and defends himself or herself against feelings of guilt by behaving provocatively toward the marital partner, aimed at inducing a rejection by that partner, and thus assuaging the existing guilt. This may lead to a result opposite to the one intended by the partner carrying on the extramarital relationship, one that finally destroys the couple. Generally, relentless aggression as an unconscious plea for acceptance and as the expiation of guilt triggered by that very aggression may not be contained by the partner.

Boundaries and Time

The boundaries separating the couple from its social environment protect the couple's equilibrium, for good or otherwise. Extreme social isolation of couples with perverse developments at the sexual, emotional, and/or superego levels may gradually worsen their destructive relationship because they lack corrective interactions with the environment and lose the normal capacity of couples to "metabolize" in their social life aspects of the aggression generated in their interactions (Kernberg 1980). Extremely sadomasochistic couples in social isolation may become very dangerous to the masochistic partner. On the positive side, the normal boundaries protect the couple's intimacy not only from triangular invasion from the surrounding social environment but also from their "private madness," the necessary discontinuities in their relationship.

Certain common boundaries of couples become significant at different stages of the couple's life. A first one is the relationship with their children, a subject too vast and complex to explore at this point, except to stress the importance of maintaining the boundaries that separate the generations. One of the most typical manifestations of unconscious guilt over the implicitly rebellious and defiant quality of any intimate relationship (representing oedipal fulfillment) is a couple's not daring to maintain firm boundaries of intimacy in relation with their children. The proverbial absence of a lock on the bedroom door symbolizes the parents' unconscious guilt over sexual intimacy and the unconscious assumption that parental functions should replace sexual ones. This regressive fantasy, projected onto the children as a fear of their reactions to being excluded from the parental bedroom, reflects the underlying fear of identifying with the parental couple in the primal scene, and the unconscious collusion between the two parents in abdicating from their rights to identify fully with their own parents.

A second boundary is that with the network of couples that constitutes ordinary social life. Relationships with other couples are normally infiltrated with eroticism. Here, among the friends and the spouses of friends, are the feared rivals and the desired and forbidden sexual objects; in unconscious collusion, these social networks maintain the erotic quality of their relationships. In fact, the teasingly exciting and forbidding boundaries among couples are the typical scenarios within which direct and reverse triangulations are played out.

The boundary between the couple and the group is always a "combat zone." "Static warfare" is represented by the group's pressure to mold the couple into its image and is reflected in conventional morality and in ideological and theological ritualization of love, commitment, marriage, and family tradition. From this viewpoint, the couple who exists from early adolescence or even childhood on, gathered by the corresponding relatives and sanctioned by everybody's benevolent perception of the two, actually lives in a symbolic prison, although it may escape into a secret love relationship. The mutual temptations and seductions in the network of adult couples represent a more "dynamic warfare," but also, at times, the potential salvation for individuals and couples entrapped in relationships that are drowning in mutual resentment and aggression.

As I have pointed out in earlier work (1980), the group needs the couple for its own survival, for the reassurance that an oedipal triumph, the breaking away from the anonymous crowd, is possible. And the group envies and resents the couple's success as contrasted with the individual's loneliness in that anonymous crowd. The couple, in turn, needs the group to discharge its aggression into the environment. Projective identification not only operates within the couple but in subtle ways includes third and fourth parties as well. David Liberman (1956) has described how a patient's bitter complaints to the analyst about the marital partner may be part of a subtle acting out. The analyst becomes the repository of the aggression against the marital partner, and the patient withdraws into a "saved" relationship with the partner while abandoning the relationship with the analyst.

This is a particular example of the more general phenomenon of the "lavatory" analyst whom Herbert Rosenfeld (1964) described. A couple's intimate friends may serve that function: the confidants are often not aware that they have become the carriers of the aggression that would otherwise become intolerable for the couple.

A couple that seems to be functioning well evokes inordinate envy within an unstructured social group. The envy that is usually kept under control by the rational and mature aspects of interpersonal relationships and friendships among a network of couples becomes immediately apparent in large unstructured groups. I refer to such formal and informal organizations as extended travel groups, local political parties, professional societies, or communities of artists. A couple's unconscious awareness of a group's envy may take the form of guilt-ridden public mutual attacks to soothe those who are envious, or an external behavior of defiant total harmony while mutual aggression remains hidden from public view. Sometimes a couple manages to hide from others how close their relationship really is.

And a third boundary, the dimension of time, is the frame for both the full development of a couple's life as such and for the limited nature of that life because of death and separation. Death becomes an important consideration for couples in the later years. Fear of aging and illness, fear of becoming unattractive to the partner, fear of becoming excessively dependent on the other, fear of being abandoned for somebody else, and the unconscious tendency to defy or deny the reality of time—for example, by a reckless neglect of one's physical health or that of one's partner—may become the field within which aggression from all sources is played out. Here, concern and mutual responsibility derived from ego and superego functions may play a major role in protecting the survival of the couple, in contrast to the unconscious collusion with dangerous self-defeating patterns, such as the neglect of illness or financial irresponsibility.

Men may be particularly sensitive to the aging process in women, much more so than women in their relationship to men, because of a deep relationship between the idealization of the surface of mother's body as one origin of eroticism, on the one hand, and the fear of the content of mother's body as expression of unconscious projection onto her of primitive aggressive tendencies, on the other (Meltzer and Williams 1988). This may sexually inhibit men as well as women in advanced stages of their life and reactivate or reinforce oedipal prohibitions against their sexuality. The affirmation of a couple's sexual intimacy at advanced stages of their life is a final test of their sexual freedom. The conventional denial of the sexual life of the aged is the final edition, so to speak, of the child's efforts to deny the sexuality of the parents and the parents' corresponding guilt-ridden renunciation of their own sexuality. And the concern for the loved person, the companion of a lifetime, may become an increasingly important factor in mediating and controlling the couple's enactment of dissociated aggression.

The changes in a couple's mutual relationships of power and authority related to changes in their prestige within their social environment, in the relative income of both partners, and in professional and work developments not only may affect their emotional equilibrium by the meanings unconsciously attributed to these changes but, paradoxically, may often represent the unforeseen effects of unconsciously determined factors. A classical example is that of the nurse who puts her husband through medical school, secure in her role as a maternal provider while gratifying his dependency needs, only to experience later the negative consequences of his success as a physician. He now expresses resentment for his dependency on mother by searching for a relationship in which he is the dominant father for a little girl–mistress while his wife struggles with her resentment over the loss of her maternal function and her unconscious resentment toward powerful men (at bottom, penis envy) activated by his professional success.

Or a narcissistic man establishes a relationship with an adoring, inhibited, unsophisticated girl and stimulates her to study and work so she can live up to his expectations for a narcissistic twinship, only to discover that her blossoming activates his deep envy of women and resentment of her independence. He subsequently devalues her and their relationship is destroyed.

Behind these scenarios, however, we find, again and again, an inability to tolerate the discontinuities of contradictory relationships to be expected between partners. These contradictory relationships reflect the predominance of a specific pathogenic conflict of the past and the two major sources of aggression in the couple: the preoedipal narcissistic conflicts centered on unconscious envy of the other sex and the oedipal sense of guilt over a full identification with the parental couple in its sexual, parental, and generative roles.

But time operates not only destructively. The search for reactivation of past conflicts to heal their wounds (to use Martin Bergmann's expression [1987]) may be successful in that their love is maintained in spite of the violence of mutual aggression; in fact, the survival of the couple may expose the fantastic exaggerated nature of their unconscious fears over repressed or dissociated aggression. To be able to attack one's partner sadistically and yet witness the survival of his or her love and to experience in oneself the transition from relentless rage and devaluation to guilt, mourning, and repair constitute invaluable experiences for the couple. When sexual intimacy and pleasure incorporate the reparatory efforts linked to such awareness, guilt, and concern, then sexual excitement and emotional intimacy increase, together with the expansion of the couple's commitment to joint responsibility for their lives.

And then, there are the accumulated experiences of a shared life that include mourning the loss of parents and youth and becoming increasingly aware of a growing past left behind and a future becoming steadily restricted. Normally, emotional growth implies an expanding identification with all the stages of life, a bridging of the boundaries that separate age groups, and, by the same token, a transcendence into the continuity of generations—into the past beyond the personally experienced one and into a future the couple will not live personally. These mourning processes imply the building up of a shared internal world that exists as long as the couple survives and, increasingly, only within the shared memories of the couple and, finally, in the mind of the partner who survives the other. This joint life becomes the depository of their love, a powerful bridging force that provides continuity throughout the discontinuities of daily existence.

At the end, the faithfulness to the other becomes the faithfulness to the internal world. The growing awareness of the limitation of all relationships through death highlights the importance of this internal world. The denial of one's personal death is limited by the awareness of the necessary end, at some point, of the joint life of the couple, which initiates a mourning process that again enriches life lived together and after the death of the person one loves. The surviving member of the couple carries the responsibility for the continuation of the life lived together. The woman whose husband has died and who joins their old network of couples with a new husband activates this mourning process within the entire group.

Pathological Role Fixation

I have explored perversity in love relations that takes the form of destroying the sexual couple (a) because aggressive elements predominate and control sexual excitement, (b) because sadomasochistic patterns dominate and control their emotional relationship, and (c) because persecutory and sadistic features dominate and control mutually projected superego functions. One additional form of perversity of love relations is the freezing of the relationship in one pattern of actualized unconscious complementary object relationship from the past, in contrast to the normal interplay of enactments from the past and realistic relations in the couple's present interactions.

To illustrate this contrast between normal flexibility of shifting roles adopted by both partners and pathological role fixation, I shall mention typical shifts in the partners' interactions with each other. For example, in a man's unconscious relation to his wife, he may shift from the role of the sexually dominant and excited male penetrating his wife and symbolically enacting the loving and sexually accepting father to the role of the satisfied infant who has been nourished by mother, symbolically represented by the woman who has given him the gift of her orgasm. He then may become the dependent child of a maternal woman who tucks him in, feeds him, and puts him to sleep; or he may actively shift into a fatherly role toward a dependent daughter by repairing a broken lamp, for example, which she cannot do (or pretends not to be able to do). He may shift from the role of a guilt-ridden boy who is scolded by a perfectionistic mother to the envious little boy watching the mysteries of adult female concerns and interests; or he may become resentful of a woman's dedication to her profession or to their baby because he feels like a neglected child, the counterpart to a woman's unconscious resentment of her husband's professional success because it reactivates early envy of men.

A wife may shift from the role of adult sexual partner to dependent daughter of a protective mother or to the motherly woman who feeds her little boy–man. She may become the guilty little girl who is seduced by a sadistic father to have sex; or she may be "raped" in her fantasy during sexual intercourse, thus confirming her lack of guilt for sexual enjoyment; or she may ashamedly exhibit herself, thus expiating for her sexual pleasure while obtaining the gratification of being admired by the man who loves her.

These and other role enactments may be mutually gratifying because they express both love and hatred and the integration of aggression within a loving relationship. But these unconscious collusions may break down, and aggression may be expressed in unconsciously "fixating" the self and the sexual partner in a particular role, leading to the typical scenarios that become the conscious subject matter of chronic marital conflict: for example, the dependent, clinging, love-hungry woman and the narcissistic, indifferent, self-centered man; or the dominant, powerful, and controlling woman who, though she feels frustrated by her insecure, childlike boy-man and wants an adult man as her partner, has difficulty in perceiving the self-perpetuating nature of their relationship; or the "sex-hungry" man who cannot understand the limited sexual interest of his wife; or, of course, the guilty partner and the blaming one in all their varieties.

Usually rigid role fixations reflect underlying enactments of dissociated scenarios by a couple unable to accept or carry out the ordinary functions of discontinuity mentioned before, and their utilization of such fixed situations for the gradual enactment of scenarios related to oedipal guilt or narcissistic fixations. One may raise the question, of course, whether simply a lack of harmonious correspondence of unconscious enactments may bring about clashes of contradictory expectations, so that while a man tries to be a protective father, he enters in collision with a competitive mother; or else, both participants are frustrated in their mutually dependent expectations. In practice, however, the unconsciously fine attunement in the couple's unconscious awareness of each partner's disposition makes it abundantly clear to each how he or she will be perceived by the other. What appears as simple misunderstanding on the surface is usually deeply determined by unconscious needs.

The assumption that the dominant problem of a couple is their lack of mutual communication only touches the surface of these developments. To the contrary, sometimes a very full communication may serve to enact barely controlled aggression. This does not mean that an effort to consciously communicate mutual needs and expectations is not helpful; but when deeper unconscious conflicts come into play, the communicative process itself may be contaminated by them, and open communication may serve only to accentuate the conflicts.

A final word about the couple's boundary with social and conventional value systems. I cannot examine here the complex relationships among conscious aspirations of the couple for their life as such, their cultural values, and those of the surrounding social system and culture (Henry Dicks [1967] has clarified these issues), but it may be helpful to mention one aspect of these aspirations. I believe that there are no "objective" rules about what value systems should determine the couple's relationship, particularly their way of dealing with conflicts. The ideological dimension of all cultures, I believe, is implicitly directed against a couple's full intimacy. It is in the very nature of conventional culture to attempt to control the basically rebellious and implicitly asocial nature of the couple as it is perceived by the unconscious conventional social environment. The couple's independence, therefore, from social conventionality may be crucial in their survival under conditions of conflict—and a couple's therapist's nonconventionality essential in his or her role with them. It is true, of course, that under conditions of extreme distortions in the enactment of dissociated object relations from the past that become threatening to the physical or emotional integrity of one or both members of the couple, ordinary social reality may protect the partners from a dangerous, even life-threatening deterioration. In contrast to the minority of cases in which that comes true, however, there is a large majority of couples whose unconscious conflicts take on the surface mimesis of ideological battle cries of the moment, further complicating their relationship as conventional standards become rigid slogans that further reduce their flexibility to deal with their conflicts.

References

Alberoni, F. 1987. *L'erotisme*. Paris: Ramsay.
Anzieu, D. 1986. "La scene de menage." In *L'amour de la haine, nouvelle revue de psychoanalyse* 33:201–09.
Bartell, G. D. 1971. *Group Sex*. New York: Signet Books.
Bergmann, M. S. 1987. *The Anatomy of Loving*. New York: Columbia University Press.
Bion, W. R. 1967. "The Imaginary Turn." In *Second Thoughts: Selected Papers on Psycho-Analysis*. New York: Aronson, 3–22.
Braunschweig, D., and Fain, M. 1971. *Eros et Anteros*. Paris: Payot.
———. 1975. *Le nuit, le jour: Essai psychanalytique sur le fonctionnement mental*. Paris: Payot.
Dicks, H. V. 1967. *Marital Tensions*. New York: Basic Books.
Fairbairn, W. R. D. 1954. *An Object-Relations Theory of the Personality*. New York: Basic Books.
Freud, S. 1954. *The Origins of Psychoanalysis*. New York: Basic Books.
Green, A. 1986. *On Private Madness*. London: Hogarth Press.

Grunberger, B. 1979. *Narcissism, Psychoanalytic Essays.* New York: International Universities Press.

Kernberg, O. F. 1980. "The Couple and the Group." In *Internal World and External Reality.* Northvale, N.J.: Aronson, 307–31.

———. 1985. "The Relation of Borderline Personality Organization to the Perversions." In *Psychiatrie et psychanalyse: Jalons pour une fecondation reciproque.* Quebec: Gaetan Morin Editeur, 99–116.

———. 1988a. "A Theoretical Frame for the Study of Sexual Perversions." In *The Psychoanalytic Core: Festschrift in Honor of Dr. Leo Rangell,* ed. H. Blum and E. Weinshel. New York: International Universities Press.

———. 1988b. "Between Conventionality and Aggression: The Boundaries of Passion." In *Passionate Attachments: Thinking about Love,* ed. W. Gaylin and E. Person. New York: Free Press, 5:63–83.

———. 1988c. "Sadomasochism, Sexual Excitement, and Perversion." Presented at a panel on Sadomasochistic Perversion at the Midwinter Meeting of the American Psychoanalytic Association, New York, December. *Journal of the American Psychoanalytic Association,* in press.

Liberman, D. 1956. "Identification proyectiva y conflicto matrimonial." *Revista de Psicoanalisis* 13:1–20.

Meltzer, D., and Williams, M. H. 1988. *The Apprehension of Beauty.* Old Ballechin, Strath Toy, Scotland: Clunie.

Person, E. 1988. *Dreams of Love and Fateful Encounters.* New York: W. W. Norton.

Rosenfeld, H. 1964. "On the Psychopathology of Narcissism: A Clinical Approach." *International Journal of Psycho-Analysis* 45:332–37.

Chapter Nine

Perversions and Deviations in the Psychoanalytic Attitude

Their Effect on Theory and Practice

Joyce McDougall, D.Ed.

I do not wish to arouse conviction; I wish to stimulate thought and to upset prejudices. . . . we do not even demand of our patients that they should bring a conviction of the truth of psychoanalysis into treatment or be adherents of it. Such an attitude often raises our suspicions. The attitude we find most desirable is a benevolent scepticism.
—Sigmund Freud, *Introductory Lectures on Psychoanalysis* (1917, *S.E.* 16)*

S INCE the practice of psychoanalysis inevitably involves two active participants, on which side of the fence should one look for signs of perverse or near-perverse manifestations in clinical practice? At analysands? Or at analysts?

* Quoted by Esa Roos (1986) in "The Part Analysis Plays in Psychoanalysis" in the *Scandinavian Psychoanalytic Review.*

Ideally, of course, we try to look at both sides of the fence at once. We might, for example, ask whether there is such a thing as a perverse psychoanalytic relationship, or whether countertransference might be infiltrated with perverse elements, thereby creating undetected complicity with the analysand. Others may have observed, as I have done, that what is pronounced by analysts as "perverse" (and the same may be said of "psychotic") in a given individual's psychic structure frequently reveals a tendency to speak of the so-called pervert—or the so-called psychotic—as the one who is on the *other* side of the fence. These clinical considerations are less frequently dealt with in psychoanalytic writings than are questions pertaining to the theoretical aspects of what constitutes the perverse and near-perverse in psychoanalysis.

Having written a number of papers over the years on the unconscious significance of deviant sexualities (McDougall [1972] 1978, 1982, 1986a, 1989), I have had ample occasion to question my own intellectual investment, as well as that of my colleagues, in these particular clinical manifestations. I am reminded of a time when a small group of Parisian analysts, including myself, decided to meet regularly to discuss our findings with regard to sexual deviations; at the time I was rather struck by the specific libidinal interest each of us displayed in certain aspects of human sexual behavior—probably those that had received the least attention in our personal analyses. One colleague, who did not participate in the book we eventually published (Barande et al. 1972) and who may therefore remain anonymous, recounted the many hours he spent at the local zoo carefully studying what he called "zoo perverts." After reading Helen Meyers's subtle chapter on furtive enactments, I found myself thinking that my colleague would have been an interesting subject for her. This colleague gave us a candid camera vision of his observations with such exquisite detail that I sometimes wondered who was the more excited—the boys who, under the guise of studying monkeys, were furtively masturbating or he who, under the guise of scientific interest, was furtively observing?

We might at this point question Freud's own fascination with human sexuality and his ceaseless exploration of its myriad complications and deviations. Perhaps we owe his momentous discovery of the unconscious and the meaning of dreams to the fact that he himself suffered from sexual problems, but was curious enough and honest enough, to want to understand how these had come about.

This reflection raises the complex question of the potential relation between symptom formation and creativity. In an early paper on the subject of creation and sexual deviation (McDougall [1972] 1978), I remarked that Freud's definition of *perversion* ([1905] 1953) was substantially the same as his definition of *sublimation* in that both terms were used to connote activities in which component sexual impulses are deflected from their original instinctual aim or object. Was my zoo-attracted colleague, absorbed in his observation of the boys and the monkeys, engaged in a perverse or a sublimatory activity? Although we who are analysts are quick to recognize the link between the voyeur and the graphic artist, the sadomasochist and the surgeon, the exhibitionist and the actor, or the fetishist and the philosopher, we are less inclined to dissect the instinctual roots behind our own choice of profession. Have we replaced our voyeuristic wish to surprise the secrets of the primal scene with the admirable desire to know? Or the wish to possess the phallic and female fertile capacities of our parents with the desire to understand and create explicative theories about our patients? Have we replaced our guilt about having perpetrated fantasied attacks against the significant objects in our inner world by the need to heal and repair the psychic world of others? And to what extent are we constantly dealing with unacknowledged parts of *ourselves* uniquely through *others* in our analytic work? What of our disavowed homosexual, narcissistic, criminal, and megalomanic tendencies? To what extent do we use theoretical beliefs as a defense against too close an identification with our patients?

With regard to this book's subject matter, perhaps it could be said that perversion, like beauty, is in the eye of the beholder. There is little doubt that the leading "erotogenic zone" is located in the mind! This holds for analyst as well as analysand. It is the analyst's eye that observes and subsequently creates the labels that define what is and what is not "perverse or near-perverse" in human sexuality and in everyday life. Analysts must remember that, from the viewpoint of their patients, their deviant or near-deviant behavior—whether expressed in the choice of sexual acts or objects, in addictive sexual pursuits, or in the perversity of their character traits—is invariably experienced by them as *ego syntonic,* even though they may suffer from the awareness of public censure regarding their predilections. When the observing specialists, the "sexperts," proclaim this or that behavior, relationship, act, or fantasy to be "perverse," upon what grounds do they make these pronouncements? And according to whose norms and value judgments? Their own? Those of Freud? Those of psychoanalytic institutes? Those of society?

In recent years much has been written about the ethics of psychoanalysis, whereas the extent to which theory and practice are affected by the *value judgments* of its theoreticians and practitioners, and the intrinsic value system that may be thought to underlie the discipline as a whole, are, with few exceptions, infrequent topics of investigation—as though the goals and values to be attributed to the metapsychology and its implied treatment aims were self-evident. Of course, like any other art or science, psychoanalysis incorporates the fundamental values of Western culture of which it is an emanation, as Ethel Person (1983) remarked in a thought-provoking paper on value judgments and sexism in psychoanalysis.

Freud claimed that the most essential value to psychoanalytic thought and practice was the search for truth. But this is not unique to psychoanalysis; the dedication to truth is the basic ethic of all scientific research. We might recall in this respect the position of Karl Popper (1959) who claimed that though theories must make predictions that can be tested, tests can never verify a theory; they can only falsify it. One value is certain: psychoanalysis, whether considered as an anthropological science or as a therapeutic art, has been acknowledged from its inception as a discipline that seeks constantly to question the obvious, to take issue with established beliefs, and to reveal the unconscious elements that lend passion to social, political, cultural, and religious options. Psychoanalysts, and psychoanalysis itself, would surely not refuse therefore to submit to the same rigorous examination (Person 1983).

Person's article on Freud's own value judgments and their effect on his theories of female sexuality demonstrates the extent to which Freud himself was marked by the value judgments of the Victorian era. Person suggests that he mistook the Victorian woman of his epoch for the enduring model of femininity. Although believing himself to be an objective observer, Freud's two famous articles on female sexuality reveal in limpid fashion the extent to which he was imbued with the moralistic attitudes of his day where women were concerned. In his defense, we might recall that he waited until he was seventy-five years old before publishing these two papers and that toward the end of his life he proclaimed, with his usual honesty, that he had lived long enough to discover that he understood nothing about women and their sexuality. Furthermore, Freud believed that all psychoanalysts, once analyzed, would thereby become completely free of moral judgments toward their analysands. Was this not a pious hope? Despite our respect for the Freudian ideal, is it even possible to conceive of such freedom from personal value judgments?

Goals and Values

With regard to the concept of psychoanalytic values in relation to the perverse or near-perverse in clinical practice, I shall address the following questions regarding the analyst's vulnerability to deviating or perverting the psychoanalytic ideal of nonjudgmental neutrality:

- What effect do analysts' value judgments have upon the construction of their psychoanalytic *theories* regarding deviant sexual and near-perverse behavior?
- What is the effect, explicitly or implicitly, of such value judgments upon their *clinical* work?
- Given the considerable divergence that exists among the many schools of psychoanalytic thought, might there not be some question of the extent to which their thought and practice may be subtly perverted through the *idealization* of theories and theoreticians?
- Over and beyond the dedication to truth, which it is hoped inspires the work and research of every analyst, and over and beyond the different psychoanalytic schools of thought, is it possible to discern an ideal, in terms of both stated goals and their implicit value judgments, that would be specifically *psychoanalytic*—that is, a fundamental value or system of values over and beyond the inevitable sociocultural values that leave their mark on all scientific and artistic disciplines?
- If such a fundamental approach can be discerned, to what extent would analysts' own acknowledged and, more particularly,

unacknowledged value judgments deflect them from such an ideal, thus permitting a measure of perversion to affect their clinical work?

- To what extent would such an ideal coincide with or deviate from *society's* value judgments? Are analysts to judge *themselves* perverse if they find they are in opposition to society's judgment of what is perverse and what is not?

What do practicing analysts see as their goal when they offer potential patients, perverse or otherwise, the possibility of engaging in the psychoanalytic adventure? Most would agree that the overall aim of psychoanalysis and psychoanalytic therapy is directed toward the acquisition of self-knowledge. They hope that their patients will use this knowledge to good account and that, as a result, life will seem a worthwhile venture despite the suffering and disappointments that are part and parcel of human existence.

If we examine Freud's topical and structural models of mental organization in order to detect the specifically analytic goals concealed within them, we might say, following Freud, that there are the aims, first, of making that which is unconscious conscious and, second, of gaining insight into the ego-superego structures and the oedipal organization to which they have given rise. The implied goal might be stated as that of permitting the individual, who discovers for the first time the truth about his infantile incestuous wishes and their attendant fears as well as the truth concerning his megalomanic narcissism and destructive impulses, to be better placed to make judgments about himself and about his relationships to others including the society of which he is a citizen. The implicit value attached to these goals would presumably be that the self-knowledge thus gained is not only an intrinsically worthwhile possession but also a useful acquisition in the service of living.

The intrinsic value attributed to self-knowledge, however, like the dedication to truth, is in no way unique to psychoanalysis. Clearly analysts need to look beyond these if they wish to find a more basic value (concealed within their stated aims and goals) that may underlie a specifically psychoanalytic way of thinking and working, a dimension that, consequently, might be considered an original contribution to the value judgments of our culture. This may, at the same time, open a further perspective on their clinical work with patients described as having perverse characteristics.

Freud was, of course, the first to broach the subject of psychoanalytic goals and values. In his paper "Types of Onset of Neurosis" ([1912] 1958), he proposed as a definition of mental health "the capacity for achievement and enjoyment, which is on the whole unrestricted." Toward the end of his life, in "The Question of a *Weltanschauung*" ([1933] 1964), Freud concluded that psychoanalysis would be incapable of producing a Weltanschauung of its own and in any case had no need of one; being a science it could adhere to the scientific Weltanschauung. He nevertheless proposed that the aim of psychoanalytic treatment was to enable the individual "to love and to work" (it being understood in both cases, with pleasure). At first sight, these goals appear to be founded on unattackable values. Who would challenge them? But how do they apply to those who can achieve a love relationship only if it is submitted to deviant sexual conditions such as sadomasochistic or fetishist behavior? Should it be an analyst's goal to enable patients to discover their fetishistic and sadomasochistic potentialities? And what of those whose work and earning power is based, for example, on activities that are illegal? (In this connection I recall the distress of one of my colleagues when he discovered that his patient, a young medical doctor, was paying for his analysis by performing illegal abortions.)

As for the capacity to love, years of psychoanalytic experience have affirmed that there are analysands who need to become aware of their *hatred*—and to be able to handle and use wisely the aggression that then becomes available to the ego. Beyond the hatred that lies deeply buried in man's heart for all that thwarts and frustrates him, there are also external circumstances that require an honest appraisal of their hateful aspects (as Freud would certainly have admitted).

In the same vein, with regard to the "relatively unrestricted capacity for achievement" and the right to work, there are patients who need to learn how to *stop working,* that pleasure in their work hides a compulsive, perhaps even a perverse dimension—those, for example, who use their work as others use drugs, to escape mental pain rather than reflect on the factors that have caused it. Numerous individuals who are constantly preoccupied with "doing" rather than "being" leave no space for imagination and dreaming. They discover in the course of analytic treatment that the latter activities are unconsciously felt to be either forbidden (leading to thoughts that are considered sexually taboo), dangerous (a potential path to madness), or terrifying (in that they may open onto a total void). In defending the "imaginary," I am reminded of a film of Woody Allen's, *The Purple Rose of Cairo*. It tells of a young married woman whose life is devoid of any gratification and who falls passionately in love with a cinematographic image; he detaches himself from the screen, although retaining all his imaginary characteristics. There comes a moment when the young woman must choose between the reality of the actor and her screen-image lover. She chooses reality—and loses everything.

In opposing "illusion" to "truth" and "fantasy" to "reality," Freud reveals an ambiguous attitude to imaginative life, whether expressed in perverse or in sublimatory ways. When fantasy life is portrayed as a personal pleasure not destined to be expressed in the form of creative acts, he tends to treat it as a symptomatic avoidance of external reality. Even his pleasure in creative works carries a note of sanction—for example, when he talks of having "succumbed" to the charm of Leonardo da Vinci's creative genius, as though it were a weakness. He appears to liken the seductive charm of creative work to a transgression, an avowal for which he must excuse himself.

Thus a closer look at Freud's ideal of enabling individuals to love and to work without hindrance may reveal that the underlying values, like those concerning femininity, are covered with a thin veneer of Victorian duplicity and reflect hidden moral judgments regarding pleasure derived from the world of fantasy. (The same may be said of Freud's ambiguous attitude toward masturbation—it is seen, on the one hand, as an integral part of human sexuality and, on the other, as a pathological manifestation.)

In attempting to understand those of my analysands who constantly flee imaginative life, consuming every second in action, I have come to refer to them as "normopaths" in that their apparent and admirable normality often hides a pathological defense against psychotic forms of anxiety (McDougall 1978, 1982). Moreover, in many cases they brutally impose their symptom on others through constant criticism, with the aim of making the less active among us feel guilty. Taking Robert Stoller's definition of perverse behavior (see chapter 2) as that which seeks to harm, and as pertaining to a "dehumanizing" goal, might not such individuals be considered, from this viewpoint, as displaying near-perverse behavior? Borrowing Stoller's metaphor regarding the ambiguous nature of the near-perverse, we might say that the normopath does *everything* in the missionary position. It could be added, parenthetically, that these interminable toilers, who can be included in the category of work addicts, display a form of psychic functioning that frequently increases psychosomatic vulnerability.

Since Freud's time, many other analysts, influenced by the theories of their period, and the charismatic quality of certain theoreticians, have attempted to formulate additional analytic goals with their attendant value judgments. These include "the attainment of genitality," "adaptation to reality," "the acquisition of autonomous ego functioning," "the capacity for stable object relations," "the desire to become a parent" (especially for girls!), "the enjoyment of healthy narcissism," and so on. While there is no reason to take exception to the "attainment of genitality," for example, as a possible aim in psychoanalysis, it is necessary to know according to which model this genital sexuality is to be judged: the normative approach of Freud ([1905] 1953) as defined in the "Three Essays"? "Adaptation to reality" has an equally acceptable ring to it, but this presupposes a concept of what constitutes "reality," for reality as recognized by any given individual's ego is a construct, slowly created by the discourse of parents and society from childhood onward; it is not an immutable given. Whose definition of reality, therefore, and whose subsequent reality-sense, is to be the standard? The same criticism might apply to standards of narcissistic health. As for the goals of achieving stable relationships and desiring parenthood, though an individual analyst may personally value these, it is not for analysts to wish for, or implicitly impose upon their analysands, either partners or offspring. If analysts unwittingly promulgate these normative standards, are they not being more than a little perverse, self-idealizing, or omnipotent?

Clearly we need to look beyond surface values, such as genitality, adaptation, and narcissistic gratification, if we wish to define a more specifically psychoanalytic goal. Of the different values enumerated, the most valid and the freest from personal value judgments remains the search for truth—provided we can define it. Bion (1965, 1970) is the analytic thinker who has the most consistently elaborated Freud's conception in this respect. He proposes that the psyche has the capacity to recognize truth since, according to his theory, it is the impact of emotion that gives the ring of truth. For Bion affect is at the heart of *meaning* and thus is the most precise indicator of true experience and judgment; it therefore becomes an essential goal of analysis to reveal "psychic reality" in these terms. He also develops the idea that the psyche is capable of attacking true thoughts and, consequently, may generate lies that will then be used in the service of destructive and death-dealing impulses.

In spite of my interest in Bion's conceptions I still find it necessary to look beyond the pursuit of truth and reality, even if these achieve dignity by being qualified as psychic. In fact, these goals are all basically *normative* and to this extent might not qualify as the essential part of a "psychoanalytic" attitude. On the contrary, they may *pervert* it. To make such aims into fundamental psychoanalytic values risks the danger of analysts imposing on their patients ethical values of a moral, religious, aesthetic, or political nature. As such, these would hinder their functioning as analysts and put pressure on their patients to fit in with the analysts' system of values instead of discovering their own system and assuming or modifying their own values in consequence. This could constitute an outstanding perversion of the psychoanalytic ideal of neutrality—and yet, in certain respects, it is unavoidable. For example, psychoanalysts in a given society are not usually in opposition to the fundamental sociocultural values of the community to which they (and their patients) belong. Any society that seeks coherence and continuity will make laws to maintain a set of ethical values, considered—rightly or wrongly—as being essential to the survival of the society. But psychoanalysts, given the nature of their work, can scarcely avoid questioning the place of deviancy and its near-perverse qualities in their society.

Deviancy and Psychoanalysis

When is deviancy to be considered normal? When, on the contrary, might it be judged as pathological? To censure all deviant behavior, in no matter what social institution, would be equivalent to putting an end to any progress in the domain in question. If, on the other hand, one were to admit, potentially, any deviation, the survival of the institution or of the society in question would be threatened. Thus, analysts cannot elude the problem of social values.

Nevertheless, psychoanalysis runs the risk of being judged *subversive* (if not perverse) in that its practitioners profess neutrality. Analysts do not seek to judge their patients—either to command or to condemn them. Their only avowed aim is to understand and to communicate their understanding, with the hope that analysands, in consequence, can assume their own choices and thus take full responsibility for their acts. The practice, the basic ethic, of psychoanalysis is limited to helping each patient become conscious of his repressed fantasies and conflicts with the result that hitherto unacknowledged sets of values, formerly accepted as basic truths, may lead to the questioning of religious, political, ethical, and aesthetic beliefs as well as sexual choices and practices.

The continuation of psychoanalysis itself as a doctrine or practice, however, might be endangered if the stated goals of rendering people more aware of their formerly unconscious conflicts (and therefore more apt to question standard social beliefs) were considered *deviant* and felt to threaten the existing order. As everyone knows, there are countries in which it is forbidden to practice psychoanalysis.

At the same time, if analysts implicitly accept any compromise with values that *threaten their essential neutrality* toward their patients and also impede the elaboration of their theoretical reflection, then they run the risk of losing their identity and becoming assimilated to a religious or a political group rather than a scientific one. I shall return to this question later when considering quasi-religious attitudes toward theoretical concepts and schools of thought that may infiltrate and perhaps subvert psychoanalytic goals.

In matters of sexual deviation society too has its word to say. In the inevitable concern for safeguarding its ethical structure, society tends to treat as an illegal offense any sexual act that is thought to threaten the welfare of its children or infringe upon the rights and liberties of its citizens. It is understandable, for example, that the sexual seduction of minors and sexual behavior that is forced upon a nonconsenting person (such as exhibitionism or rape) are acts that are usually punishable by law.

Other sexual deviations, such as fetishistic or sadomasochistic practices between consenting adults that affect no one but those who engage in them, do not come within the scope of the law.

The controversial question of homosexuality also arouses further reflection. In societies where homosexuality has been or still is declared illegal, even in some cases being judged as a crime that warrants the death sentence, the homosexual preference has presumably been considered a threat to the society in question. We might assume in that case that it has been assimilated to a contagion that, if not circumscribed, may spread among the community, thus endangering its survival. Less than cursory observation, however, will confirm that heterosexuals do not become homosexual merely by contact with those who are—nor vice versa.

It is surprising to discover that analysts sometimes fail to distinguish between that which is deviant and that which is delinquent. This is particularly manifest in the field of sexual deviation. For example, last year I received (along with some two hundred other analysts throughout the world) an invitation to collaborate with a small group of analysts and well-wishers who wanted to combat "perversion." The founders of the movement had secured both the funds and the interest of highly placed political figures for an effort to ban all pornographic and erotic expressions in the media, particularly cinematographic. I protested that this was not necessarily a perversion nor was it the role of psychoanalysts to decide which films adults should or should not watch, that the project might be better pursued individually by those who felt personally concerned rather than by psychoanalysts. In response it was explained to me that erotic films were causing the breakup of happy marriages. To support this contention I was sent a "case history" in which a woman in her mid-fifties, who described herself as highly religious, complained that an entirely harmonious marriage had been broken because her husband began to watch pornographic movies in which the sexual act was exhibited "in all its crudity" (I am quoting from the document in question). The erotic movies had "disgusted" the wife and were considered by her to be the cause of her husband's beginning a love affair with another woman. When I expressed doubt that an "entirely harmonious marriage" of thirty years' standing could be set asunder by watching erotic films and suggested that perhaps the marriage had not been as harmonious as the lady proclaimed, I was furnished with a second reason to support the move-ment—namely, that young children were being employed to play roles in pornographic films. I was very shocked to hear this (and equally dis-turbed to realize that such employment would also require the complicity of parents), but again I protested that this was a problem beyond the scope of psychoanalysis and, indeed, a scandal in which the intervention of legal protection for these children should be sought. It seems to me that confusions of this kind, in spite of the good intentions behind such movements, stem as much from unconscious fears and wishes as they do from psychological or legal concerns.

When an analyst, or any other individual, proclaims that this or that theory, practice, or person is "perverse," he may in fact be saying: "Don't look at me, the very model of normality, but cast your eyes over there." The pervert is always someone else! If analysts fail to interpret their own splits and projections with the same assiduity as that required for analyz-ing the projections of their patients, they may easily appear a sententious and moralistic community.

Acknowledged and Unacknowledged Value Judgments of Analysts

Let us return to the two above instances (sexual practices that are de-clared illegal and homosexuality) in which the analyst's personal value judgments, despite his conscious adherence to "benevolent neutrality," may lead him to deviate from the analytic ideal. With regard to the sexual activities that are condemned by law (child abuse, exhibitionism, rape), any analyst is liable to discover that one of her patients is, for example, a pedophiliac or a voyeur capable of sadistic attack upon the objects of his observation. Even though she may listen with apparent equanimity to the analysand's associations around the theme and concentrate on its uncon-scious significance, the analyst at the same time tends to identify with society's protective aims toward its citizens. Once, when I broached this subject among a small group of venerable analysts discussing ethical questions, one or two members protested that "one should never take such patients into treatment." But, of course, analysts are rarely in-formed in advance of a patient's sexual predilections when these are not the reason for seeking psychoanalytic help. The protesting colleagues then said that such analysands should immediately be thrown out of treatment. Others (including myself) contended that this way of sliding out of the problem was not in conformity with an analytic attitude, supposedly dedicated to comprehension, not condemnation.

It seems necessary, therefore, to emphasize that when an analyst finds a pedophiliac, exhibitionistic, or sexually sadistic patient on the couch, he is obliged to study his own countertransference attitudes closely if he wishes to interpret with equanimity the lawless dimension in such a patient (almost invariably linked to the history of a missing or abusive father and sometimes a sexually arousing-and-rejecting mother). This will enable him to maintain a strict analytic frame, which, though particularly resented by such patients, is deeply reassuring as a paternal presence; he can then interpret the fragmented pregenital impulses with empathy and link them to the incoherent erotic relationship with the mother of early childhood. Analysts may also find themselves having to analyze unconscious incestuous wishes toward their own children or be led to explore their own unacknowledged sadistic, voyeuristic, or exhibitionistic tendencies. The fact that these have been successfully repressed or sublimated should not prevent them from probing more deeply into their unconscious selves—indeed, this is essential if analysts hope to further their self-understanding as well as that of their patients.

With regard to homosexuality the question is somewhat different since in most Western societies this version of sexuality is no longer regarded as illegal between consenting adults. Even where homosexuality is not punishable by law, however, one still comes across some analysts who harbor a secret desire to transform their homosexual patients into heterosexual ones; this raises inevitable questions regarding countertransference attitudes. Such a wish would be comprehensible if the desire to live a fully heterosexual life were consciously sought and specifically stated *by the analysand,* and perhaps equally understandable in the case of patients who might be termed "latent heterosexuals"— those whose homosexuality represents primarily a defensive structure against the fantasized dangers of any heterosexual attraction (this is not the case, however, with the majority of homosexual men and women). Richard Isay has published many pertinent papers on this countertransference potentiality to which he gives the name of "homophobia" (1986,

1989). Limentani (1977) and Leavy (1985) have also made notable contributions concerning the same phenomenon.

In the absence of a specific or a discovered wish for sexual reorientation, the analyst needs to ask what justification there might be for his imposing his own sexual preferences on patients with other predilections. Even if many analysts (again not all) believe that homosexuality indicates a *symptomatic* solution to internal conflict, such "solutions" frequently reflect the best adjustment the child of the past was able to make in the face of circumstances unfavorable to heterosexual development. These often involve difficulties in understanding sexual roles or in facing sexual realities with their concomitant renouncements and narcissistic wounds, as a result of the parents' unconscious problems and their subsequent effect upon the family discourse. If one takes this standpoint into consideration, it becomes understandable that if a homosexual solution is undermined, it may give rise to depressive phenomena or even to serious disturbance in identity feeling.

Again, some prominent analysts maintain that homosexuals cannot be treated psychoanalytically. Two experienced colleagues, one from Europe, the other from North America, related an almost identical incident. Each had prepared a paper dealing with aspects of homosexuality and illustrated with a clinical case. Both were asked publicly how they justified having taken such people into treatment and why they referred to their work as "analysis" since "homosexuals are not analyzable." Of course, some homosexuals are unanalyzable—and some heterosexuals, too.

When analysts overlook such factors, this may be due to a certain idealization of heterosexuality. Yet they are well placed to know that heterosexuality is no protection against psychological disorders. They would also do well to recall, in this context, that most sexual perversions, such as fetishistic or sadomasochistic practices (which I prefer to call "neosexualities" to distinguish them from the different homosexualities; McDougall 1986a), are attempts to achieve and maintain a *heterosexual* relationship.

In the absence of the above-mentioned determinants, should an analyst maintain heterosexual goals for homosexual patients that the patients do not have for themselves, or maintain that analysis is not for the homosexual, it is probable that these countertransference attitudes are linked to unconscious homosexual fears and wishes in the analyst, giving rise to values of a normative and, in view of the analytic ideal, near-perverse kind. The analytic couch must not become a procrustean bed.

With regard to a genuinely psychoanalytic attitude within the analyst-analysand relationship, it would seem justifiable to state that an analyst shall never wittingly impose upon his patients *his* system of values, *his* sexual preferences, *his* political opinions—or the theoretical convictions of *his* particular school of psychoanalytic thought. Any other attitude is a perversion of the analytic role. I cannot claim that all analysts respect this particular ethic, but I am stating the ideal, much as it was promulgated from the beginning by Freud.

Before concluding this discussion concerning respect for *patients'* personal value systems, let us look at the respect that analysts display—or do not display—toward one another. Although they may preach impartiality as a value in regard to other people's ideals and options, they may not necessarily apply this standard to the theoretical and clinical beliefs of their colleagues—especially if they happen to run counter to their own. Theoretical convictions, of whatever cast, are usually the fruit of serious clinical research and long years of experience. Nevertheless, the various schools of analytic thought seem always to be in danger of adopting a quasi-religious attitude toward their concepts and their leaders; their findings are treated as articles of faith rather than scientific theories. A theory, by definition, is nothing more than a set of postulates that has never been proved and that may remain forever incapable of proof. If it were otherwise, conceptual models would no longer be theories, but laws. *Is it not a major perversion, then, for an analyst to believe that he holds the key to the Truth?*

Freud, in his own way, led a crusade against what he called "religious illusions," but at the same time, although aware of the danger, he tended to replace religious faith with faith in psychoanalysis ([1927] 1961, [1930] 1961). The situation of psychoanalytic theory and practice today is even more complex in that the various schools protect their theories as though they were religious doctrines, idealize their leaders as though they were priests, and treat other clinicians and theorists as though they were heretics. Although theory is essential to any science, one does not find in other professions the same passionate defense of theories as one finds in psychoanalysis. How might we explain this?

One reason may be that psychoanalysis differs from other sciences in that very few of its theoretical concepts are demonstrable. (In this respect they bear a resemblance to religious beliefs—they lack hard data to support them.) But beyond that explanation, perhaps a transference phenomenon is at work here. The experience of personal analysis, as well as the close teacher-pupil relationship that characterizes the transmission of psychoanalytic knowledge, are both marked by strong positive and negative transference affects. And these, if not recognized, may readily be used in near-perverse ways. They certainly contribute to the violence that so often accompanies theoretical and clinical divergences. The sanctification of concepts and the worship or denigration of their authors appear to me to be sequels to unresolved transference ties. Adherents become *disciples* who no longer question their theoretical models or engage in creative personal research. When reading Louise Kaplan's chapter in this book, "Women Masquerading as Women," I wondered whether unquestioning disciples might not be "analysts masquerading as analysts" in that their dedication to their analytic schools may prevent their truly hearing their patients and searching for further insight when the patients do not fit the theories. In certain respects, they are like Kaplan's patient "Janet" who had "stolen" her femininity from her mother, without any true introjection and identification to her role as a mother or as a sexual partner and lover.

Another disturbing aspect of psychoanalytic sects is the fact that their theoretical beliefs frequently prevent the converts of whatever persuasion—Hartmanian, Kleinian, Lacanian, Winnicottian, Sullivanian, Kohutian, Bionian—from profiting from one another's discoveries. Instead they spend their energies trying to convert the others. "Free thinkers" run the risk of excommunication, a sort of intellectual terrorism that takes on an aspect of religious persecution of the infidel who dares to question the true doctrine. In this respect, a comparison might also be made with those who have constructed deviant sexual scenarios which they forcefully protect, claiming that theirs is the true sexuality and that the "others" are unwilling to admit it.

Theory and Observation

In spite of the danger of perverting the psychoanalytic attitude through the idealization of theories and thinkers, one must face the paradoxical relation of theory to practice. It is evident that theoretical convictions play a fundamental role in no matter what field of science or art. No one can practice psychoanalysis without a solid theoretical basis; in fact, without the Freudian metapsychology it would be impossible to *think* psychoanalytically. Observation, in whatever domain, can never be free of theory—it is always directed to proving or disproving some existing theoretical standpoint. There is no such thing as "pure" observation (Roos 1982, 1986), a point of view that has been consolidated over the years in the writings of Popper (1959), Kuhn (1962), and Feyerabend (1975).

Thus, theoretical convictions and the values attached to them are bound to leave their mark on theoretical and clinical discoveries. Trying to confirm existing theory is an integral part of any scientific discipline, and it is a fact that dedicated researchers, in no matter what field, tend to find what they are seeking. In psychoanalysis, as in any other science, until such time as changing clinical problems force practitioners to question their existing concepts, *they are only able to discover that which their theories permit them to find.* Perhaps where research is concerned the saying "I'll believe it when I see it" should read "I'll see it when I *believe* it." This reflection is particularly appropriate to schools of psychoanalytic thought: cherished concepts frequently appear to be self-confirming. Nevertheless, the part played by the desire to confirm existing concepts must be accepted as a given when research is undertaken; it does not necessarily pervert or invalidate the value of the findings in question. There are many roads to clinical truth and in this respect researchers resemble the blind men describing the elephant.

Thus analysts explain that psychic change and symptom cures are due—according to their theoretical school—to the fact that some part of what was unconscious has become conscious, that "where Id was, Ego has come to be," that the patient has "worked through the depressive position," that the "basic signifiers of desire" have been revealed, that "beta" elements have developed into "alpha" functioning, that a "transitional space" has been created where none existed before, that the self has been liberated from its "grandiosity and self-objects," or that the "internal theater" has been reconstituted to the satisfaction of both analyst and analysand. No matter which analytical explanation is proffered, each reveals that the account of an analysis is always a narrative written by two people.

It is not astonishing, then, to observe that patients effect important psychic change in their way of functioning, even though they are in treatment with psychoanalysts holding widely divergent theoretical concepts. It would be inaccurate to imagine that it is the *theories* that bring about psychic change and symptomatic cure. Nevertheless, analysts cannot work without them, although they must be ready to challenge them when observation no longer fits their concepts. Theories are *needed* to help analysts bring order out of the chaos of mental functioning, to help them understand why psychic change should occur at all as a result of the "talking cure," and to help them face the uncertainties that besiege them daily in their clinical work. Moreover, they give some protection against the inevitable feeling of solitude that the clinical situation creates. In belonging to a school of psychoanalytic thought, they are members of a family and are less alone with anything that escapes them—for there will always be such elements in any given psychoanalytic session.

Therefore, I am not denigrating the value of theory nor regretting the diversity and apparent contradictions evident in the different schools of analytic research. All analysts belong to the same family to the extent that they are interested in *the psyche and its ways of functioning, or its failure to function.*

Before attempting to discern a more global psychoanalytic position that might *override* theoretical differences, I should like to digress a moment and discuss value systems in relation to psychoanalytic paradigms. Thomas Kuhn, in his seminal study *The Structure of Scientific Revolutions* (1962), defined *paradigm* as a constellation of beliefs, techniques, and values that are shared by all members of a given scientific community. The question of a paradigm shift with regard to psychoanalytic metapsychology merits a fuller exploration than I am able to give here. But suffice it to say that psychoanalytic research may well be in a period of transition from which new paradigms will emerge. Although the creators of the major schools of psychoanalytic thought have brought many important modifications to Freud's basic concepts—sometimes extending his thought, sometimes reducing it in scope—there has been no true paradigm shift in psychoanalytic theory (as defined by Kuhn) since the publication of Freud's life work.

Nevertheless, if we consider that diagnostic categories form part of a psychoanalytic paradigm, then there *has* been a shift in that psychoanalysis was originally designed to study and treat the so-called classical neuroses and not borderline, psychotic, addictive, and psychosomatic states, nor the subtle forms of perversity with which this volume is concerned. Today, these form a considerable part of many an analyst's caseload. I shall leave aside the query as to whether neurotic states, as classically defined, ever existed in a pure form (except perhaps in the mind of the psychoanalyst), as well as the inadequate nature of their conceptualization if limited to the phallic-oedipal level of psychic structure. The complex unity that represents a human personality can with difficulty be comprehended within this one dimension. This said, it is evident that the continually widening scope of psychological problems that patients bring to psychoanalysis is forcing analysts to reexamine their conceptual frameworks and the theoretical modifications that these entail.

Before leaving this topic I should like to emphasize one point. There has been a tendency to refer to analysands suffering from psychosomatic, narcissistic, borderline, or psychotic manifestations, as well as the kinds of persons presented in this book, as "difficult patients" (it would probably be more appropriate to refer to difficult encounters between analyst and analysand), but we should recognize that neurotic problems, and the organizations from which they arise, still provide many mysteries and present as many difficulties in the course of analysis as do the more primitive systems of defense that characterize the clinical categories mentioned above. In my opinion, there is no such thing as an "easy" psychoanalytic patient. The fact that an analysand's unconscious conflicts and fantasies may be simple to understand does not mean that they are simple to analyze. Many a psychotic delusion is also relatively simple to decode, but the analytic process is not rendered any easier for this reason.

What Ensures Psychic Survival?

I now return to the question of a fundamental value underlying our theories of psychic functioning and clinical practice, particularly in respect to the analysis of perversions and the near-perverse in everyday life. I propose the following idea: if societies, as has been claimed, seek primarily to safeguard *social* survival, and if medicine seeks fundamentally to safeguard *biological* survival, might psychoanalysis not claim as its ethic the goal of safeguarding, above all, the factors that contribute to the *psychic* survival of human beings?

Obviously I must define this term before proceeding further. What are the elements of psychic functioning that enable us to maintain our sense of ego identity in both its subjective and its sexual dimensions, and to maintain our feeling of narcissistic value even though levels of self-esteem are constantly affected by fluctuating circumstances? In answering this question, of course, theorists run the risk once again of falling into the trap of their own unconscious and its perverting influence on their judgments. What is and what is not considered essential to psychic survival in human beings? How do analysts judge the psychic organization of an individual whose survival techniques differ widely from theirs or from those of the majority of citizens? And even if we set aside the problem of unconscious collusion in making these value judgments, the mere definition of what constitutes "normal psychic health" is still no easy matter. As with physical health, it is always simpler to point to what is "abnormal" than to define the "normal," yet we cannot elude this question.

The concept of "symptom" is in itself a normative one—it is "normal" to be free of neurotic or psychotic symptoms. Perverse and near-perverse manifestations, by the very use of the terms, are included in the category of symptoms. At the same time, all symptoms are childlike attempts at self-cure in the face of unavoidable mental pain. (I am not claiming that all analysts would give this conception a dominant position in their own scheme of psychoanalytic values, and I must make allowances for its potentially deviating effect on my own thinking and practice.) There is, from the beginning, a paradoxical demand in the mind of the prospective patient who comes to treatment in order to get rid of his suffering. Even if certain philosophies and religions hold to the idea that life on earth is a vale of tears and that suffering is the normal lot of human beings, the social values of the last two centuries suggest that people are not "supposed" to suffer. Not only therefore does the suffering of the future analysand make no sense since its source is unconscious; it is also judged "normal" socially to be *free* of suffering. The fact that symptoms are the result of our own strenuous efforts to survive psychically and at the same time to function in an adult world invalidates much of the psychic energy used to combat them. The analysand's expressed desire to lose his symptoms concerns only conscious aims. The reasons that originally rendered necessary, perhaps vitally so, any symptomatic construction, including perversions and near-perverse behavior, are unknown to the analysand. Their discovery will become one of the goals of treatment and, it is hoped, will bring about psychic change and a modification in the patient's mental suffering to the extent that it is exacerbated by these factors.

Although the elements that contribute to the psychic survival of a given individual and that of humanity as a whole do not totally coincide, we can discern certain commonalities. My own perspective (that psychological symptoms and inhibitions, including perverse and near-perverse behavior, are all attempts at self-cure in the face of conflict and the obligation to find solutions to the difficulties of being human) applies equally to object choices and activities that are not judged perverse or near-perverse because they are acceptable to society, for our sublimatory activities are also attempts at healing ourselves psychologically. The universal traumata to which the young are exposed are composed of unpalatable realities such as the existence of otherness, the discovery of the difference between the sexes and the generations, and the inevitability of death. Admittedly, some solutions to these conflictual situations are more acceptable than others. Those who seek the help of psychoanalysis bring with them the sequels of *failure to deal with the universal traumata of human life,* particularly when the struggle has been intensified and deepened by the unconscious conflicts of parents and their problematical solutions to these same realities (McDougall 1985). In some cases the incoherences and perversions within societies themselves (civil clashes, warfare, Holocaust horror) have had a traumatic impact on individuals, forcing solutions to overwhelming anxiety and depression from which the parents could not shield their children. Erotization is one of these means (as Jacob Arlow and Sheldon Bach both demonstrate convincingly in their chapters in this book). For whatever reasons, events leading to shock or strain traumata have obliged the child of the past to make sense of what was unacceptable or senseless in order to preserve his right to exist and to invest his self-image and personal life with meaning. That the meaning thus created is called by others a perverse or near-perverse symptom does not invalidate its purpose—the drive to survive. This inexorable search for the means of psychological survival seems to me as ineluctably rooted in the human being as is the instinctual thrust to biological survival. We might also add that when our techniques of psychic survival are put out of action, *biological survival itself might be endangered* in that the sudden failure of symptomatic defenses can lead to people's dying for the wrong reasons such as suicide or psychosomatic death.

This perspective is no mere metaphysical position. As with any other value attributed, explicitly or implicitly, to psychoanalysis, it leaves its mark on both the development of theory and the way of conducting analytic treatments. In turn, diagnosis and prognosis will be affected, as well as the nature of interpretations, and the choice of what to interpret and what to pass over in silence. Thus it is subject, in turn, to the criticisms already formulated regarding other theoretical perspectives. However this may be, most analysts would agree that their patients will always tend, in spite of their suffering, to protect their past solutions to mental conflict and psychic trauma, while hoping, of course, to find others that are less destructive and will provide an enlarged spectrum of creative satisfactions, gratifying relationships, and pleasure in living. The analyst, whose aim is not to "socialize" or to "normalize" his analysands, will consciously strive to treat with deep respect the precarious equilibrium constructed by the distressed and anxious child that is hidden within every adult. Manifestly, such an approach requires analysts to probe carefully into their *own* neurotic bastions, social façades, perverse dimensions, and psychotic cores.

If psychic survival is to be accepted as a fundamental psychoanalytic value, this will require reflection not only upon the distinction between deviancy and delinquency, the similarities and differences between perversion and creation, and the problems of the criminal mind but also upon those that arise from borderline and psychotic organizations as well as the criminal, borderline, and psychotic parts of everyone's psychic structure. Today's research is increasingly involved in understanding the complexities of the narcissistic economy and the nature of psychotic thought. Thus, interwoven with the inevitable problems concerning psychosexual organization and the desires and frustrations that form an ineluctable part of normal adult life is the intricate question of the factors that threaten the sense of identity. Here the struggle is no longer centered on conflict concerning "the right to love and to work" but on "the right to exist."

In 1937, speaking of the problems arising from the difference between the sexes and generations, from castration anxiety and the nature of the oedipal organization, Freud proclaimed that the "bedrock" with which we had to contend was anatomy. Perhaps today we might conceive of the bedrock as also including the drama of *otherness* that gives rise to annihilation anxieties of a narcissistic or psychotic order. This may be considered as a prototypic form of castration anxiety, linked to the inherently traumatic discovery of the existence of one's enduring dependence upon, and inevitable submission to, the existence and wishes of others.

It follows that when there is failure to meet these universal traumata by the self-healing attempts implied in the construction of neurotic and perverse symptoms, the psyche has recourse to more primitive defense mechanisms such as splitting, pathological projective and introjective identifications, disavowal, and the extreme form of psychic defense that Freud designated as foreclosure (*Verwerfung*). These must now replace, and try to accomplish, the work of repression.

Love, Hate, and Indifference

When the solutions found tend toward neurotic, perverse, or psychotic organizations, in each case the struggle between love and hate predominates. As already indicated there is a tendency for neurotic and perverse organizations to restrict the effect of this struggle to perturbation in adult sexual and narcissistic wishes, whereas the psychotic outcome is concerned with the protection of individual existence and the sense of identity. We might add that the psychotic sectors of the individual are more vividly marked by the forces of hate and destructivity and that, in addition, these run the risk of being turned back upon the subject himself.

But at this point we may become aware of a *third* outcome in the exhausting fight against effective flooding and mental pain, when difficulties in the maintenance of significant relationships and in the achievement of narcissistic satisfactions are encountered. The passions of love and hate, although in opposition, are nevertheless both *on the side of life.* Otto Kernberg, in chapter 8, makes a passionate plea for the recognition of both in any true love relationship; he would therefore agree, I think, that the veritable contrary to love is not hate but *indifference.* Love and hate, in their myriad forms and the innumerable transformations to which they give rise—creative and sublimatory activities, neurotic, psychotic, perverse, and characterological solutions—are all protective barriers against the danger of the final defense, which is the destruction of affect and, with it, the meaning of relationships. Disinvestment of the psychic reality of others, as well as of one's own psychic reality, leads to the disturbing symptom that we might call "disaffectation" (McDougall 1984). The disaffected state that follows this disinvestment makes the world and one's relation to it meaningless. Perverse, neurotic, and psychotic constructions are all desperate attempts to give meaning to life. Indifference and disaffectation render the individual concerned *invulnerable to psychic suffering.* People then run the risk of falling prey to the call of nirvana and to the consequent danger that an individual may cease to deal with mental conflict by simply destroying the messages and their meaning, thus gliding toward psychological and, potentially, biological extinction.

Although at this point the curtain may rise upon acts of a psychotic or a suicidal nature, analysts more commonly observe that the "empty fortress" of psychosis, behind which the secret self attempts to survive, is transformed into a false battlement with destruction and *true emptiness* behind it. Psychotic compromises are still striving, blindly, to find a solution to mental pain through dislocating language and meaning, whereas the ejection from the psyche of any mental presentation capable of mobilizing affect leads to the destruction of the very *awareness of suffering.* Since affects are the principal messengers between body and mind, the destruction of many, perhaps of all, psychic presentations accompanying affective arousal tends to result in a radical split between psyche and soma (McDougall 1978, 1982, 1986b). In regressing to the preverbal world of the infant, the psyche, deprived of word-presentations, has no protection against what Freud named thing-presentations. This unconsciously contrived organization against mental pain requires neither a cautious retreat from the world (as in the schizophrenias) nor recourse to paranoid or depressive shields against the relationship with others, or to perverse modes and manipulations as a way of keeping some form of relationship to outer and inner objects.

When human relationships have been *emptied of their libidinal and narcissistic significance,* the individual thus affected will go about his life with "false-self" adjustments in which he will seek, by watching others, to discover the clues to living and react in the way that the world is felt to demand. In all probability he will be neither perverse nor even near-perverse. These are the "supernormal" (that is, pseudonormal) personalities who are more vulnerable than others to addictive solutions, fatal accidents, and psychosomatic death.

We all harbor a "normopathic" dimension of this kind within ourselves; provided, however, that other psychological survival techniques exist, the danger to biological survival is lessened. Analysts must be aware not only of their own normopathic aspects but also of the normopathic part of their analysands, which, if not detected and rendered analyzable, may lead to interminable analyses or the outcomes noted above. Analysts may even, somewhat perversely, be reassured to discover the existence of deviant sexual or characterological creations as a childlike attempt to combat the forces of castration and death rather than face the danger of psychotic or psychosomatic pathology.

Parenthetically, let me note in this context that even severe psychosomatic pathology, though it so often leads to death, presents a paradox in relation to the life impulses. The capacity of the psyche to capitulate before the forces of antilife—which leads individuals to die for reasons that are not programmed by their biological clocks—is, nevertheless, *also constructed in the service of survival.* Individuals, in spite of their suffering and their wish to find more creative solutions to their psychic conflicts, will always have difficulty in leaving their survival techniques, even those that potentially lead to death. This paradox invites further exploration of the debatable theory of a "death instinct." Is the psyche that appears to espouse deathlike wishes imbued with aggression and hate? Or with a profound longing for a state of nondesire and nothingness? Or with a desperate *will to live?* Perhaps here we catch a glimpse of a paradigm shift to come.

Taking as their fundamental value the need to ensure psychic survival will sooner or later oblige analysts to confront their own neurotic and normopathic façades and awaken their recognition of their own perverse, near-perverse, and psychotic parts, as well as alerting them to the danger of allowing feelings of giving up, of psychic death, to be installed within them when they are faced with the disaffected world of some of their patients. This requires constant and sometimes violent incursions into their own countertransference attitudes if they wish to maintain, as a fundamental part of the psychoanalytic attitude, the respect for each personal equilibrium, however precarious, that has been constructed by the defensive child within each adult. Only in this manner may analysts hope to liberate this child's desire to live as fully as possible an adult life in which love, hate, and suffering will no longer be *feared* and can therefore fulfill their profound life-preserving functions.

To conclude, analysts must remember that they too are psychic survivors, that their work, apart from the fact that it enables them to earn a living, also allows them every day to confirm the compromises they have created to deal with their own past psychic traumata. Indeed, it is frequently those very traumata that have given birth to their wish to become analysts, as well as stimulating their curiosity with regard to the mysterious workings of the mind. (It seems highly probable from this viewpoint that intelligence itself should be regarded as a symptom!) In turn, their patients also enable them to maintain and to continue their insight into their own neurotic, perverse, psychotic, and normopathic aspects. Thus, with each analysis and with every analysand, the analyst rediscovers *his* analysis and psychoanalysis itself.

References

Barande, I.; Barande, R.; McDougall, J.; de M'Uzan, M.; David, C.; Major, R.; and Stewart, S. 1972. *La sexualité perverse.* Paris: Payot.
Bion, W. 1965. *Transformations.*London: Heinemann.

———. 1970. *Attention and Interpretation.* London: Heinemann.

Feyerabend, P. 1975. *Beyond Method.* London: Verso.

Freud, S. [1905] 1953. "Three Essays on the Theory of Sexuality." In *Standard Edition,* 7:125–145.

———. [1912] 1958. Types of Onset of Neurosis. In *Standard Edition* 12.

———. [1927] 1961. "The Future of an Illusion." In *Standard Edition* 21.

———. [1930] 1961. *Civilisation and Its Discontents.* In *Standard Edition* 21.

———. [1933] 1964. "The Question of a *Weltanschauung.*" In *Standard Edition,* 22.

———. [1937] 1964. "Analysis Terminable and Interminable." In *Standard Edition* 23:209–54.

Isay, R. 1986. "Homosexuality in Homosexual and Heterosexual Men." In *The Psychology of Men,* ed. G. Fogel, F. Lane, and R. Liebert. New York: Basic Books.

———. 1989. *Being Homosexual.* New York: Farrar, Straus, and Giroux.

Kuhn, T. 1962. *The Structure of Scientific Revolutions.* Vol. 2 of *International Encyclopedia of Unified Sciences.* Chicago: University of Chicago Press.

Leavy, S. 1985. "Male Homosexuality Reconsidered." *International Journal of Psychoanalysis and Psychotherapy* 22:116–24.

Limentani, A. 1977. "The Differential Diagnosis of Homosexuality." *British Journal of Medicine and Psychology* 50:209–16.

McDougall, J. [1972] 1978. "Création et déviation sexuelle." In *Plea for a Measure of Abnormality.* New York: International Universities Press.

———. 1982. *Théatres du je.* Paris: Gallimard.

———. 1984. "The Disaffected Patient: Reflections on Affect Pathology." *Psychoanalytic Quarterly* 53:386–409.

———. 1985. "Parent Loss." In *Trauma and Reconstruction,* ed. C. Rothstein. New York: International Universities Press.

———. 1986a. "Identifications, Neoneeds, and Neosexualities." *International Journal of Psychoanalysis* 67:19–31.

———. 1986b. "Un corps pour deux." In *Corps et histoire.* Paris: Les Belles Lettres, 9–43.

———. 1989. "The Dead Father." *International Journal of Psychoanalysis* 70.

Person, E. 1983. "The Influence of Values in Psychoanalysis: The Case of Female Psychology." *Psychology Update* 1:36–50.

Popper, K. 1959. *The Logic of Scientific Discovery.* London: Heinemann.

Roos, E. 1982. "Psychoanalysis and the Growth of Knowledge." *Scandinavian Psychoanalytic Review* 5:183–99.

———. 1986. "The Part Analysis Plays in Psychoanalysis: A Historical Perspective." *Scandinavian Psychoanalytic Review* 9:31–55.

Part IV

Cultural and Literary Issues

Chapter 10

Reflections on the Smile of Dionysus

Theatricality, Specularity, and the Perverse

Ellen Handler Spitz, Ph.D.

Go, O Bacchus . . .
with smiling face cast your noose;
under the deadly herd
of maenads let him fall!
—Euripides, *The Bacchae*, lines 1020–22

TRAGEDY, like therapy, has to do with the project of attempting to wrest meaning from the ambiguities, arbitrariness, and devastation of human life. Thus, it seems worthwhile to retell its tales and to reinterpret them in each generation according to changing priorities and frames of reference (see Segal 1982, 1986; Simon 1978, 1988; Spitz 1988, 1989). Just as the dramas of the ancient Greeks inspired Freud in his day (see Rudnytsky 1987), so they continue to possess an enduring power to enrich clinical understanding; in addition, they enable clinicians to

The author gratefully acknowledges the support of her work by a grant from the Fund for Psychoanalytic Research of the American Psychoanalytic Association, 1988–89.

locate their endeavors on a continuum that reaches back into historic time.

Among the extant masterpieces of Greek tragedy, the most fecund and explicit in its representations of perverse fantasy is *The Bacchae* of Euripides. Here bisexuality, cross-dressing, humiliation, voyeurism, orgiastic revelry, and mutilation are dramatized through spectacle and spoken word. Thematizing the figuration of the perverse in this play, I shall in this chapter offer a series of meditations with several foci of interest. First, I shall consider *The Bacchae* as reflecting a world in which cultural upheaval engenders perverse enactments as attempted solutions to the paradoxes of human sexuality and generation—a theme that can be explored through its repetitive images of doubling, overturning, and falling. Second, I shall read key scenes in the play as perverse scenarios that recapitulate a violent birth trauma evoked in the opening lines of the play and referred to throughout. Central to this theme are issues of identity, disguise, and méconnaissance (failures of recognition)—especially within the mother-son dyad. Third, as a leitmotif, I shall reflect on the trope of visualization that figures so prominently in this play as it does in the perversions generally, where staring, furtive glancing (see Meyers, chap. 5, this volume), revealing, and concealing are often implicated and where the sight of the phallus (or lack thereof) may carry overwhelming signification. As a part of this third theme, I shall consider choices made here as to the relative merits of representation by spectacle and onstage enactment versus representation by word alone (see Aristotle, *Poetics*, 1455a, lines 23–37; see also Fried 1980; although Fried's argument considers visual art in terms of theater and I have reversed the terms, his work has stimulated my thinking with regard to this topic).

Because my critical discussion meanders, I shall begin with a focused summary of the dramatic action and offer details from certain background myths that are alluded to within it and relevant for what follows.*

Background and Argument of the Play

Dionysus, god of theater, festival, wine, and revelry, has returned to Thebes, site of his ancestral home. Standing before the Theban palace,

---

* The following précis draws heavily on Rose (1959) and on the commentaries of Kirk (1970). For a later comparative retelling in Latin, see Ovid, *Metamorphoses,* Book III.

he speaks his first lines directly to the audience. Even before hearing him, we notice he is young, beardless, and effeminate (almost hermaphroditic) in appearance, with long golden curls and a fawn skin; he wears (and will wear throughout the play) a smiling mask. This emblematic mask evokes uncanny feelings, for, ostensibly betokening comedy, it appears grotesque in a context so redolent of tragedy—a stage set wherein a ruined, still-smoking house and vine-covered tomb are displayed. Thus, before words are uttered, theater works through visual spectacle to create strange juxtapositions and ominous forebodings. This aspect of the drama bears stressing with regard to the theme of this book, for spectacle is likewise often central to perverse experience.

Dionysus, soliloquizing, identifies himself as the son of Zeus but then says that he is in disguise as a mortal, a foreign stranger. Significantly, he immediately tells the story of his traumatic birth, an event that, as I shall show, haunts the entire play. In the account, Semele, his mother (a daughter of Cadmus, the dragon-slayer and founder of Thebes), because she was beloved and impregnated by Zeus, brought down upon herself the jealous wrath of Hera, who, in disguise as an old woman, teased and cajoled her into asking the sovereign god to reveal himself so she might *see* his splendor and thereby ascertain beyond all doubt the divine identity of her lover. Semele did so but, as Hera had foreseen, proved unequal in her mortal state to the revelation. She was destroyed by the Olympian lightnings of Zeus, and her fetus, snatched up from her ashes, was implanted by him in his own thigh and delivered therefrom after the full period of gestation (see *Bacchae,* lines 88–93).* Thus, Dionysus is a male born from a male, a child abandoned and unrecognized by his mother, a son whose father has destroyed his mother, a male deeply scarred by a perverse birth, a child humiliated in utero by a murderous and powerful female (Hera)—a persona of complex and bewildering identity.

Dionysus informs us that he has come to Thebes in mortal disguise (paradoxically) in order to legitimize himself as a god, for his identity has

---

* Except where otherwise indicated, all line references are to Euripides, *The Bacchae,* trans. Geoffrey S. Kirk (Englewood Cliffs, N.J.: Prentice-Hall, 1970). This translation was chosen for its fidelity to the original Greek text, and I am grateful to Professor Lowell Edmunds, Classics Department, Rutgers University, for his counsel on this decision. I am also indebted to Professors Peter Jelavich, Helene P. Foley, and Charles Segal for their generous and illuminating readings of various drafts of this essay.

(also) been publicly challenged. Rumor has it that his mother Semele, in fact, cohabited not with Zeus but with another mortal and contrived the story of Zeus as a front; her death then is explained as a punishment by him for her falsehood (lines 26–31). Manifestly, therefore, Dionysus returns to establish his patrimony, to insist on (dramatize) his identity as son of Zeus (line 1), and to institute his rites of worship in Thebes. His obvious opponent in all this is Pentheus, his antagonist in the play, son of another of Cadmus' daughters, Agave, and brash young ruler of the city, who has not only neglected his worship but condemned it and denounced him as an impostor.

Beyond the manifest content here (the wish to be recognized and affirmed), the psychoanalytically minded reader can discover other levels of meaning for the return of Dionysus to Thebes. One particular motive, which organizes on a fantasy level the action of the plot and bears directly on clinical notions of perversion, is the powerful need of a traumatized child to replay his trauma, often by staging a series of scenarios through which, by displacement, reversal, and projective identification, he can simultaneously identify with and triumph over its original participants (see McDougall 1986). This will be one of the frames through which I shall examine key scenes of *The Bacchae*.

Pentheus, having declared Dionysus an impostor, rages that the women of Thebes, under his corrupt influence, have flocked to the hills to engage in frenzied bacchic orgies. Unable to prevent them, he plans to use military force to return them to the city. When Dionysus arrives in his disguise as a Lydian stranger, Pentheus has him captured, manacled, and arraigned before him, and then, despite warnings by his grandfather Cadmus and the blind seer Teiresias, cast into the palace dungeon. In an apocalyptic scene, which I shall discuss below, the stranger (Dionysus) is miraculously delivered, destroys the palace in a thunderous explosion, and appears to the frustrated Pentheus as a bull.

Chastened but unyielding, Pentheus again confronts Dionysus who, still in disguise, actively and with ironic delicacy begins to direct his diabolical play within the play. Masterfully, he seduces the young ruler into abandoning his regal interests and following out the perverse implications of his own unacknowledged erotic desires. Persuaded to disguise himself as a woman, Pentheus willingly goes to spy on his mother, his aunts, and the other Theban women in order to see for himself what actually transpires in their secret rites on the mountain beyond the city walls (to "see the maenads' shameful deeds," as he puts it, line 1061; see also Segal 1986, 311).

Through back alleyways (see Foley 1985), lest he himself be seen, the costumed and excited Pentheus is led by Dionysus to a tall tree in which he can hide and watch the women. A fateful reversal thwarts this voyeuristic plan, however. Alerted by Dionysus, the women—the bacchae—instead behold him in his exposed perch against the sky. Crazed, they fall upon the tree, pelt him with branches, shake him down, rush frantically upon him, and rend him limb from limb—his mother playing the role of principal assassin.

Gradually, in an exquisitely crafted closing scene (discussed below), Agave is brought by her father's gentle words to a recognition of her deed and to a state in which she can lament the death of her son and her own terrible part in it as well as other losses—the fall of the house and extinction of the line of succession, the impending familial separations, and their retaliatory banishment from Thebes.

Background Myths

Before turning to commentary, I will supplement this retelling with several details from background myths that bear on what follows and provide a fuller familial context for the tragedy. Cadmus had, according to myth, four daughters, two of whom we have met. In addition to Semele and Agave, there are Autonoe and Ino, both characters mentioned in *The Bacchae*.

Autonoe is the unhappy mother of Actaeon who had angered the chaste goddess Artemis by spying on her in her bath or by boasting that he was a better hunter than she or by proposing to marry her after bringing offerings to her shrine (we can trace all these alternative themes in the narrative of *The Bacchae;* on hunting, see Vidal-Naquet 1986). In her fury, Artemis changes this young man into a stag, whereupon he is felled in a ghastly scene and dismembered by his own hounds. Thus, Autonoe's story prefigures that of Agave and Pentheus, but with greater displacement. The murder here is not performed at the hands of the mother herself; rather it is arranged by her proxy, another (in fantasy) chaste and, to the son, unavailable, woman. This barely disguised theme of erotic and murderous relations between a mother and son is thus deeply implicated in the drama of *The Bacchae* and also treated parenthetically by Euripides in two earlier, closely related plays, *Hippolytus* and *Medea* (on *Hippolytus,* see, among others, Segal 1986; for a recent psychoanalytic commentary on *Medea,* see Simon 1988).

Ino, the fourth daughter of Cadmus, has an analogous albeit more complex history, again with several alternate versions. As sister to the dead Semele, Ino is called upon to nurse the infant Dionysus. In the meantime, however, she has married and borne two sons of her own. Hera, enraged at this latest subversion of her plot for the total destruction of Semele and her offspring, takes revenge now on Ino by driving her mad. Ino apparently disappears, and in her absence, her husband believes her dead and remarries, siring two more sons by his second wife. Discovering at length, however, that Ino is still alive, he brings her back with her children, whereupon his second wife, Themisto, plots secretly to kill these stepchildren who pose, as she believes, a threat to her own sons.

The detailed narrative of this attempted slaughter is interesting because it emboldens the theme of mother-child violence and nonrecognition that etches so deep and lasting an imprint on the play. Themisto, the would-be murderess, arranges to have her own children dressed in white and those of Ino in black so that she can tell them apart in the darkness of night. Learning of this, however, Ino reverses the colors. Thus (prefiguring Dionysus' role in *The Bacchae*), she arranges for Themisto to destroy her own children, whereupon the latter, horror-stricken, commits suicide. Hera now reenters the tale and finishes things off by again inducing madness (another prominent theme of *The Bacchae*), this time in both Ino and her husband. The latter (anticipating Agave's role in *The Bacchae*) mistakes one of their two remaining sons for a deer or a lion and kills him; Ino, in order to escape his unreasoning violence, clasps her remaining child in her arms and races to a nearby cliff whence she leaps into the sea, destroying both herself and the only remaining child. Clearly, this story foreshadows Euripides' narrative not only in *The Bacchae* but in *Medea* as well. In both of these dramas, however, infanticide by the mother "comes out," so to speak, and parades itself in all its perversity on the lighted stage—a macabre theme for open portrayal with no more disguises, displacements, or substitutions.

Commentary

To meditate on the action of *The Bacchae* is to experience a kind of vertigo, almost as though the very notion of perversion (from the Latin, *pervertere*) were turning itself upside down. I mean by this that, whether we choose to conceive of perversion as an opposition of the presumably unnatural to the natural or the supposedly immoral to the moral, the invented world here permits no stable referents. Again and again, the play shows us a convergence between apparent opposites and offers images of irony and contradiction that leave us uneasy: "Do not be too confident that sovereignty is what rules men" (line 310); "This beast we found was gentle" (line 436); "He who talks wisdom to an ignorant man will seem out of his senses" (line 480); "'This male womb of mine'" (line 527); "Am I to stop being a man and join the ranks of women?" (line 821); "You will be hidden with the hiding that is appropriate / for one who comes as a furtive spy" (line 955); "The god has ruined us, justly, but to excess" (line 1249). Riddling and prodding, it addresses with uncanny urgency our modern conscience.

The Bacchae reflects a turbulent moment in ancient history when the Peloponnesian Wars had caused a violent upheaval in established customs and beliefs (see Harsh 1979; Fine 1983; de Romilly 1985). Participating fully in the tempestuousness of its epoch, the play with its ambiguities brings to mind a thoughtful passage by Ernst Kris, who speaks of art as being characterized by greater ambiguity during periods when "systems of conduct ideals are in doubt or social values are in process of transition." Art produced under such circumstances reflects, he suggests, "the uncertainties and equivocations in the culture of which it is a part," and his own era, he indicates, is one of this kind (1952, 262). Thus, *The Bacchae* speaks to us across the centuries as we grapple today with the disorientations of our own time and the fluctuations in our mores and values. For us as well as for Euripides, stable notions are suspect, and the referents for our most cherished shibboleths cast in doubt. Yet my approach here is neither historical nor ahistorical, for I seek to consider *The*

Bacchae psychologically as a work for our time rather than to locate it within its own epoch or remove it from history altogether.

The play makes its impact directly on us through its panorama of sliding signifiers; its images shift as readily as does Dionysus himself, who, though sporting only the one smiling mask, appears in many guises: as an ambiguously gendered stranger, a roaring and thundering god, a clever sophist and seducer, a theatrical director, a bull, a snake, a lion, and finally a terrible avenger. *The Bacchae* defies fixity. It is given over in large segments (both concretely and metaphorically) to movement and to dance—to turnings, twistings, and fallings; its rhythmical coda ("Many are the shapes of things . . . ," line 1387) valorizes unpredictability and a bewildering plurality of signification.

Generating classical commentaries that have sprouted as lavishly about it as the ivy and vines sacred to Dionysus himself, *The Bacchae* was written, it is thought, in the seventh decade of Euripides' life. It occupies a place in his canon comparable to those of *Oedipus at Colonus* and *Oedipus Rex* in the oeuvre of Sophocles—the former by virtue of its having also been produced at the end of the author's career when he was in exile and first performed posthumously (within a year of *The Bacchae*), and the latter because of its consummate artistry and obvious parallels, both structural and thematic, with this play. Elusive and complex, *The Bacchae* distills culminating reflections by its master on themes that had engrossed him in earlier works, particularly, as noted above, in *Medea* and *Hippolytus*—namely, themes centering on the erotic and hostile attachments between mothers and sons, a motif of moment in the clinical literature on male perversions (see, among others, Chasseguet-Smirgel 1985; Stoller 1985). Beyond this, its preeminent stageability has given it the magnetism of a lodestone, attracting reinterpretation not only by scholars and literary critics but by directors and performers.

Mimicking, however, the partial blindness figured in its text, interpretations have occasionally fallen to one side or the other of a false divide (see Harsh 1979). They have, on the one hand, envisioned the play as principally a glorification of Dionysus and all he apparently stands for (theater, ritual, festival, wine, voluptuousness, transcendence, reunion with nature) and, on the other, privileged a condemnation of the above, with the additions of licentiousness and brutality—this latter position being supported by the final scenes in which the tragically linked fates of Dionysian victims Pentheus and Agave are rendered with pathos and empathy. It is worth noting, however, that the noxious character traits of both Pentheus and Dionysus create a partial disidentification between each of the protagonists and the audience such that a kind of mutual exculpation results. Thus, as in a typical perverse scenario, neither of the parties—indeed, no one who has colluded in the event (including here the audience)—need feel guilty or be judged so by the end (see Arlow, chap. 3, this volume).

In what follows, I shall press for an attempt to hold both such positions in place without losing grip on either, for to do otherwise would constitute, in my view, a seduction by part elements of the play, whereas to follow through on the doubling devices that riddle its text and keep ambiguity alive without giving up on notions of frame and boundary is, rather, to engage interpretively with a central problem posed by the play as a whole—namely, the intimate relations of paradox to perversion.

To experience *The Bacchae* is to be struck by a strange thought, namely, that paradox, both emotional and intellectual, can be conceived as the underlying traumatic state out of which perversion crystallizes. Perversion, distinguished by mechanisms of splitting and doubling, engenders, at least here in the Euripidean text, a dazzling repertoire of failed attempts to master paradox—paradox understood, however, not solely as aberrant but as deeply intrinsic to the human condition and as horrifyingly obdurate to more than momentary hallucinatory solution.

Early in the action of the play, Pentheus rails at his grandfather Cadmus and at the aged seer Teiresias who form a twosome (line 198) to join the Dionysian revels that the young king overtly despises but covertly envies and desires. Enraged, he threatens to punish Teiresias by "turn[ing the latter's throne] upside down [and] mix[ing] everything up in utter confusion" (lines 347, 348). This wishful punishment, however (turning things upside down and mixing them up), is concocted out of a desire to set things right in the face of Dionysian madness, which he considers perverse. Yet the punishment precisely recapitulates the very dynamic of perversion (see Chasseguet-Smirgel 1985). Thus, the penalty Pentheus conceives for Teiresias is identical to the crime of which he accuses him, and here, as elsewhere in the tragedy, Pentheus conflates weapon with enemy and means with end. This is supremely so when eventually he goes garbed as a woman to spy voyeuristically on women (lines 821–39). Unwittingly, he colludes with and is coopted by what he professes to despise. Such mergings, as they occur throughout the play, problemize the notion of perversion by revealing that norms are often indistinguishable from what apparently deviates from them.

To confuse implies a contrasting state—namely, one of clarity or distinctness. To overturn or turn away (pervert) implies a right side up or a baseline. But it is precisely such "normal" states—of rectitude, stability, reliability—that *The Bacchae* calls in question. Deeply hidden within the notion and experience of negation lies, as Freud ([1925] 1953) taught us, affirmation. Similarly, couched within the notion of perversion are implicit sexual and social norms upon which its meaning depends (Freud [1905] 1953a; Stoller 1985). Thus, in the double sense that negation is both the obverse of affirmation and simultaneously equatable with it, so perversion may be seen not only as an overturning of sexual and social norms but also, in a different sense, as equatable with sexuality itself (Bersani 1986). This doubling, a recurrent feature of the Freudian text, is anticipated in the Euripidean text of *The Bacchae,* where, as we shall see, it figures as a major trope. To foreground the proliferation of such doubling devices in the play is thus to observe the way in which the very notion of perversion is both explored and at the same time rendered problematic.

Reversals, ironies, and transformations abound. Dionysus, although purposing to prove his divinity, disguises it. Appearing first as a Lydian stranger, "his hair all fragrant with light-brown tresses, /with ruddy cheeks and the charms of Aphrodite in his eyes, who daylong and nightlong mingles with young girls/holding out before them his rituals of holy joy" (as described by Pentheus, lines 235–38), he later on becomes a raging bull. Pentheus, however, intent on hiding fatefully from himself, fails totally to penetrate either of these ruses (lines 501–06). This is so because of and despite the fact that bull and curls are symbols that unite the two young men.

It was as a bull that Zeus had raped Europa, sister to Cadmus, grandfather of both protagonists, and it was as an outcome of Cadmus' search for his sister that eventually the dragon seeds were sown and Pentheus' father Echion (snake-man) sprang from the earth. Thus, in taking on the shape of a bull, Dionysus "becomes" his bestial rapist father and instantiates that animal part of himself that Pentheus must so strenuously deny. Likewise, the flagrant bisexuality of Dionysus, both tantalizing and repugnant to Pentheus, annoys him because it prevents him from successfully evading his own conflicted sexuality.

Dionysus, in the scene where he has become prisoner to Pentheus, asks, "Tell me what I must suffer—what is the dreadful thing you will do to me?" Pentheus replied, "First I shall cut off your delicate locks" (line 493), a wish that can be read in its double sense, paradoxically, not only as castrative but also as an effort to foreclose doubleness by attempting to force Dionysus into a strictly masculine gender role.

Next, Pentheus commands Dionysus to hand over his thyrsus (ivy-tipped wand), and it is at this point, with the other's response, that the brilliant seduction begins. Dionysus says, "Remove it from me yourself" (line 496). In so saying, he implicates Pentheus in the latter's own disavowed desire, forces him to play out actively his own forbidden wish. He refuses him a place outside the action, prohibits him from disowning his own lust. Silently, as Pentheus takes the thyrsus into his hand, the roles reverse. From this point on, it is Dionysus who commands and orchestrates and Pentheus who must unknowingly obey. By handling the thyrsus, he is now in the hands of Dionysus. Although he has gloated earlier that when he finally captures this sensual "worshipper of Dionysus," he will "cut his neck clean off from his body" (line 241), it is Pentheus himself who in the end appears onstage as an impaled and severed head. Thus Euripides creates chilling ironies that overturn the expected and even exceed the unexpected.

This centrality to paradox and its inextricability from perversion characterizes both actor and spectator in *The Bacchae*. Its protagonists, Pentheus and Dionysus, though manifestly human and divine, respectively, are perceivable as *doubles* (see Foley 1985). They are cousins, for their ill-fated mothers, Agave and Semele, were sisters. Heirs, therefore, to a bizarre and intertwined genealogy, the two young men seek to establish and secure a stable identity despite family histories tainted with repetitive blots of rape, murder, infanticide, and suicide. Paired in their mutual acts of sadism, they seek to humiliate each other and by so doing to replay and repair their own past wounds. Colliding and eliding, their enmity figures a twinship that is revealed paradoxically through role reversals that occur both within their individual personae and in the libidinized and hostile (sadomasochistic) relations that obtain between them.

Pentheus, the hunter, for example, swiftly becomes Dionysus' quarry; Pentheus, the keeper, is metamorphosed into Dionysus' prisoner; the would-be observer of perversion becomes an actor in it, fully costumed and implicated; this "actor" is quickly transformed into an "actress," and the one who most rigidly defends his boundaries of self, a victim of *sparagmos,* of violent physical dismemberment and death. Like the matched groups of women, the onstage chorus of bacchae from Lydia and the offstage Theban bacchae in the hills outside the city, the god Dionysus and his doubles are participant-observers.

Similarly, we, as audience to *The Bacchae,* are compelled to partici-pate with its characters in an observing that is simultaneously an enacting. Always potential objects to ourselves, we are fated to seek, rediscover, and lose, both inside and outside their intense theatricality and perver-sity, the double vision of our own human condition.

The genius of the play, therefore, lies at least partly in its brutal insistence on the necessity for, but the utter impossibility of, some species of double vision. Relentlessly, it parades before us the disasters attendant on our penchant for the unilateral and the polemical, the too sharply delineated, the logically bounded or statically conceived. Pentheus' deep-ly felt human need, for example, to wall things off (line 653), to demarcate by means of chains (lines 356, 444, 446, 644) or by fastening down with iron nets (line 231), figures a type of partial blindness we can find in ourselves. When, however, he relinquishes the walls of Thebes and, fol-lowing Dionysus, plunges "in drag" into a hallucinatory maelstrom out-side the seven gates, we almost lose him. Clutching arrogantly at his prerogatives of masculine gender and socially conferred power but be-traying latent bisexuality and infantile passivity, he finally gives up the narrowly conceived identity to which he has previously clung and, ventur-ing out beyond civilization, is threatened with, and suffers, annihilation.

These extremes are the choices dramatized by *The Bacchae*. They are extremes meant, however, to be experienced by us as our own.

In *The Bacchae*, the centrality of double vision to perversion, though continually evoked, leaps into full awareness at the moment when Pentheus is dressed as a woman and led by Dionysus to his death at the hands of women (lines 911–76). The rigidly tyrannical young king, his fiercely guarded identity now thrown visibly into question and eager, as Dionysus ironically hints, to see what he should not see (line 911), suddenly exclaims:

> Look—I seem to myself to see two suns
> and a double Thebes, a double seven-mouthed fortress;
> and you appear to lead on ahead of me as a bull,
> and on your head horns seem to grow!
> Were you a beast before? For you are certainly a bull now!
>
> (lines 918–22)

Thus, the male who dresses in female garments doubles his identity, instantiates his bisexuality, demonstrates in his person the central paradox of gender and of human sexuality. Replaying with erotic excitement an original and possibly on some level universal trauma of passivity and humiliation at the hands of woman, Pentheus enacts a fantasy of identification and aggression, while all the while, under the disguise of the castrated image, he preserves his intact phallus and masculine persona, of which however, he is only intermittently aware. This point is conveyed in lines 924–63, where he first asks, "What do I look like, then? Do I not seem to have Ino's way of standing, or that of Agave, my mother?" But then, moments later, he commands, "Convey me through the middle of the Theban land—/for I am the only man of them to dare this deed." Such oscillations between knowing and not knowing impart a tension and suspense, a thrill of anxious pleasure, and intermittent sense of mastery and terror—one doomed in the end, however, to be ephemeral, tragic, even fatal.

It is fascinating that, to Pentheus' hallucination of the double image, Dionysus, now his torturer in earnest (though still himself disguised), responds, "Now you see what you should see" (line 923). Thus, the

bifurcated, dissociated world of perversion—where one fixed set of images is hyperidealized at the expense of another set that remains too
dangerous to contemplate (see Bach, chap. 4, this volume)—stunningly
erupts in this scene. The audience, through spectacle and onstage enactment, experiences a kind of dual transvestism in the twinned figures of
the disguised young men barely distinguishable now except for their
antithetical masks—one smiling and the other unsmiling, or tragic (see
Foley 1985)—while speech and language simultaneously exhort us to
share in their diplopia.

Dissociation of imagery is, however, nowhere dramatized with more
consummate impact than in the final scenes of *The Bacchae* where the
crazed Agave, having murdered her son, is brought to awareness by the
words of her grieving father. Here we see the Euripidean overturning—
the equation between madness and sanity, deviation and norm—as Cadmus, understanding not only that his grandson has been murdered but
that Agave, having committed the act, does not comprehend her deed,
must choose between allowing her to remain in her manic state or help
her to a reality that can only be more painful than her present condition.
He laments, "O sorrow unmeasurable and *beyond seeing*" (line 1244;
italics mine) and continues:

> Alas! If you all [Agave and her sisters] realize what you have done
> you will grieve with a dreadful grief; but if to the end
> you persist in your present condition,
> though far from fortunate, you will think you are free from
>   misfortune.

> (lines 1259–62)

Taking the role of the good parent (or therapist, see Devereux 1970;
Segal 1982), he accepts the responsibility *to make her see,* to bring her
dissociated worlds of imagery together, to return her to what will be for
her forever a tormented world. And here, as elsewhere, we hear the
leitmotif of seeing and knowing, image and word. Agave, believing she
has hunted and destroyed a wild beast and is holding its head in her
bloody hands, must come to recognize this object as the severed head of
her beloved child. Cadmus, in helping her achieve this, does so by *direct-*

ing her gaze. Thus, he concretizes the metaphors that link vision with knowledge:

CADMUS: (*pointing*) First turn your gaze on this sky above.

AGAVE: There: why did you suggest I look at it?

CADMUS: [*Asking her to monitor the alterations in her perceptions*] Is it the same, or does it seem to you to be changing?

AGAVE: [*Turning symbolically from the benighted vision, the dream, the hallucination, to the light of daytime and of commonplace reality*] It is brighter than before and shines with a holier light.

CADMUS: [*Asking her to become aware of her changing affects as secondary to her changing perceptions*] And is this passionate excitement still in your heart?

AGAVE: I do not understand this question—and yet I am somehow becoming in my full senses changed from my previous state of mind.

CADMUS: [*Calling upon her faculties of reason, her ego functioning*] So you could understand a question and give a plain answer?

AGAVE: [*Her altered state of consciousness dissociated now from the more normal state*] Yes, except that I have forgotten what we said before, father.

CADMUS: [*Reconnecting her with her past history, with the flow of sequential time, a dimension absent in her former manic state*] To what household did you go at your marriage?

She responds appropriately, and Cadmus asks her what child she bore.

AGAVE: [*Remembering but still dissociating this thought from her perception*] Pentheus, through my union with his father.

CADMUS: [*Now making the final move of reconnecting thought with percept*] Whose head, then, are you holding in your arms?

AGAVE: [*Denying by avoidance, by* not looking] A lion's—at least, so the women hunters said?

CADMUS: Now consider truly—*looking* costs little trouble [italics mine].

AGAVE: (*violently agitated*) Ah, what do I *see*? What is this I am carrying in my hands? [italics mine].

CADMUS: *Look hard at it and understand more clearly* [italics mine].

AGAVE: [*Describing her affect before being able to connect it with her visual perception or to pronounce the name of her child in this altered context*] What I see is grief, deep grief, and misery for me!

CADMUS: [*Reminding her of her former hallucinatory perception which has now become dystonic*] It does not seem to you to resemble a lion?

AGAVE: No, but it is Pentheus' head I am holding, unhappy woman!

CADMUS: Yes, Pentheus', bewailed before you recognized him!

Thus, Euripides, with a sensitivity to psychological process that annuls the passage of time, implicates us in a scene of recognition that is not described but enacted onstage before our eyes. It is a scene again that of Pentheus "in drag," that confronts us with the double vision of the human condition, a double vision intensified by the perverse scenario but by no means peculiar to it. Agave must go on to face herself as the unwitting agent of her child's death and to learn that she will be separated not only from him but from her father and her birthplace.

I should like to comment on the fact that these two scenes—Pentheus led into the perverse scenario and Agave being brought out of it—are enacted onstage rather than retold and described to us. This is not the case with other major scenes in the drama, such as the bacchic orgy on the mountain and the death of Pentheus. Speculating on this choice between representation by spectacle versus representation by word alone, I would suggest that, based on the interpretive frame of this essay, when the scene occurs *within* the perverse fantasy per se, Euripides has chosen narrative, whereas when the scene involves *moving* from one modality or state of consciousness to another, he has favored enactment plus word. Thus, in the moments located within the perverse fantasy, each member of the audience is given more freedom and privacy to imagine the scene according to individual need (for example, Pentheus and the maenads on Mount Cithaeron), whereas the representation of passage from one state or mode to another is rendered, vis-à-vis the audience, with greater precision. Made intuitively, such artistic decisions have counterparts in clinical practice, where different modes of intervention are likewise chosen and matched with levels of material presented. One wonders further as to the etiology of such choices beyond the clinic in the realm of perverse psychopathology per se—where words and images are often used to achieve similar effects.

Dissociation and splitting continue to be developed in *The Bacchae* by a doubling in the characterization of women. In a series of passages given to numerous speakers including the chorus, images of women in the daytime, at home, under their roofs, seated quietly at their looms, are contrasted with images of women at night, in the hills, in motion, shrieking, dancing, or running.

The Theban women on Mount Cithaeron, for example, abandon their looms and roofs (line 38) to roam the hills outside the city. Their behavior, both literally and figuratively, is out of bounds (in Pentheus' words, their madness "exceeds all bounds," line 785). Having transgressed the limits of the seven gates, they loosen their hair and perform orgiastic revels that include the imbibing of wine, milk, and honey—a reversal of the usual feminine role as provider to others of such nourishment. Tapping magically with their thyrsi, they exorcise these liquids from the earth and voluptuously suckle young deer and wolf cubs, thus violating the boundary that separates human from animal. At a certain point, sensing ambush by the followers of Pentheus, they, like Pentheus and Dionysus, suddenly "fall" and, yet again, turn "everything/upside down" (lines 753, 754). Inverting their previous nurturant behavior, they pounce on live animals and tear them to pieces, snatch children from their homes (lines 735–55), and transform themselves from magical imbibers and providers with powerful phallic appendages into monstrous predators. Bearers and givers of life, these women are seen by the spying males as wanton slaughterers. Thus, they prefigure the scene of Pentheus' death. The description of them ends with snakes licking drops of blood from their cheeks.

Paradoxically, however, this entire scenario (Messenger's speech, lines 677–769) begins with an emphasis on the women's orderliness: they are "a miracle of discipline to behold,/women young and old and girls still unmarried" (lines 693, 694). Thus, just as Pentheus in the name of order threatened to overturn Teiresias' throne at the beginning of the play, so here, states of rectitude or propriety against which confusion can be measured turn into their opposite. The seemingly composed bacchae disorganize; pattern erupts into anarchy; apparent structure proves a deceptive veneer over chaos.

Such portrayals of women cannot be left unconnected with Semele, the dead mother, whose onstage presence is evoked by her burned house and tomb. Dionysus, in returning to Thebes, has returned to his mother in the form of this tomb and, in so doing, must relive the trauma of his birth. Reading the narrative of *The Bacchae* this way, we see in it a turning of passive into active by Dionysus who, having suffered a perverse birth, here foists a similar but more ghastly return upon his cousin Pentheus, for Pentheus, too, by the end of *The Bacchae,* is made to reencounter the scene of his birth, which also now becomes a tomb—namely, the person of his mother, Agave, and a maternal bereavement. In Dionysus' restaging of the trauma, however, it is not a live son who returns to the tomb of a dead mother but rather a live mother who is forced to contemplate in horror the body of her dead son. Thus, by masterminding and directing this perverse scenario, Dionysus revenges himself both on his enemy Pentheus (who had refused to recognize him) and on his mother, Semele (who died before recognizing him), and identifies both with his father, Zeus (through powerful acts of sexualized violence and destruction), as well as with Hera, the aggressor par excellence, while, as a double for Pentheus, he also experiences, via this proxy, his own victimization and maternal abandonment.

Thus, though his divinity had truly been called in question by Pentheus and a prevalence of rumors had accounted manifestly for his insistence on announcing himself as being beyond all doubt the son of Zeus, yet Dionysus has had all along a further agenda—namely, to master the outrage he has suffered *for the sake of his mother, Semele,* to reenact their joint trauma by proxy. Thus, he has forced Pentheus to be outraged *by his mother.* In designing and witnessing this destruction of another son and mother (for Agave is, in the end, psychologically shattered), Dionysus momentarily redresses his own and Semele's still-smoldering humiliation.

Forsaken by the first woman in his life in a disaster plotted by another woman, Dionysus seeks vengeance on all females. Simultaneously, however, he identifies with them in his Maenadic band. Unique among male divinities in this involvement with women, Dionysus reveals an ambivalence toward women that we see operating also in Pentheus. This identification and hatred, on both divine and human planes, figures perhaps a fundamental ambivalence toward the mother (Charles Segal, letter of March 8, 1990). Maddening his followers, the bacchae, Dionysus enthralls them ("So them I stung in madness from their homes / and they dwell on the mountains stricken in their wits . . . all / of the women, I maddened," lines 32–36) as well as, by a more proximate displacement, Agave. Her misfortune is that she was born sister not only to the woman who deserted him but to the woman who did so blindly before affirming or acknowledging him as her child.

Recognition matters deeply here, for the theme of *recognition* is central not only to *The Bacchae* but to all tragedy (see Aristotle, *Poetics,* 1452, 1455). Without recognition, there can be no identity—no sexual or generational identity. Thus, Dionysus demands that the audience *recognize* him ("I have come, the son of Zeus, to this land of the Thebans, / I, Dionysus, whom once Cadmus' daughter bore, / Semele, brought to childhood by lightning-carried fire," lines 1–3). His very compulsion to proclaim his identity in terms of both parents belies the confusion, puzzlement, and pain that underlie it—which he betrays by announcing that he has problemized his own identity by donning a disguise:

> Exchanging my divine form for a mortal one
> I am here, by the streams of Dirce and the waters of Ismenus;
> And I see the tomb of my mother, the thunderbolt-struck
> her by the palace, and the ruins of her house
> smoldering with the still-living flame of the fire of Zeus—
> Hera's undying outrage against my mother.
>
> (lines 4–9)

Thus, the effeminate disguise is linked with images of the dead mother, which kindle living rage within him, rage externalized by the ruins on the stage—signs given to the audience before we ever learn of his ostensible reason for the return to Thebes.

These parental identifications with father and mother reverse themselves later in the play in the apocalyptic scene when, as prisoner to Pentheus, Dionysus causes the Theban palace to tremble and fall. Significantly exchanging the order of these first identifications, here his mother's name comes *before* his father's ("again I speak,/the son of Semele, the son of Zeus!" line 581). Thus, this catastrophic scene, read as a restaging by Dionysus of the primal scene, the paternal assault (also accomplished with pyrotechnics and thunder), shows us, if we focus on the reversed order of the referents, that as a child of both parents he must identify deeply with the destroyed as well as with the destroyer—that, indeed, it is as much his deeply felt congruity with the humiliated Semele as with the potent Zeus that has made him the cruel avenger he is.

Furthermore, in his initial scene of sadistic seduction, when he begins to lure Pentheus step by step to his death, Dionysus again brings issues of recognition and identity to the fore—identity and vision—twinning himself with Pentheus. For Pentheus, duped by his disguise, asks him at one point where Dionysus is (line 501). Ironically, he replies:

DIONYSUS: Even now he is close by and *sees* what I suffer.
PENTHEUS: Well, where is he? *He is not visible to my eyes.*
DIONYSUS: Here, with me; but you, because of your impiety, *do not behold him. . . . You do not know what your life is–neither what you are doing nor who you are.*
PENTHEUS: [I am] Pentheus, son of Agave and Echion as father. (lines 500–07; italics mine)

Thus, identity is reintroduced and reproblemized here, its paradoxes brought home to the core of the tragedy, juxtaposed with the vexed equations of vision equals knowledge and blindness equals ignorance. Foisting his own dilemma on Pentheus, Dionysus reveals their deeper twinship, for Pentheus, in fact, does *not* know who he is. Confined within his limited, overly defended persona—walled, like the city he rules—he is, as we have already seen, both inwardly and outwardly blind. Like and unlike Oedipus, he can recognize neither his interlocutor nor himself.

Identity and recognition, however, surge into preeminence almost unbearably in the scene in which Pentheus has fallen from the tree and is about to be sacrificed. Ripping off his feminine disguise, he begs Agave to acknowledge him as her child and to spare him. Touching her cheek, he pleads:

Look, it is I, mother, your child
Pentheus, whom you bore in the house of Echion!

Take pity on me, mother, and do not by reason of my
errors murder your own child!"

(lines 1117–21)

Like the dead mother of Dionysus, however, she cannot at this crucial
moment *see* him. Her blindness and her inability to affirm him matter
focally to the perverse scenario, for Dionysus' revenge must be taken not
only against Pentheus but, on a deeper level, against the lost mother. Had
she lived to know him as her son, her recognition and affirmation would
have made it imperative (in fantasy) for Pentheus and others to have done
likewise.

Exploiting, at key moments, the trope of falling, *The Bacchae* presents a
world in which moderation appears only as a chimera hallucinated by the
chorus, while its principal human subject plummets from extreme to
extreme, living out with erotized intensity the paradoxes of his mortality.

Descending images abound, only culminating in Pentheus' final fall
from the treetop (lines 1111–12), but we may take this one as a stunning
metaphor for libidinal regression—regression as applied to the fate of
Pentheus in his participation in the Dionysian trauma. Hurtling from his
phallic tree, he is propelled into a sadistic orgy of dismemberment and
then, at the very end, exposed to one horrible moment of primitive oral
aggression when his deranged mother actually suggests that he be eaten
("Partake then of the feast!" she says, holding up his impaled head; line
1184).

From the start, falling figures as a trope. Worrying that it might be
topsy-turvy for old men like himself and Cadmus to join the young at their
bacchic revels, but pointing out that Dionysus makes no distinction between the generations (line 206), Teiresias requests his friend to "support
my body, as I will yours. / It is shameful for two old men to *fall*" (lines 364–
65; italics mine). Thus, falling, perceived as disaster, can be momentarily
averted by the device of doubling—a point echoed later, ironically, when
Pentheus perceives the two suns over Thebes.

Furthermore, when Dionysus, in imitation of his father, demolishes
the palace (lines 585–607), the female chorus is awestruck by his display
and, in their terror, replay vis-à-vis him the role of Semele to Zeus: like
her, they fall to the ground (lines 600–11). Thus, in this falling scene as

well, the infantile trauma is reenacted. Pentheus, stumbling helter-skelter in helpless confusion and bewilderment (lines 625–30), rehearses in this repetition of trauma the role of the unborn child. Moreover, the palace, symbolizing "solidity," may be interpreted as figuring the secure adult self, which collapses in ruins at this moment to reveal the helpless child beneath (Segal, letter of March 8, 1990).

Falling images figure physical disaster, grief, terror, even ecstasy, as when the frenzied bacchae are described as hurling themselves to the earth in the throes of their worship (lines 135–36). Thus, the world of *The Bacchae* is one of almost perpetual descent, even unto the final imagery, where the venerable but impotent Cadmus is transformed by Dionysus into a snake as a closing humiliation. Destined henceforth to touch the earth with all his body parts, he thus reverts to the chthonic being of the family ancestry, barred forever from siring future kings. In terms of the totality of the myth, his achievement as a civilizing hero is thus undone.

In meditating on these images, we realize that fear of falling is basic to the human species. The most primitive of our fears, it is the one that causes every infant to grasp reflexively and against which every good mother protects by her holding hands and cradling arms. Adumbrated here throughout *The Bacchae,* this fear is actualized in a supreme moment of perversity. For Pentheus drops not *from* but *into* his mother's *un*sustaining, life-threatening hands. Losing his grip on the tree that supports him and reaching the ground, he is, as we know, deprived of life by the one who gave him life—rent in a total fragmentation of body and mind.

The male child, by achieving merger with and humiliation of the mother through his cross-dressing and voyeurism, thereby relinquishes the masculine identity by which he can be recognized by her. In falling from his precarious phallic perch to the earth, he must be passively and violently undone. Nightmarishly, this scene enacts the deepest level of male fantasy—that terror of annihilation for which castration anxiety itself is but a façade.

Thus, to accomplish its overturning of the overturned, *The Bacchae* has, by its final choral piece, produced reversals, transformations, and violations of established boundaries. In what has transpired here, I have attempted to mirror the text by locating and dislocating several of the notions of perversion discoverable there. By pointing to specific types of imagery, I have demonstrated how one traumatic event, evoked in the first moments, spawns a set of new editions that both erupt into and propel the tragic action. I have indicated that, despite florid pathology figured in the story and its background legends, Euripides' tragedy speaks directly to us today.

Perverse solutions are attempted answers to riddles that compel, in troubling times and in fantasy, only the most extreme of deeds. To read or see *The Bacchae* is to confront ourselves; for Euripidean theater, like and unlike Artaud's, is a theater of cruelty—and a theater of truth.

In autumn 1980, an English version of *The Bacchae* was performed in New York with Irene Papas in the role of Agave. Anyone with a passion for Greek tragedy would have found it unforgettable. Onstage throughout, a great bronzed disk caught and reflected the lights. Continuously in view, it glowed, glowered, leered, grinned, and grimaced at both audience and players. Seductive and unsettling, its haunting presence seemed to blur comedy and tragedy. Although it was meant perhaps as an amalgam of the two suns over Thebes, I saw in it only the diabolical smiling mask of Dionysus.

References

Note: In addition to the references cited in the text, I have included below a few additional works that might prove of interest to other psychoanalytically minded readers of *The Bacchae* and of Greek tragedy generally.

Aristotle. 1964. *Poetics.* In *Philosophies of Art and Beauty: Selected Readings in Aesthetics from Plato to Heidegger,* ed. A. Hofstadter and R. Kuhns. Chicago: University of Chicago Press.

Artaud, A. 1976. *Selected Writings,* ed. Susan Sontag. Berkeley and Los Angeles: University of California Press.

Bersani, L. 1986. *The Freudian Body: Psychoanalysis and Art.* New York: Columbia University Press.

Chasseguet-Smirgel, J. 1985. *Creativity and Perversion.* New York: W. W. Norton.

de Romilly, J. 1985. *A Short History of Greek Literature,* trans. L. Doherty, Chicago: University of Chicago Press.

Détienne, M. 1979. *Dionysus Slain,* trans. M. Muellner and L. Muellner. Baltimore: Johns Hopkins University Press.

Devereux, G. 1970. "The Psychotherapy Scene in Euripides' 'Bacchae.'" *Journal of Hellenic Studies* 90:35–48.

———. 1976. *Dreams in Greek Tragedy: An Ethno-Psycho-Analytic Study.* Berkeley and Los Angeles: University of California Press.

duBois, P. 1988. *Sowing the Body: Psychoanalysis and Ancient Representations of Women.* Chicago: University of Chicago Press.

Euripides. 1959. *The Bacchae,* trans. W. Arrowsmith. In *Euripides,* vol. 5, ed. D. Grene and R. Lattimore. Chicago: University of Chicago Press.

———. 1970. *The Bacchae,* trans. G. S. Kirk. Englewood Cliffs, N.J.: Prentice-Hall.

Fine, J. V. A. 1983. *The Ancient Greeks: A Critical History.* Cambridge: Harvard University Press.

Foley, H. P. 1985. *Ritual Sacrifice: Poetry and Sacrifice in Euripides.* Ithaca: Cornell University Press.

Freud, S. [1905] 1953a. "Three Essays on the Theory of Sexuality." In *Standard Edition* 7:125–245.

———. [1905] 1953b. "Psychopathic Characters on the Stage." In *Standard Edition* 7:305–10.

———. [1925] 1953. "Negation." In *Standard Edition* 19:235–39.

Fried, M. 1980. *Absorption and Theatricality: Painting and Beholder in the Age of Diderot.* Berkeley and Los Angeles: University of California Press.

Green, A. 1979. *The Tragic Effect: The Oedipus Complex in Tragedy,* trans. A. Sheridan. Cambridge: Cambridge University Press.

Harsh, P. W. 1979. *A Handbook of Classical Drama.* Stanford: Stanford University Press.

Kris, E. 1952. *Psychoanalytic Explorations in Art.* New York: International Universities Press.

Loraux, N. 1987. *Tragic Ways of Killing a Woman,* trans. A. Forster. Cambridge: Harvard University Press.

McDougall, J. 1986. *Theaters of the Mind: Illusion and Truth on the Psychoanalytic Stage.* New York: Basic Books.

Ovid. 1955. *Metamorphosis,* trans. M. M. Innes. Harmondsworth, Middlesex, England: Penguin Books.

Rose, H. L. 1959. *A Handbook of Greek Mythology.* New York: Dutton.

Rudnytsky, P. 1987. *Freud and Oedipus.* New York: Columbia University Press.

Segal, C. 1982. *Dionysiac Poetics and Euripides' "Bacchae."* Princeton: Princeton University Press.

_____. 1986. *Interpreting Greek Tragedy: Myth, Poetry, Text.* Ithaca: Cornell University Press.

Simon, B. 1978. *Mind and Madness in Ancient Greece: The Classical Roots of Modern Psychiatry.* Ithaca: Cornell University Press.

_____. 1988. *Tragic Drama and the Family: Psychoanalytic Studies from Aeschylus to Beckett.* New Haven: Yale University Press.

Slater, P. E. 1968. *The Glory of Hera: Greek Mythology and the Greek Family.* Boston: Beacon Press.

Spitz, E. H. 1988. "The Inescapability of Tragedy." *Bulletin of the Menninger Clinic* 52:377–82.

_____. 1989. "Psychoanalysis and the Legacies of Antiquity." In *Freud and Art.* New York and London: Abrams.

Stoller, R. J. 1985. *Presentations of Gender.* New Haven: Yale University Press.

Vernant, J.-P., and Vidal-Naquet, P. 1981. *Tragedy and Myth in Ancient Greece,* trans. J. Lloyd. Atlantic Highlands, N.J.: Humanities Press.

Vidal-Naquet, P. 1986. *The Black Hunter: Forms of Thought and Forms of Society in the Greek World,* trans. A. Szegedy-Maszak. Baltimore: Johns Hopkins University Press.

Chapter 11

The Hard-Boiled Dick

Perverse Reflections in a Private Eye

George Stade, Ph.D.

I would confess from the onset that I am contributing to this volume under false pretenses—if only I knew what a true pretense was. About perversion in itself I have nothing, or almost nothing, to say. My subject, rather, is perversion as reflected in the nervous and fascinated gaze of straights. There are reasons. For one thing, my understanding of perversion, or my lack of it, is not based on clinical experience, and without clinical experience you are nowhere. All analysts to that extent agree with the Master, even when they agree with him or each other about little else, even now that upstarts routinely make their bones by showing how little the Master himself understood his own clinical experience, even when clinical experience turns up such phantasmagoria as fecal penises and phallic mothers.

But if a layman is nowhere when it comes to understanding perversion, it is not clear, exactly, where the experts are—all over the place, maybe. It used to be that a pervert was simply a guy who made love to old shoes, say, and that was that; but no longer, not if you read the people with clinical experience. One last thing about which the experts agree is that a pervert is not a pervert by virtue of what he does, sexually speaking, or by virtue of what he does it with, but by virtue of the frame of mind in which he does it: with deplorable fantasies of degradation and revenge, according to Robert J. Stoller;* with "the urge to regress to a preoedipal fixation in which there is a desire for and a dread of merging with the mother in order to reinstate the primitive mother-child unity," according to Charles W. Socarides,† who writes with a brick; or with a desire to bring about an "erosion of the double difference between the sexes and the generations, in fact. . . . to reduce the universe to faeces," according to Janine Chasseguet-Smirgel,‡ who writes with a whip.

To Dr. Stoller I would only pose a question that he himself entertains, though not for long: would humans bother with sex at all if you were to take away their fantasies of degradation and revenge? To Dr. Socarides, I'd point out that men as a matter of course fall in love with stand-ins for their mothers and that if they don't want to merge with them, I'm damned if I know what they want to do. And to Dr. Chasseguet-Smirgel, I'd observe that a pretty fair definition of what humanity has been up to, and for some time now, is precisely to turn the world into feces. If everybody does it, it can't be perverse. Besides, to uncover such longings, you need clinical experience, which, as I may have mentioned, I don't have.

For these reasons, then, my subject is the attitude of straights toward perverts, rather than perversion itself. With straights we are on firmer ground. We all know who the straights are. They are us, never mind the bizarre things we do in the name of "foreplay." And straights, unless they have been reading the experts, know who the perverts are. Precisely because they know who the perverts are, straights know who they are. A pervert is to a straight what according to Saint Paul sin is to the law: without the one, you would not know the other. Straights and perverts, then, define themselves and each other reciprocally in opposition, harden each other in their ways. To study the attitudes of the one is therefore

* Robert J. Stoller, *Perversion: The Erotic Form of Hatred* (New York: Pantheon Books, 1975).

† Charles W. Socarides, *The Preoedipal Origins and Psychoanalytic Therapy of Sexual Perversions* (Madison, Conn.: International Universities Press, 1988), 42.

‡ Janine Chasseguet-Smirgel, *Creativity and Perversion* (New York: W. W. Norton, 1984), 2, 4.

also to study the other, so long as we keep in mind certain complications. Not all perverts, for example, consider themselves perverted. No doubt there are necrophiliacs who feel that coprophilia is disgusting, but that necrophilia is nice. And no doubt within every straight is a pervert of some kind, maybe of every kind, moaning to get out, as within every pervert there is a killjoy straight he has to appease. And no doubt there are ways of being straight that are perverted, as we shall see.

For my evidence I did not turn to life. I turned to literature, which I prefer, and with which I have had clinical experience, so to speak. Among kinds of literature, I did not turn to the good stuff, but to schlock, because people actually read it. Among the popular genres, I turned to the detective novel, because it is the most enduring and popular and resonant subspecies of schlock. That it is also my favorite kind of bedtime reading, a goodnight kiss to build a dream on, has nothing to do with it. Among detective novels, I turned to the American hard-boiled type, rather than to the English genteel type, because who cares what the English think about perversion? Among Americans, I turned to Mickey Spillane, because he is the all-time best-selling American crime writer of the century. Of the thirty best-sellers of all kinds published in America between 1895 and 1965, Mickey Spillane wrote seven. Dashiell Hammett, Raymond Chandler, and Ross MacDonald did not even come close. Among novels by Mickey Spillane, I turned to *I, the Jury* (1947), his first and the best-sellingest American whodunit ever. For nonreaders, there are two movie versions.

Who bought all those copies of *I, the Jury* is not known—people such as the writer and readers of these remarks, I imagine. What we found in the novel that made it worth reading is by no means obvious. It was certainly not clean-cut prose or a lock-step plot of memorable caricatures or ingenious detecting or an invigorating ethos or witty dialogue or a moralized urban landscape or the inside dope—the usual come-ons—because none of those things is there to be found. The novel's hero and narrator, the private eye Mike Hammer, has lots to say (it's a talky novel) about such matters as the criminal justice system, police procedure, ballistics, forensic medicine; about organized crime, corrupt politicians, the numbers game, the heroin trade, drug addiction, white slavery, prostitutes, the management and clientele of whorehouses; about pornography, psychoanalysis, hypnotism, beekeeping, college life, and, of course, perversion—and he gets all of it wrong. On the basis of this novel it would be reasonable to assume that Mickey Spillane has no factual knowledge about anything whatsoever.

Detective novels are usually solicitous of the otherwise thrown-away facts and objects of everyday life; these are redeemed, brought back into consciousness, by their potential status as clues; the writer directs the reader's inner eye toward them until they glow with possibilities—but not in Mickey Spillane. Mickey Spillane *never* has his eye on the ball. In one scene Hammer observes the marks of a whetstone on a knife held across his neck and under his chin (47),* although nowhere are we told that his jaw is transparent. With one sniff of the bore, he can tell that a pistol has not been fired during the previous month (40). On the first page of the novel Hammer arrives at the scene of a murder. He asks the presiding cop, his old friend Pat Chambers, when the murder occurred. Chambers answers in these words: "'The coroner places it about five hours before I got here. That would make it about three fifteen. When I get an autopsy report we may be able to narrow it down even further'" (10). An autopsy report would narrow it down to three-twelve and twenty-two seconds maybe.

The murder victim, by the way, is a one-armed man named Jack Williams, another private eye and Hammer's best friend. Hammer deduces that after being shot in the belly, Williams "tried to drag himself along with his one arm" (6); but Hammer also deduces that the poor guy was "trying to keep his insides from falling out with his hand" (13) while he dragged himself along. Either Williams had one arm with two hands, or we have a very unusual case of the phantom limb syndrome.

This blurred focus, these lapses in attention, this distracted gaze, this vacant stare, extends even to the descriptions of women, although Hammer insistently reiterates his enthusiastic admiration for shapely female flesh. About the appearance of his secretary, Velda, we are told only that "she had million-dollar legs, that girl, and she didn't mind showing them off," and that "she kept her coal-black hair long in a page-boy cut and

* All references are to the twentieth anniversary edition of the New American Library reprint of the original E. P. Dutton edition of 1947.

wore tight-fitting dresses that made me think of the curves in the Pennsylvania Highway" (12). About the appearance of another alleged beauty, Esther Bellemy, a suspect, all we are told about her physical appearance is that she is athletic-looking and that "she was another one to make your mouth drool" (146).

But the main Pavlovian stimulus—a woman who has legs, Hammer says, of a "kind that make you drool to look at" (14)— is Hammer's heartthrob, his eventual fiancée, Charlotte Manning, a Park Avenue shrink. Here is Hammer's first look at her in the flesh:

> She was delicious. There was a lot about her that couldn't be put into words. Charlotte Manning was sitting at her desk, hands folded in front of her as if she were listening for something. Beautiful was a poor description. She was what you would expect to find in a painting if each of the world's greatest artists added their own special technique to produce a masterpiece. (31)

You are free to imagine, I suppose, a body by Breughel, limbs by El Greco, eyes by Picasso, and a complexion by Jackson Pollock, or anything you want. Spillane's interest is elsewhere.

A clue to the direction of his interest is provided by a remark Hammer makes about Charlotte Manning: "she could have sued me if she knew what went on in my mind" (31). Spillane's descriptions of objects, events, and characters are governed by the principle that you do not have to look at a thing closely if its sole raison d'être is to generate a fantasy. In the scene with Charlotte, as everywhere, Mike Hammer is the reader's intermediary, medium, and model. The focus of the novel is not on what he sees but on how he reacts to what he sees. *I, the Jury,* in fact, is a disguised manual of conduct. Its informing motive is to teach men through the example of Mike Hammer how to conduct themselves. And that is why Hammer is so exquisitely self-conscious, so studied in all his motions, as though he knew he were the cynosure of every eye. Here is how the novel opens:

> I shook the rain from my hat and walked into the room. Nobody said a word. They stepped back politely and I could feel their eyes on me. Pat Chambers was standing by the door to the bedroom trying to steady Myr-

na. The girl's body was racking with dry sobs. I walked over and put my arms around her.

"Take it easy kid," I told her. "Come on over here and lie down." I led her to a studio couch that was against the far wall and sat her down. She was in pretty bad shape. One of the uniformed cops put a pillow down for her and she stretched out.

Pat motioned me over to him and pointed to the bedroom. "In there, Mike," he said.

In there. The words hit me hard. In there was my best friend lying on the floor dead. The body. Now I could call it that. Yesterday it was Jack Williams, the guy that shared the same mud bed with me through two years of warfare in the stinking slime of the jungle. (5)

And so on. What follows during the rest of this chapter is a number of tirades by Hammer about how he feels— "there was so much hate welled up inside me I was ready to blow up" (7)—and about what he will do to the killer— "Some day, before long, I'm going to have my rod in my mitt and the killer in front of me. I'm going to watch the killer's face. I'm going to plunk one right in his gut, and when he's dying on the floor I may kick his teeth out" (8).

That is how you behave when your friend has been murdered; how you behave on other occasions we learn from the full array of Hammer's dispositions and traits. He is the only character who has traits to speak of; he is the novel's paragon and paladin; everything about him is exemplary. His favorite meal, for example, is fried chicken and potatoes; complicated food is for sissies. Similarly, he drinks only bourbon and beer. He smokes Luckies, which somehow always get crumpled. For a hat, he wears a "battered felt" (28), as he wears a "wrinkled ruin of a suit" (30), although it has been altered to accommodate his government-issue Colt .45 pistol. He drives a "heap" or "jalopy," within which is a souped-up motor (59). His "mug," as he calls it, is not handsome, but women cannot resist him, for, as with his suit and his car, beneath the roughed-up exterior is a hidden source of violence and power.

Hammer's first impulse, on meeting another man, is to slap him around. As you might expect from someone who drools, when he hugs or kisses a woman, he hurts. "I felt like reaching out and squeezing her to pieces" (102), he says of Charlotte. And when Hammer feels like doing something, he does it: "I knew I was hurting her," he says on this occasion, as on another he says, "it was a wonder she could breathe" (138), and on still another he says, "I squeezed her arms so hard my hands hurt" (65). Intensity of feeling in Hammer always leads to someone else's pain. Charlotte seems to go for this sort of thing: "You love hard, too, don't you Mike?" (65), she says admiringly.

It does not bother this cultivated and educated woman that Hammer has plebeian tastes; that he says he cannot follow the big words in her books; that when he goes through magazines, he looks only at the pictures and ignores the text; that on Sundays he throws away the news and reads only the funnies; that he needs his secretary's help to tie his tie. Nor does it bother Charlotte, in spite of her clinical experience—she's a psychoanalyst, remember—that Hammer's attitudes toward sex are full of warning signs. He is both prudish and prurient, both lustful and bashful, a firm believer in the double standard.

He is upset, for example, when Velda utters a mild obscenity, "the kind you see scratched in the sidewalk by some evil-minded guttersnipe" (18). When Velda fusses about his intention to visit a cathouse (on business), he reassures her with the usual brag that he doesn't have to pay for it and that, in any case, as he says, "After all those pictures the army showed me of what happens to good little boys who go out with bad little girls, I'm afraid even to kiss my mother" (74). The madam of the cathouse, by the way, "looked like somebody's mother" (77). As he leaves, having declined a quickie offered by one of the girls, he again says "a silent thanks to Uncle Sam for showing me those posters and films" (83).

In general, Hammer does not like forward women. He likes to do the pursuing himself. "I like to do some of the work myself," he says, "not have it handed to me on a platter" (64). Mary Bellemy wants to peep at his beefcake, but he puts her off with an "'I don't get undressed in front of women'" (145). Charlotte Manning, by then his fiancée, needs a little loving. "'Mike,' she whispered, 'I want you,'" but he says no. "'No, darling,'" he says; "'it's too beautiful to spoil'" (103). He also tells Charlotte that once they are married, she will have to give up her job, although she is raking it in while he is not. He explains himself with his customary savoir faire:

"No wife of mine is going to work. I want her home where I know where she is" (141).

None of this bothers Charlotte, who reaches down into the abysmal recesses of her clinical experience to explain why:

> "When you came in to see me I saw a man that I liked for the first time in a long time." She sat down and continued. "I have hundreds of patients, and surprisingly enough, most of them are men. But they are such little men. Either they had no character to begin with or what they had is gone. Their minds are frail, their conception limited. So many have repressions or obsessions, and they come to me with their pitiful stories; well, when you constantly see men with their masculinity gone, and find the same sort among those whom you call your friends, you get so you actually search for a real man."
>
> "Thanks," I put in.
>
> "No, I mean it." Charlotte went on. "I diagnosed you the moment you set foot in my office. I saw a man who was used to living and could make life obey the roles he set down. Your body is huge, your mind is the same. No repressions." (61).

You might think that Charlotte is putting Hammer on, but later events will prove that she is speaking from the heart.

I, the Jury, then, is a manual of conduct; more specifically, it is a show-and-tell treatise on masculinity. We are shown by his conduct and told by other characters that Mike Hammer, otherwise an ordinary Joe, is extraordinary only in being all man. Never is he more polemically a man than when confronted by his moral opposites, or negative definers. These are criminals, forward women, and perverts, all of whom, by the end of the novel, have been equated.

Hammer's first stop on the track of his partner's killer is at a Westchester mansion. It is owned by a broken-nosed tough guy, an ex-bootlegger, now a numbers racketeer, one George Kalecki. Hammer gains entrance by browbeating the butler. Kalecki comes on strong, but, says Hammer, "I lit a butt and blew the smoke at him" (20). Backing down, Kalecki offers an alibi: "I sneered in his face," says Hammer. Turning pale, Kalecki protests that the police have cleared him: "I spat in his face," says Hammer, who then tosses Kalecki around a bit. At this point Kalecki's partner in crime, Hal Kines, enters and tries to brain Hammer with a vase. "I let fly a wicked punch that landed low" (21), and as Kines doubles over, Hammer lays him out with a head butt. Kines, we learn later, only looks young; he is the beneficiary of good bones and frequent face lifts. Equipped with these, he will register at some college for a month or a term, get some coed to fall for him, ruin her, and then deliver her over to a life of prostitution. Worse than that, George Kalecki and Hal Kines are homosexual bedmates. Hammer guesses as much right away, although no clues to their perversion in their speech or appearance or behavior is ever given to the reader. Their homosexuality, one gathers, is merely a shorthand signal to the reader that these guys have sunk as low as you can go. It also sets off Hammer, of course, and prepares us to accept their violent ends as poetic justice. "That kind of guy," Hammer says later of Kines, "ought to be hunted down and strung up by the thumbs. I'd like to do it personally" (84). Someone beats him to Kines, kills him with the same .45 that gut-shot Jack Williams, but Hammer does manage to waste Kalecki with his own beloved .45.

Kalecki and Kines are the only male suspects, but there are a surprising number of other perverts in Hammer's environs. Whenever Spillane wants to flesh out a scene, he brings out a pervert or two for Hammer to bash, verbally or physically. When Hammer learns, for example, that there is to be a sex show at a certain den of iniquity, he has no difficulty picturing those who will attend: "Rich jokers of both sexes who liked smut and filth and didn't care where they got it. A pack of queers who enjoyed exotic, sadistic sex. Nasty people" (81). As Hammer watches the audience arrive, his imaginings are made flesh. A taxi pulls up, and "a young punk in a double-breasted suit stepped out and gave a hand to the fat boy with him. A greasy slob." Another car drives up, and

> a pair of dillies climbed out. The man, if you could call him that, was done up in a camel's-hair coat, his skinny neck protruding above a flaming-red ascot. He had a marcel that was brand new. His companion was a woman. The only way you could tell was by the skirt. The rest of her was strictly male. She walked with a swagger and he minced his way to the sidewalk holding on to her arm. Fruit. (85)

Wherever Hammer looks, high or low, he sees the same kind of people. Late in the novel, for instance, he has a chance to observe the life-styles of the rich and famous when he visits a Westchester estate for a tennis party thrown by the glamorous Bellemy sisters, twin heiresses. Hearing a racket outside the window of his room, Hammer leans out to see what is going on:

> Direct beneath me two underweight males were having a hair-pulling match while four others egged them on. What a place. The two boys hit the dirt together and followed by a slap or two. I grinned. A couple of pansies trying to decide who would be Queen of the May. I drew a pitcher of water from the sink and let it go on their blonde heads.
>
> That ended the fight. They both let out a falsetto scream and got up running. The gang saw me and howled. It was a good gag. (146)

Spillane thinks that gag is so good that he brings the butts of it on stage again, so that these "tootsies" or "pansies" can try to pick Hammer up while he sits at the bar. One of them gets too close, but, says Hammer, "all it took to get him out was a strong hand on the seat of the shorts and another around his neck. The whole deal was getting very monotonous" (147).

Well, yes, the whole deal is monotonous in the way of all obsessions. Hammer's, or Spillane's, obsessions take on more questionable shapes, become even more agitated and sinister, in the novel's treatment of its six main female characters, three of whom, in Hammer's eyes, are more or less perverse. These female heavies, as though perched on the end of a seesaw, elevate the three straight women they face across the novel's moral fulcrum. The three straights are Velda, Hammer's secretary; Myrna Devlin, a reformed prostitute; and Eileen Vickers, a prostitute, who is unreformed but repentant. If you stand back and squint, Velda shows only as a shadow cast by Hammer's self-regard. She, too, has a P.I. license, packs a semiautomatic, and is prone to violence: "she could whip off a shoe and crack a skull before you could bat an eye" (12), says Hammer. Her main function in the novel is to wear her heart on her sleeve; her crush on Hammer and Hammer's affection for Velda amount to requited self-love, as though when you kissed the mirror, it kissed back. Velda's female form saves Hammer, and Spillane, from unmanly displays of narcissism. Velda is all right.

The other two female straights are treated with a combination of maudlin sympathy and prurient interest. They are worn down and out by their occupations; they are not forward women; they are prematurely aged, actively passive, victims more than victimizers, Myrna in that she was made first into a drug addict and then into a prostitute by a criminal combine, Eileen in that she was ruined and turned out by Hal Kines. Essentially, they are all right, too. They are all woman, which in this novel means that there would be nothing left over were you to take away from them their roles as sexual servitors to men. At the same time, their association with sexuality makes them dangerous and culpable, for runaway fantasies are not reined in by contradiction. Myrna and Eileen are killed off by bullets from the same .45 that put the quietus to Jack Williams and Hal Kines.

The Bellemy twins, Esther and Mary, are dangerous enough, suspects from the start, but they are not killed off, except to the extent that they are aspects of Charlotte, who is. Esther is never seen clearly; she hovers on the periphery of the novel's field of view, slightly out of focus. About her we learn only that she is muscular, that she could make you drool, that she is always calm, cool, and reserved, even when bedlam and murder erupt around her, that she has no sexual interest in Hammer, that, as Charlotte puts it, "she has a tendency to turn away from love affairs" (128). It is enough, in this novel, to make her perverse. The implication is that she is frigid or, more likely, a lesbian. Her sister, Mary, is something else. According to Charlotte's diagnosis, which is based solidly on her clinical experience, Mary is afflicted with nymphomania—a malady, alas, that seems not to exist outside of literature.

On his first visit to Mary, still not on the trail of his buddy's killer, Hammer is immediately struck by her physique: "I was facing a woman that had athlete written all over her. . . . Her arms and shoulders were as smooth-muscled as a statue's" (45). Hammer is by no means put off by the brawn: "Me, I like them husky" (40), he says. A few minutes into their conversation, Mary remembers that she left the bath water running, an unlikely story. She runs out only to reappear in a "sheer pink negligee" (46) through which Hammer can see the "smooth parallel rows of light muscles, almost like a man's" (47). She informs Hammer that the only physical difference between her and Esther is that one of them has "'a small strawberry birthmark on the right hip.' " "'Which one?' " says Hammer. "'Why don't you find out?' " says Mary. Hammer demurs. "'Don't be a sissy,' " Mary says. The following scene ensues:

> Her eyes were blazing into mine. They were violet eyes, a wild blazing violet. Her mouth looked soft and wet, and provocative. She was making no attempt to keep the negligee on. One shoulder had slipped down and her brown skin formed an interesting contrast with the pink. I wondered how she got her tan. There were no strap marks anywhere. She uncrossed her legs deliberately and squirmed like an overgrown cat, letting the light play with the ripply muscles in her naked thighs.
>
> I was only human. I bent over her, taking her mouth on mine. She was straining in the divan to reach me, her arms tight around my neck. Her body was a hot flame; the tip of her tongue searched for mine. She quivered under my hands wherever I touched her. Now I knew why she had never married. One man could never satisfy her. My hand fastened on the hem of the negligee and with one motion flipped it open, leaving her body lean and bare. She let my eyes search every inch of her brown figure.
>
> I grabbed my hat and jammed it on my head. "It must be your sister who has the birthmark," I told her as I rose. "See you later." (48)

That is how to conduct yourself with forward women, a grand arousal followed by the great refusal. We are supposed to admire Hammer for his interruptus, although it is not usually considered admirable in a man for him to be a cockteaser. Mary Bellemy, on the other hand, is turned into a figure of fun for a sexual appetitiveness that conventional taste finds more seemly in men and that Hammer finds threatening. She preempts Hammer's role, thereby earning his churlish response, thereby proving herself a menace. Later in the novel, during the tennis match, Mary leads Hammer away from the lights and into the dark night of the woods. He does not know that she has undressed until he feels all those delicious muscles pressed against him. He succumbs; but it is while they are rolling in the shrubbery that Myrna Devlin, whom Hammer has pledged himself to protect, is killed. Mary is technically innocent of Myrna's death, but she is guilty by association.

For if you once again stand back and squint, Mary begins to look like a split-off aspect of Charlotte Manning, who turns out, of course, to be the novel's criminal mistress-mastermind. Mary, that is, takes on the aspect of a forward woman; her sister, on the other hand, takes on the aspect of Charlotte implied in her last name, "Manning." The three women look alike in Hammer's fascinated but myopic glances; the words used to describe them are fairly interchangeable. Hammer first sees Charlotte not in the flesh but in a photo. Here is what he sees:

> The picture was taken at a beach, and she stood there tall and languid looking in a white bathing suit. Long solid legs. A little heavier than the movie experts consider good form, but the kind that make you drool to look at. Under the suit I could see the muscles of her stomach. Incredibly wide shoulders for a woman, framing breasts that jutted out, seeking freedom from the restraining fabric of the suit. . . . I felt like whistling. (14–15)

Hammer is smitten. "Even her eyes had cupids in them" (60), he says at one point. Better or worse, "she radiated sex in every manner and gesture" (32), he says at another. Charlotte is the embodiment of sexual allure, an unmixed blessing you would think, but not for Hammer, to whom she is a pipedream and a daymare at once. "'You remind me of something,'" he says. "'What?'" she says. "'A way of torturing a guy'" (60).

Hammer is unsettled by something uncanny about Charlotte. It is not just that she is replicated in the Bellemys or that she saps masculine resolve—that old black magic that she weaves so well. In part it has to do with her profession. In this novel, as perhaps in life, psychoanalysis is in itself uncanny, its adepts mind readers equipped with the evil eye. "'You have an incredible mind,'" says Hammer to Charlotte; "'somehow you think of everything at once. . . . That comes of being a psychiatrist'" (172). From the time of their first meeting, Charlotte confides to Hammer, "'I made it my job to look into your character. I wanted to know what a man like you is made of. It wasn't hard to find out'" (63). Hammer is startled by how easily she finds out what he is made of; "she was clairvoyant," he exclaims (61). Charlotte, however, disavows mind reading, although she admits that she "'can study people, observe their behavior and determine what lies underneath' " (104)—which amounts to the same thing. It is no wonder, then, that Hammer breaks off one of his ferocious tirades when he notices Charlotte "listening intently, her eyes wide. She was making a typical study of me as though she was hearing the story of a confessed murderer and trying to analyze the workings of the mind" (107). What Charlotte can do to an individual, she can do to a crowd; we later learn that she murdered Myrna and got away with it, despite the crush at the tennis party, through the application of something Hammer calls "mass psychology" (173): she knew what everyone was thinking and what they would do.

Through sexual and psychoanalytic black magic, then, Charlotte reads minds and casts her spell. She is also a stealer of souls, a Park Avenue Circe who turns the men who attend her into subhuman figures of appetites only she can assuage. She began with her patients, runs the charge in Hammer's final indictment. "'Yes, you treated them, eased their mental discomfitures—but with drugs. Heroin. You prescribed and they took your prescription—to become addicts, and you were their only source for the stuff and they had to pay through the nose to get it. Very neat' " (168). In her therapeutic reliance on drugs, Charlotte is ahead of her times, but in other respects she is old-fashioned. She is an expert hypnotist, for example, as well as an amateur photographer with her own darkroom—in both cases, the better to capture your soul. While they were still courting, Charlotte had shown Hammer a photo she took of one of her patients. "'What's the matter with him? The guy looks scared to death,' " says Hammer. "'He's in a state of what is commonly known as hypnosis' " (137), said Charlotte. And it was through hypnosis that Charlotte had gotten control over Hal Kines. Once when he was posing as a student and she was gathering clinical experience, she hypnotized him and thereby, in Hammer's words, "brought to light every dirty phase of his life" (168). Pumped up with this knowledge, Charlotte tried to muscle her way into the Kines-Kalecki criminal combine. After such knowledge, what forgiveness?

Certainly Hammer is not in a forgiving mood, when in the novel's last pages, he confronts Charlotte with her crimes. He is about to make good on a promise to avenge his buddy's murder. That makes him feel good: "There was a crazy joy bubbling inside me that made me go alternately hot and cold" (164). But good is not the only way he feels and his buddy's murder is not all he is out to avenge. He loves, hates, and fears Charlotte, all for the same reason, her bewitching allure. If he were an actual person, rather than a character in fiction, we would gather that this allure reveals something about Hammer that Hammer does not want known or to know. And, as a rule, the more you have something to hide, even if only from yourself, the less you want your mind read, but the more you fear that someone is reading it. And the less you want your soul bared, the surer you are that someone is stealing it, the better to expose it. A murderous hate follows such fear, as implacably as "doom" and "tomb" rhyme with "womb."

The final scene is so much an imaginative coup, so insanely apt, so resonant and fitting a climax, that all of Spillane's gaucheries fade. This passage instantly certified him as the idiot savant of detective fiction. In it, as Spillane's private eye strips Charlotte morally, she removes her clothes. The paragraphs in which Hammer, sitting in a chair, bares Charlotte's villainies, one after another, alternate with italicized paragraphs in which Charlotte, silent, standing before Hammer, exposes her body, one thing after another. In the trembly web of analogies that this novel has been spinning from within itself, what Hammer discloses to Charlotte and what Charlotte exposes to Hammer amount to the same thing: the sins that justify his role as judge, jury, and executioner.

When Hammer levels his .45 "straight at her stomach" and announces that he has seen through her cover, Charlotte just stands there *"like a soldier,"* he says. *"Her stomach was so flat against the belt of her skirt. . . . Her lips wanting to silence mine with a kiss. . . . I couldn't let her speak or I would never keep my promise."* While Hammer unveils her unprofessional use of drugs and hypnosis, Charlotte unbuttons her blouse. By the time he has revealed how she shot Jack Williams, how, says Hammer, "'while he tried to pull himself toward his gun you made a psychological study of a man facing death,'" Charlotte has removed her blouse. *"She wore no bra,"* Hammer notes. *"Lovely shoulders. Soft curves of hidden muscles running across her body. . . . Soft, yet so strong."* Probably we should not make too much of Charlotte's muscles, which in some uncanny way are both prominent and hidden, or of the direction of Hammer's gaze, which is toward Charlotte's broad shoulders, away from what an-

other man might consider more worth looking at. While Hammer un-
covers the motives behind Charlotte's murder of Hal Kines and Eileen
Vickers, Charlotte removes her skirt and slip. Hammer cannot take his
eyes off her nutcracker legs: "*Legs that were all curves and strength and
made me see pictures that I shouldn't see any more. . . . Heavier than you
see in the movies. . . . All that was left were the transparent panties. And
she was a real blonde.*"

Charlotte becomes naked entirely at the moment Hammer finishes
dressing her down. But he adds that no one else has seen what he has
seen. No one else knows what he knows, nor would anyone believe him if
he tried to tell it. "'No jury would ever convict you,'" he says. But she will
not get off. "'No, Charlotte,'" Hammer says. "'I'm the jury now, and the
judge, and I have a promise to keep. Beautiful as you are, as much as I
almost loved you, I sentence you to death.'" But Charlotte is not finished
either. To Hammer she looks like "a sun-tanned goddess giving herself to
her lover. With arms outstretched she walked toward me. . . . She leaned
forward to kiss me, her arms going out to encircle my neck." Here is how
the novel ends:

> The roar of the .45 shook the room. Charlotte staggered back a step.
> Her eyes were a symphony of incredulity, an unbelieving witness to truth.
> Slowly, she looked down at the ugly swelling in her naked belly where the
> bullet went in. A thin trickle of blood welled out.
>
> . . . Her eyes had pain in them now, the pain preceding death. Pain and
> unbelief.
>
> "How c-could you?" she gasped.
>
> I had only a moment before talking to a corpse, but I got it in.
>
> "It was easy," I said.

No doubt Charlotte has been a bad girl. But as I read the novel,
Charlotte's crimes add up to no more than Hammer's pretext for killing
her. Her crimes read to me as merely the symptoms and consequences of
something far worse. Here is how Hammer, just before their striptease à
deux, described to Charlotte her original sin, from which all her other sins
followed:

> Your profession started it. Oh, you made money enough, but not
> enough. You are a woman who wanted wealth and power. Not to use it

extravagantly, but just to have it. How many times have you gone into the frailty of men and seen their weaknesses? It made you afraid. You no longer had the social instinct of a woman—that of being dependent upon a man. (167)

Compared to that offense, such are the operative values, murder is a mere indiscretion, like urinating on a man's hedge after you have burned down his house. Indiscretions aside, Hammer kills Charlotte because in his blood-dimmed eyes she is a pervert. That she is a manly woman is bad enough; but worse, there are times when as in an afterimage or double exposure Charlotte is also uncannily like a womanly man. Consider Spillane's reworking of *I, the Jury* in a novel he published three years later.

Vengeance Is Mine (1950) differs from *I, the Jury* only in incidentals. Once again the action is triggered by the murder of a wartime buddy of Hammer's. Once again his quest for revenge takes him into a diversified criminal enterprise involving prostitution, perversion, and dirty pictures, for starters. Once again a gorgeous forward woman in heat tries to ensnare Hammer by surprising him in the buff. Once again, he leaves her to her own devices. Once again, the leading forward lady is a big, muscular, bewitching blonde beauty with whom Hammer all but falls in love. Once again she turns out to be a multiple murderer, "the brains of the outfit," the most villainous of the villains. But this time her name is Juno Reeves, "queen of the lesser gods and goddesses," as Hammer puts it, otherwise a director of a modeling agency. And this time Hammer declines her sexual advances not because their relationship is too beautiful to spoil but because again and again, at the moment of truth, Juno reminds Hammer of Charlotte Manning.

These reminders blow in on emotional storms that leave Hammer awash in a kind of fugue, his hands shaking, knees trembly, spine atingle, head buzzing, eyes glazed, reality erased by a vision of Charlotte's physiognomy. Hammer can't figure it out: "Maybe she reminded me of something else I could never have. Never," he says. The pronouns are confusing. The "she" is Juno, but is the "something else" Charlotte . . . or something else? The climax of the novel gives us a clue. Once again Hammer confronts his adversary in love and hate with her sins, his pistol pointing. "'I'm going to shoot you where it will hurt like hell,'" he says.

Once again he knows what no one else will believe. "There wasn't a single shred of evidence against her that could be used in a court and I knew it," he says. "But I could kill her." This time, however, his resolve crumbles under the force of an involuntary memory: "My eyes burned holes in my head and my whole body reeled under the sickening force that pulled me to her. . . . I was seeing Charlotte's face instead of [Juno's]. I went crazy for a second. Stark, raving mad." When he comes out of it, "panting like a dog," he decides to turn Juno in rather than shoot her and tucks away his weapon, enough being enough.

But not for Juno: she takes the measure of Hammer's distraction, jumps him, and proceeds to beat the bejesus out of him. Only by dint of a superhuman effort ("my madness saved me,") does he manage to get a grip on Juno, who (no mere human either) twists free, leaving her dress in Hammer's hands. As he looks over Juno's "beautiful body," which is "stark naked except for the high-heel shoes and sheer stockings," his pistol once more cocked and at the ready, Hammer begins to recover himself. "I forgot all my reservations about shooting a woman then," he says. So he shoots, not once, but until his magazine is depleted: "The rod was jumping in my hand, spitting nasty little slugs that flattened the killer against the wall with periods that turned into commas as the blood welled out of the holes." The last words of *Vengeance Is Mine* come close to outdoing those of *I, the Jury:*

> I spit on the clay that was Juno, queen of the gods and goddesses, and I knew why I'd always had a resentment that was actually a revulsion when I looked at her.
>
> Juno was a queen, all right, a real live queen. You know the kind.
>
> *Juno was a man!*

It's moments like this that shake the professional self-confidence of analysts, whether of literature or of life. Could it be that Spillane does, after all, know what he is doing? Is it possible that the man does, after all, have a sense of humor, one so diabolically sly, in fact, that it never tips its hand? Can he have anticipated our dirty-minded suspicions, the better to rub our noses in them? The possibility is awful to contemplate. But no, there is too much evidence to the contrary. Too many other things would be different if Spillane knew what he was doing. Books like his are written in a daze or not at all.* And they depend for their effect on being read in a reciprocating uncritical doze. Such novels work only if you do not attend to what is working on you.

But now that we have attended, I hope you will agree that the inner workings of *I, the Jury* are perverse. I hope you will agree further that they are dangerously unstable, volatile, on a hair trigger, like Hammer's .45 caliber extension of his masculinity. It is not just in literature that people are killed when emotions like Hammer's are vented. They require, therefore, careful handling. The question is how to handle them at all. We could manhandle them by saying that Hammer is a repressed homosexual who in the familiar way kills the object of unconscious longings he consciously abhors.† Unconsciously he wants to make love to men; consciously therefore he protests (too much) his love for women. A manly woman would seem like the answer to everything, but the male part of her is compromising. So Hammer kills Charlotte, having projected onto her what he loathes in himself, his perversion. That he also hates women for the very reasons that made him a homosexual doubles his pleasure. We could say that, and find reports of clinical experience to confirm it, but I have qualms about psychoanalyzing literary characters. The countertransference may be there, but the transference is not.

We could turn from the character to the author, then, and read *I, the Jury* as one long symptom of a man haunted by a phallic mother. What Spillane needs from this reading is five sessions a week with someone like Dr. Chasseguet-Smirgel. Or, if we are more up to date, we might say that Spillane's dopamine transmitters are clearly out of whack. What he needs, rather, is a regimen of Prolixin, along with a dose of Cogentin, to counteract the Prolixin, along with some Imipramine, to counteract the Cogentin. We could say that, but it is impossible to know how much of what is in a book is also in its author, even when we have a good deal about him from other sources, as we do not about Spillane.

We could turn a little further, from the character to the author to the

---

* Spillane claims that he wrote *I, the Jury* in nine days. He also claims that he never revises. See Michael Barson, "Just a Writer Working for a Buck," *Armchair Detective*, Fall 1979, 294–99, a portion of which is an interview with Spillane.

† Malcolm Cowley, "Sex Murder Incorporated," *New Republic*, February 1952, 17, approaches this argument.

times in which the book was produced, under the assumption, very big in the academy nowadays, that the history of power relations explains everything. We would then observe that in 1947 men were looking to reclaim jobs that during the war women had occupied, that propagandists were beginning to proclaim the feminine mystique.* But none of that would explain the double-edged perversions of *I, the Jury;* nor would it answer to our suspicion that the novel has predecessors and successors in different times and places.

A little stiff in the neck by now, we could turn once more, away from the character, the author, the times, and look into the genre, assuming for the moment that Spillane is a mere mechanical producer of cultural commodities for which there is a proven demand. Sure enough, we would find that the same shadowy, tangled web of lusts and furies lurk everywhere in hard-boiled detective novels, from the most recent to the first and best of them, *The Maltese Falcon* (1929). In that novel, one more time we see the initiating murder of the male lead's fellow detective, as though there but for the grace of God goes the private eye; we see the boyish secretary with a crush on him, the forward woman (Ina Archer) who throws her shapely self at him and gets put down for her pains, the criminal conspiracy ripe with perverts and drugs, the literally stunning beauty for whom the detective falls, but who turns out to be unnatural, an exploiter of the frailties of men, a multiple murderer. But Brigid O'Shaughnessy does not remove her clothes. She does better: she declares her love for Spade, makes him sweat by saying that if he really loved her, none of her crimes would matter. And Spade does not shoot Brigid; he turns her in. He is aware, however, that as a result, she will face the gallows. We could say all that, but then we would have to explain how this web of motives and motifs got raveled into the genre.

We would have to turn, that is—never mind the vertigo—from the character, the author, the historical moment, the genre, to the audience, this time under the assumption that the conventions of the enduring popular genres take shape under pressures exerted by the desires of their consumers. A popular genre is always as you like it, we could argue, ruled

* See Kay Weibel, "Mickey Spillane as a Fifties Phenomenon," *Dimensions of Detective Fiction,* ed. Larry N. Landrum, Pat Browne, and Ray B. Browne (Bowling Green, Ohio: Popular Press, 1976), 114–23.

by the pleasure principle, unlike literature proper, in which the other principle holds equal sway. We would not have to look far for schools of historians with shoals of explanations as to why Americans, and of both sexes, are uptight about gender roles and sex. But we would have to ask them one further question. We would have to ask them why hard-boiled detective fiction, including Spillane's, has caught on in such culturally diverse places as Scandinavia, France, Japan, and Latin America, none of which was founded by Puritans or Calvinists, and only some of which still suffer the aftereffects of a vanished frontier. We might even ask, by the way, whence comes the frisson of horror, the uncanny recognitions, the tumescent rage, none of which, being emotions, is susceptible to historical explanation. There are still some things that psychology does best.

But perhaps we have mistaken our audience. Perhaps we have to step back one last time, widen our field of view, and look not to our national character but to human nature. Perhaps during the good old days before the Neolithic revolution, when men were men and so forth, when our DNA learned everything that is human about it, there were survival values in an instinctual horror of male homosexuals and manly women, who are, after all, less likely to have children. Perhaps vestiges of that disposition remain with us, one more piece of evidence that instinctual gratification is not everything. Or perhaps, with a hint of desperation, we should consult with feminists, who might agree that the disposition remains with us, all right, but that it has nothing to do with instinct, that patriarchal ideology leads inevitably to Mickey Spillane. Where, when, or how patriarchal ideology originated, though, remains a matter of dispute. Perhaps it descended from heaven. Perhaps we could simply say that *I, the Jury* is overdetermined, and leave it at that.

Our look around for the source of Hammer's attitudes toward perversion have led us everywhere and nowhere—that is, back to the eye of the beholder, which is as it should be. For every act of interpretation reveals as much about the interpreter as about his text. You could say that, I guess, so long as you applied the maxim to yourself while you were interpreting me—or better yet, while you were interpreting *I, the Jury.* If you did, you would find, I believe, pretty much what I found, that aside from the psychomachia of perverts and straights, aside from the psychodrama of Hammer's attempt to straighten himself out, there is little to keep you turning the pages. For straights, and not just for straights, perversion is an itch that will not go away, whatever its source. Turning the pages of *I, the Jury* and other novels of its ilk is one way to scratch it. Writing essays such as this one is another. Few readers of this essay, of course, will overtly endorse Mike Hammer's violent way of defining himself in opposition to perverts, if only because anyone old enough to read this essay, pervert or straight, has already in his own way defined himself, and will continue to define himself, through a sustained and covert psychomachia with his own opposing self and its uncanny projections.

Homosexuality and the other perversions remain mysterious, the causes in dispute. In that respect they are like heterosexuality, for what it is that makes one straight is equally, so far, inexplicable. Given the importance we attach to questions of sexual identity and the thrashing about of experts, one can forgive the layman for taking matters into his own hands. Whatever its sources, *I, the Jury* is a fantasy, or more precisely a stimulus to fantasy, that is impatient of mysteries—which in this novel are detected not to be solved but to be denied, unless violence is a solution. The reader who participates in the fantasy sees one unknown achieve definition by conflict with another, which also gets defined in the process. To establish his masculinity, which by definition is straight, the detecting hero must turn himself inside out and destroy what comes to light. The implication follows that masculinity is not given, but achieved, and at some cost. From the outside, no doubt, the achievement seems gratuitous, absurd, suspended over the void. But that much can be said about many human values. Whether masculinity is to be valued and perversion therefore devalued is one more question for which psychoanalysis has no answer, not to the extent that psychoanalysis is a science. Mickey Spillane does—thus, I would suppose, his popularity.

Index

Bach, Sheldon, 7, 86, 87, 89, 100, 198, 220
Bak, R. C., 139
Barande, I., 177
Bartell, G. D., 165
Beating fantasies, 77–80; in sadomasochism, 89–90
Behavior: flexible, 85; normal, 41–42
Bergmann, M. S., 154, 170
Bersani, L., 216
Bias. See Ethical bias, in definition of perversion
Biologic causes of perversion, 44–45
Bion, W. R., 161, 185
Blindfolding, in sadomasochism, 79–80
Blue Velvet (film), 32
Borges, Jorge Luis, 38
Boundaries, in couple relationship, 166–71
Braunschweig, D., 155, 158
Breast, as fetish, 30–31

Castration anxiety, 22, 30, 49, 150; obscene phone calls and, 119
Chandler, Raymond, 234
Character perversion, 21, 63–65
Chasseguet-Smirgel, J., 22, 70, 99, 100–01, 214, 215, 233
Childhood trauma, sadomasochism and, 85
"Child Is Being Beaten, A" (Freud), 99, 102
Children: in couple relationship, 167; sexual molestation of, 73
Circe fantasies, 72
" 'Civilized' Sexual Morality and Modern Nervous Illness" (Freud), 19
Classification of personalities, 39–41
Clitoral masturbation, 43
Clockwork Orange, 98
Clothes, psychology of, 70–71
Coen, S., 94, 101
Colby, K. M., 39
Collusion, in couple relationship, 162–63
Complementarity, in couple relationship, 160–61

Compromise formation, perversion as, 99–100
Conditioning, 45
Conscience, culture and, 45–46
Conscious perverse fantasies, perverse action and, 94–97
Cooper, Arnold M., 5
Coprolalia, 69
Countertransference attitudes, towards homosexuality, 189–91
Couple relationship: authority in, 169–70; boundaries in, 166–71; children in, 167; collusion in, 162–63; complementarity in, 160–61; culture in, 173–74; death in, 169; direct triangulation in, 163; discontinuities in, 158–60; dissociated aggression in, 170–71; internal world in, 171; pathological role fixation in, 171–74; power in, 169–70; repressed aggression in, 170–71; reverse triangulation in, 163; social conventionality in, 173–74; social life in, 166–68; time boundary in, 169–71; triangulations in, 163–65; twinship in, 161–62; value systems in, 173–74
Creativity, perversion and, 69
Cultural causes of perversion, 45–46
Culture: conscience and, 45–46; in couple relationship, 173–74; popular, 3; sexual instincts and, 19

Damage play, 66–67
Death, in couple relationship, 169
Death instinct, 202
Defensive splitting, 96
Dehumanization, in perversion, 23–24
Delinquency, juvenile, 63, 70
Delinquent behavior, deviant behavior and, 187–88
de Romilly, J., 213
Detective novel, 234–35; audience for, 251–52
Devereux, G., 220
Deviant behavior, delinquent behavior and, 187–88